JANE AGAINST THE WORLD

ROE v. WADE
AND THE FIGHT FOR
REPRODUCTIVE RIGHTS

KAREN BLUMENTHAL

JANE AGAINST THE WORLD

ROE v. WADE AND THE FIGHT FOR REPRODUCTIVE RIGHTS

ROARING BROOK PRESS ⬥ NEW YORK

Copyright © 2020 by Karen Blumenthal

Published by Roaring Brook Press
Roaring Brook Press is a division of Holtzbrinck Publishing Holdings Limited Partnership
120 Broadway, New York, NY 10271
fiercereads.com
All rights reserved
Library of Congress Control Number: 2019941017
ISBN 978-1-62672-165-4
Our books may be purchased in bulk for promotional, educational, or business
use. Please contact your local bookseller or the Macmillan Corporate and
Premium Sales Department at (800) 221-7945 ext. 5442 or by email at
MacmillanSpecialMarkets@macmillan.com.
First edition, 2020
Book design by Monique Sterling
Printed in the United States of America
1   3   5   7   9   10   8   6   4   2

"Unwed Fathers"
Words and music by John Prine and Bobby Braddock
Copyright © 1983, 1984 Bruised Oranges and Sony/ATV Music Publishing LLC
All rights for Bruised Oranges Administered by Downtown DLJ Songs
All rights for Sony/ATV Music Publishing LLC Administered by Sony/ATV
Music Publishing LLC, 424
Church Street, Suite 1200, Nashville, TN 37219
All Rights Reserved Used by Permission
Reprinted by Permission of Hal Leonard LLC

To Jen

CONTENTS

PROLOGUE

Jane 3

PART I
RESTRICTIONS

8

PART II
REFORM

78

PART III
ROE v. WADE

176

PART IV
AFTER ROE

272

JANE AGAINST THE WORLD

ROE v. WADE AND THE FIGHT FOR REPRODUCTIVE RIGHTS

Imagine that you're sixteen years old and still in school.
Now imagine that you have just discovered that you're
pregnant—or your girlfriend is pregnant.

What does that mean to you?

What does that mean to your life from now on?

What do you want to do?

What can you do?

What are you going to do?

PROLOGUE

Jane

Martha Scott and Jeanne Galatzer-Levy didn't set out to become illegal abortion providers.

They were just women who thought other women should have control over whether and when they had a child.

That was a revolutionary idea. For much of the world's history, girls and women had little access to reliable birth control and few safe or legal choices to address an unintended pregnancy. It was almost as true in the United States in the 1960s as it was in ancient Greece and Rome.

Until 1965, almost half the states still had laws on their books restricting the sale of birth control, and for some years after that, many doctors flat-out refused to provide it to unmarried females because they didn't believe they should have sex. In addition, for much of the twentieth century, abortion, or intentionally terminating a pregnancy, was illegal in every state unless the life of the woman was in danger. Despite that, hundreds of thousands of women—perhaps as many as a million a year—sought the illegal procedure.

In the 1960s, that began to change. Lawyers began to question why women who were victims of rape or incest, or who faced serious health issues were forced to either continue a pregnancy or endure an illegal abortion. Doctors were troubled by the increasing number of women who arrived at emergency rooms injured by or dying from backroom abortions. Attitudes about premarital sex shifted at the same time that women began to demand rights that had been denied to them. In a gathering wave, women and men, ministers and rabbis, society ladies and feminists began to insist that women be able to control whether and when they bear children.

It was an uphill battle. Medical schools had drummed into generations of doctors that abortion was both illegal and wrong, except in very specific circumstances. The powerful Catholic Church was firm in its opposition to both medical birth control and abortion, even if a woman was raped or her long-term health might suffer from a pregnancy. For everyone involved, this was a deeply personal and moral issue with little middle ground.

In the early 1970s, Scott and Galatzer-Levy (then Galatzer) joined a group of Chicago women who supported women's reproductive rights and went further than most.

Initially, the group had referred pregnant callers to reliable, though illegal, abortion doctors. But the cost was high—at least $500 a procedure, or $3,600 or more in today's dollars—and some of the providers were rude or abusive to their patients.

For a time, the group hired its own abortion provider. But he wasn't a medical doctor, and after some months, he wanted to relocate. Rather than find a replacement, he began to teach a handful of the women volunteers, including Scott, how to perform safe abortions themselves. By modern standards, that was a shocking choice. But it also hearkened back to the thousands of years that women quietly and often secretly helped each other with contraception and abortion.

Pregnant women seeking an abortion in the Chicago area learned about the service from small advertisements, doctors, and friends, who suggested they "call Jane." One group member would return the messages and others would help women through the process.

Officially, the Chicago women called themselves the Abortion Counseling Service of Women's Liberation, or "the service" for short. But everyone else called them "Jane."

For women like Sunny Chapman, who was nineteen, pregnant, and terrified, Jane was a lifesaver. "I would rather die than have a baby," she said years later. Panicked, she had tried to end the pregnancy by jumping off a friend's garage roof and taking scalding baths. She made herself sick with quinine but didn't miscarry.

She was referred to an abortion provider, but his $600 fee was "a fortune—beyond belief," equal to more than seven months of rent. "I couldn't imagine getting that much money together," she said. Finally, Jane was able to help her for what she could afford.

Some volunteers, like Galatzer-Levy, learned to be assistants, prepping women for their abortions.

On appointment day, pregnant women, their friends, their partners, and sometimes their kids would go to an apartment called "the Front" to wait. A Jane driver would pick up the women and take them to another apartment, "the Place," where the abortions were performed. With Jane members doing the work, the price fell to $100, or about $650 today. But Jane accepted whatever the women could afford to pay.

The calls increased. Married women, single women, teens, and mothers wanted help. Jane members were performing up to thirty abortions a day, three days a week. Thousands of women came through the service.

Then, on May 3, 1972, Chicago homicide detectives knocked on the door.

The police questioned those at the Front and the Place. They seized Jane's equipment. Everyone in both apartments, children included, was rounded up.

From left, Martha Scott, Jeanne Galatzer-Levy, Abby Parisers, Sheila Smith, and Madeline Schwenk volunteered with Jane and were arrested in 1972.

In one wagon heading to the police station, three Jane members ripped the day's schedule into tiny pieces. In another, one of the Jane workers pulled about thirty index cards from her purse. She and other Jane members quietly tore off the corners with their clients' names and contact details. Then, they ate the scraps to protect their clients' privacy.

Seven Jane women, from Galatzer-Levy, a twenty-one-year-old former student, to Scott, a thirty-year-old mother of four, were arrested and charged with serious crimes. They each faced the possibility of many years in prison.

But there was a small glimmer of hope. A lawsuit called *Roe v. Wade*, which challenged the Texas law prohibiting abortion, was pending before the all-male U.S. Supreme Court. The court's ruling—which would become perhaps the most famous legal decision in American history—would determine their fate and that of millions of women across America.

PART I

RESTRICTIONS

Lust defiles the body, debauches the imagination, cor-rupts the mind, deadens the will, destroys the mem-ory, sears the conscience, hardens the heart, and damns the soul. It unnerves the arm, and steals away the elastic step. It robs the soul of manly vir-tues, and imprints upon the mind of the youth, visions that throughout life curse the man or woman. Like a panorama, the imagination seems to keep this hated thing before the mind, until it wears its way deeper and deeper, plunging the victim into practices that he loathes.

—Anthony Comstock, writing about obscene publications in *Frauds Exposed*, 1880

MADAME RESTELL

1800s

More than a century before the women of Jane secretly ran their illegal service, Ann Trow Lohman ran a thriving and very public abortion and birth control business in New York City.

Lohman, a native of England who had immigrated to the United States in 1831, claimed to have learned to become a midwife from her grandmother. In truth, she may not have had any formal training. In the late 1830s, she hung out a shingle, called herself Madame Restell, and began advertising her Preventative Powders ($5 a package, for birth control) and Female Monthly Pills ($1 each, to restore missed menstrual cycles) in the local newspapers.

Customers bought her medicines by mail or came to her offices in New York—and later in Boston and Philadelphia—for a consultation or to arrange a surgical procedure. She also ran a boardinghouse for single women who were pregnant, helping them through the birth and then arranging adoptions for the babies, for a fee.

In her more than thirty years of practice, Madame Restell enjoyed an unusually lucrative business. She dressed in "elegant silks and costly furs," news accounts noted, and traveled in a carriage with two handsome horses. She and her husband accumulated a fortune that exceeded a million dollars.

She also earned a nickname: "the wickedest woman in New York."

THE FEMALE ABORTIONIST.

An illustration of Madame Restell from the *National Police Gazette,* a tabloid-like publication, in 1847.

In newspaper advertisements, Madame Restell boasted of her "experience and knowledge in the treatment of obstinate cases of female irregularity, stoppage, suppression." But there were many others doing the same thing, part of a rush of women and men who took advantage of the growing newspaper industry to aggressively hawk solutions for late or missed menstruation beginning in the 1840s.

The services Madame Restell and others offered were as old as civilization. At least since the beginning of recorded human history, women have sought to regulate their childbearing or end pregnancies. The Kahun Papyrus, the oldest medical text known from Egypt, dating back to around 1850 BCE, includes a recipe for crocodile dung and fermented dough to prevent pregnancy. (Exactly how the concoction was used isn't known.)

The Ebers Papyrus, another Egyptian medical scroll from around 1500 BCE, listed a formula "to cause a woman to stop pregnancy." The ingredients included unripe fruit of the acacia tree, colocynth (also known as bitter apple), and dates. The mixture was to be moistened with honey to form a compound and inserted into the vagina.

The pills and powders that Madame Restell and others sold in the 1800s were somewhat less exotic but still relied on herbs and plants that were believed to somehow prevent a pregnancy or cause uterine cramping that resulted in miscarriage. (Some of them, unfortunately, were also poisonous and very dangerous.)

The potions often didn't work, but Madame Restell and her competitors had plenty of customers, and in a time well before formal pregnancy tests, women had a window in which they could address their situation.

PREGNANT PAUSE:
Where Babies Come From

Today, we know that human babies come from a female's egg (or ovum) and a male's sperm, which combine to form an embryo that splits and grows. But understanding that basic fact took thousands of years and relatively advanced technology. Early on, humans figured out that sexual intercourse could eventually result in new life. But many theories persisted throughout history about how that happened, virtually all of them formulated by men who had little understanding of women's bodies. Here's a short history:

Aeschylus (Greek, around 500 BCE), in keeping with ancient Greek myths in which male gods were the creators, proposed the men provided the seed and women were the field where the seed became a child.

Aristotle (Greek, 384–322 BCE) recognized that women stopped menstruating when pregnant and theorized that male semen and female menstrual blood mixed to create an embryo.

Galen (Roman, around 150 BCE), in a theory that hung on for hundreds of years, concluded that females were just men inside out, with ovaries matching testicles and a vagina being the reverse of a penis. He believed that embryos were created from male semen and female fluid or semen.

Anton van Leeuwenhoek (Dutch) developed a crude but powerful microscope in the 1670s, and in 1677, he used it to look at his own semen. There, he saw hundreds of tiny, swimming "animalcules" for the first time.

Scientists, building on van Leeuwenhoek's work and influenced by their belief in a powerful God, concluded that minuscule fully formed humans existed in every sperm of a man and in the sperm of each of the fully formed humans in a man's sperm and so on, like Russian nesting dolls in reverse. This preexistence or "preformation" theory was embraced from the late 1600s through the 1700s.

Lazzaro Spallanzani (Italian) took the opposite viewpoint after unusual experiments in the 1760s, in which he put tiny taffeta pants on frogs to see if the nattily attired fellas could fertilize frog eggs. When only the naked frogs were successful, he theorized that tiny humans were formed inside all of a female's eggs and male semen only got the process moving. But no one knew for sure if women had eggs because no technology was available to actually see them.

Finally, **Karl Ernst von Baer (Estonian)** in 1827 discovered that all mammals have eggs, and in 1875, **Oscar Hertwig (German)** saw in his microscope the nuclei of sperm penetrate the nuclei of an egg and the two become one.

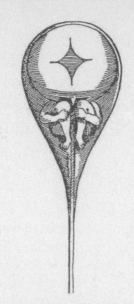

A drawing of a fully formed man inside sperm, as envisioned in 1695.

For much of history—from the ancient Greeks and early Romans, through the writing of the U.S. Constitution and well into the 1800s—a fetus wasn't considered alive or human until the woman felt the fluttering of fetal movement, a stage called *quickening*. For hundreds of years, the Catholic Church and Protestant churches considered quickening to be the point in a pregnancy when the soul entered the fetus.

Before quickening, the focus was on what was missing—a woman's monthly menstrual bleeding—rather than what might be growing. After all, the absence of menstruation isn't always a sign of pregnancy; malnutrition, stress, overwork, and any number of chronic diseases can result in females missing a period. If a woman was pregnant, though, her breasts may have become swollen and tender during those early weeks. She might have felt nauseous or unusually tired; her belly may have thickened. But the official proof of pregnancy was feeling the fetus kick, typically in the fourth or fifth month.

After quickening, aborting a pregnancy was a crime under common law, or law based on long-held understandings and court precedents rather than a written statute.

Starting in 1821 with Connecticut, however, some states began to include written laws restricting abortion as part of broad revisions to their criminal codes. Initially, the laws prohibited giving poisons to induce an abortion, a safety issue for women. Then, they became broader.

By 1840, ten of the nation's twenty-six states had some kind of abortion law on the books. Not all of them made a distinction for abortions that happened after quickening, but courts and juries almost never convicted anyone of a crime unless it was after the woman had felt the fetus move.

Despite the written laws, abortion grew more common, so much so that abortion practitioners became, according to one historian, "one of the first specialties in American medical history."

Madame Restell was at the forefront, in large part because of her advertising, which was once estimated at nearly $60,000 a year. But authorities also kept a close eye on her. In 1841, she was arrested, tried, and convicted of performing an abortion on a young woman who died of tuberculosis. She appealed and was acquitted in a second trial. She was tried again in 1847 for performing an abortion on a young woman named Maria Bodine.

Restell had urged Bodine to move in and deliver the baby. But Joseph Cook, a widower who employed her as his housekeeper and seduced her, had insisted she get an abortion. He eventually came up with the $75 that Restell charged her.

Newspapers closely followed the trial and its salacious details, especially since Bodine's morals were on the stand as well. Bodine was quizzed in detail about changes to her body during the pregnancy, how often she had sex with Cook, and whether she had been a virgin before him. One attorney accused her of being a prostitute.

In her testimony, Bodine described Restell as a concerned and involved practitioner. Once she had been paid, Restell examined Bodine and likely punctured the amniotic sac to induce a miscarriage. Painkillers weren't widely available, and antiseptics and antibiotics—to prevent or treat infections—hadn't yet been developed.

After the procedure, Restell checked on her regularly over two days and spent the second night with her. Once Bodine miscarried, Restell took care of her for another two days and then gave the tearful young woman money for transportation home.

The jury was asked to find Restell guilty of manslaughter if Bodine was "quick with child." But on the seventeenth day of the trial, the all-male panel found her guilty only of a misdemeanor, for procuring a miscarriage. Still, Restell was sentenced to a year in prison.

By 1848, news accounts were using a new synonym for abortion: "Restellism."

Advertising and the wide availability of abortion providers had a profound impact: What had been fairly rare ten or twenty years before was now almost routine. Historian James C. Mohr estimated that in the mid-1800s, there was one abortion for every five or six live births among white women.

After the Civil War, a technological revolution expanded

opportunities in growing cities, while making a living off the land grew tougher. Millions of people, including many single young women, moved from rural homesteads to expanding urban areas to find work. Many single women who became pregnant hurried to the altar with a male partner. But those who had been raped or were abandoned by boyfriends had few places to turn. If the pregnancy continued, they would lose their jobs and become social outcasts, bringing shame to themselves, their families, and their children.

In addition, more and more, white, Protestant, middle- and upper-class married women were looking to plan their pregnancies for health reasons, because they could not afford another mouth to feed, or to avoid the very real dangers of childbirth. On a farm, more children meant more workers. But in the cramped confines of city living, raising and feeding a large family was far more difficult. For help, they looked to abortion specialists when their birth control methods failed. At one point, the *New York Times* estimated that about two hundred lesser trained doctors operated in the city, handing out medicines—including fake ones—and inducing miscarriages.

Overall, the birth rate for American white women declined dramatically during the nineteenth century: In 1800, a typical woman bore seven children, though not all were likely to live to adulthood. By the 1860s, however, the average number of children delivered had dropped to close to five, and by 1900, it would fall to 3.5, half the number of the previous century.

The experience of black women, however, was very different, especially for enslaved women in the South. Many slaveholders looked at black women's bodies as a source of free labor and often forced relationships or raped enslaved women to produce more children. Generally, enslaved women who bore children were considered more valuable than those who didn't.

At the same time, the backbreaking work expected of the women, the lack of medical care and healthy food, and abusive treatment often resulted in miscarriages, premature births, and stillbirths. Those losses led some southern whites to conclude that enslaved women knew secret ways to manage their fertility.

Though the practice probably wasn't as common as was assumed, some black women did use remedies such as cotton root or looked to a black midwife to end their pregnancies. In doing so, they were asserting some control over their own bodies—and perhaps hoping to avoid the heartbreak of having a child born into slavery or sold away from the family. But the birth rate for black women didn't notably decline until after the end of the Civil War.

By the 1850s, easy access to abortion ran into fierce opposition from an unlikely source: medical doctors.

At the time, doctors who had trained at medical schools competed with many others with less formal training: botanic specialists, herbalists, homeopathic practitioners, midwives, and, of course, abortion providers like Restell, who sometimes called herself a doctor. To set themselves apart, medical doctors formed the American Medical Association in 1847 to establish expectations, create ethical standards, and oversee medical education.

The new organization gave a platform to Horatio Robinson Storer, a twenty-seven-year-old, ambitious Harvard University–educated doctor. In 1857, Storer started his medical practice in Boston, with an interest in obstetrics, like his father. His father opposed abortion because it was dangerous for women. The younger Storer, however, took a moral position: A fetus was alive and thus worth preserving, he argued, no matter how many children a woman was struggling to feed. Abortion, he wrote later, went against "nature and all natural instinct, and against public interests and morality."

At the annual AMA convention that year, the young doctor urged like-minded delegates to take a stand against the practice. In response, the organization agreed to study "criminal abortion" and asked Storer to chair the effort.

Based on that work, the AMA and medical doctors took the lead in opposing abortion. Among their first steps, in 1859, was to declare that nothing scientific happened when a woman felt a fetus move, since the fetus had been growing and changing well before that. Doctors were dedicated to preserving life, even the beginnings of life. So, they argued, both doctors and the law should drop the distinction of quickening, ending centuries of practice and expectation.

That conclusion put the power of declaring a pregnancy in the hands of doctors, who were virtually all male and who had only recently focused on women's health.

Following Storer's lead, many doctors opposed abortion except to save the life of the mother and began to lobby for changes to criminal laws after the Civil War. In response, male legislators began to revise or enact dozens of laws criminalizing abortion at any time during pregnancy—even though many Americans, including jurors hearing the cases, were slow to accept that abortion was wrong before quickening.

Storer's effort also paid off handsomely for the medical profession. With tougher abortion laws, the scientifically trained doctors over time ran many competitors out of business, including female midwives and abortion providers.

That gave doctors more control over women's bodies just as women were beginning to speak up for their own rights, including the right to own property or vote. Under the laws in place in the 1800s, a wife was her husband's property. He could beat his wife without breaking the law. He could ask for a divorce, but she often could not, nor could she get custody of her children, who belonged to the husband. He worked for wages, she raised children—and depended on him.

Susan B. Anthony and Elizabeth Cady Stanton joined up in the late 1860s to fight for a woman's right to vote. But they also lobbied for a woman's right to education and divorce. Stanton, in particular, was an advocate of "voluntary motherhood," the right of a wife to say no to her husband and choose periodic abstinence. Allowing a woman a voice in a couple's relationship was empowering and groundbreaking in itself. She also believed in "the sacred right of a woman to her own person," including the right to have fewer children.

Storer and his AMA colleagues fought against women's rights and waged an intense battle to prevent women from being recognized as doctors. From Storer's viewpoint, women existed solely to marry and bear children. "This, as we have seen, is the end for which they are physiologically constituted and for which they are destined by nature," he wrote in *Why Not? A Book for Every Woman*, published in 1866.

Storer and other antiabortion doctors also had another agenda: They worried publicly that white, Protestant, American-born women were choosing to have fewer children at a time when they should be having babies to counter an influx of immigrants.

Beginning around 1845, millions of Catholics moved to the United States from Europe. There was room in the nation's expanding West and South for "countless millions yet unborn," Storer wrote. "Shall they be filled by our own children or by those of aliens? This is a question that our own women must answer; upon their loins depends the future destiny of the nation."

The doctors often invoked the name of God in their arguments, though Protestant clergy of the late nineteenth century were largely silent on the issue. In Catholicism, abortion was a sin, but it wasn't considered murder until after quickening. That changed in 1869, when Pope Pius IX declared that ending a pregnancy at any time would lead to automatic excommunication from the church, reflecting a belief that all life was sacred beginning at conception.

Sidelined by an infection after surgery, Storer retired from his work in 1872 at age forty-two. But that very same year, Anthony Comstock joined the opposition for very different reasons. A deeply religious salesman, Comstock was shocked at the lewd pictures and books available around New York that other men seemed to enjoy. He was horrified to see advertisements in many New York newspapers for contraception—including a relatively new one, rubber condoms for men—as well as medicines aimed at women's needs, which he thought were vulgar.

Comstock began buying what he considered obscene material

at bookstores and reporting it to the police. Bookseller arrests followed.

Emboldened, he went to Washington in 1873 to lobby for a nationwide ban on sending indecent materials through the  mail—including women's pills and rubber condoms. He didn't single out contraception and abortion. He just saw anything connected to sex and human reproduction as religiously and morally wrong, even if it was legitimate medical information.

Congress agreed. That March, it banned selling or advertising obscene material by mail—as defined by Anthony Comstock. His

Anthony Comstock.

list included any products intended to prevent pregnancy or produce a miscarriage. President Ulysses S. Grant signed the legislation, which became known as the Comstock Act.

The young crusader, a stocky man with thick red whiskers on his cheeks and a shaved chin, soon was named a special agent of the U.S. Post Office, which gave him enormous power to enforce the law. He wrote letters to birth control providers across the country, pretending to be a believer in free love or a desperate woman in need of help. Then, when they responded with products, he made or arranged arrests and sought convictions.

In his first two years attacking vice, he helped arrest more than a dozen abortion providers in New York City and Albany, New York. He also confiscated 130,000 pounds of books, almost 200,000 photos and "bad pictures," more than 60,000 items made of rubber "for immoral purposes," and more than 3,000 boxes of pills and powders.

Not satisfied with the federal law, he also lobbied for and won tougher laws in New York banning any drug, medicine, or article to prevent pregnancy or end it.

On January 28, 1878, Comstock, wearing his characteristic black suit and bow tie, knocked on the door of Madame Restell's elegant New York home on Fifth Avenue at East 52nd Street. Comstock innocently asked her if she had any medicine to prevent conception.

The madam, now widowed and in her mid-sixties, brought him a sealed package that contained a bottle of dark liquid, some pills, and instructions. He asked if it would work. No medicine is perfect, she replied, but in nine cases out of ten, this was effective. The user must follow the directions, though, she said, or "it would be of no more use than so much chalk."

If the medicine failed, she went on, the woman could come see her, though treatment would be expensive—$200.

Another customer knocked, and Comstock overheard a conversation from another room that would soon make shameful testimony. A married woman with children told Restell that she had been indiscreet while her husband was away and needed some medicine. Restell sold her some and returned to Comstock, saying, "A great many ladies come to me for this medicine."

Comstock paid her $10 and left with his package.

He returned two weeks later with two officers in plain clothes and a warrant. The three searched her house, removing boxes of pills and powders, and arrested Restell. While Comstock alerted the city's newspapers, Restell was moved to a local jail called the Tombs. She was held for a few days before returning home.

New York's newspapers couldn't get enough of the sensational story of one of the city's best-known women and Comstock's trap. But while the headlines buzzed, Restell agonized about a possible

A rendering of Madame Restell after her suicide, from an 1887 book.

conviction and the possibility that she would spend her remaining years imprisoned. As a trial approached, she grew frightened and anxious, wringing her hands and pacing nervously.

On April 1, the day her trial was to begin, she rose before the sun and filled a tub with water. Once in the bath, she used a large kitchen carving knife to cut her throat from ear to ear. A housekeeper found her body that morning.

She was neither the first nor the last of Comstock's victims to take her own life—though he had little concern about that. In his case notebook, he wrote in purple ink: "A bloody ending to a bloody life."

Over the years, Comstockery, as it was dubbed, censored George Bernard Shaw's plays, James Joyce's *Ulysses*, and artists' paintings of nudes. But more than anything else, Anthony Comstock's personal moral code most deeply affected American women. His work drove basic information about reproduction and the practice of safe birth control and abortion underground and impacted women for close to one hundred years.

PREGNANT PAUSE:
A Short History of Birth Control: Ancient Times to the 1870s

Probably the oldest and most common form of birth control (even today) goes by the funny name of *coitus interruptus*. That's when a man withdraws his penis from a woman's vagina before he ejaculates, in hopes of keeping his sperm from mating with an egg. It can work, but not reliably, and requires a woman to depend on a man's willingness and discipline during sexual intercourse.

Because trying to restore menstruation before quickening was not considered an abortion, women, for thousands of years, used herbs and plants to either prevent pregnancy or bring on bleeding. Information was passed along woman to woman.

Among the most commonly used were aloes, birthwort, black cohosh, colocynth, cotton root, ergot, juniper oil (also known as savin), myrrh, pennyroyal, seeds of Queen Anne's lace, rosemary, sage, tansy, and thyme. Some of these were poisonous and deadly in the wrong quantity.

Women also tried douches, or injections of water, vinegar, or other fluids into the vagina.

A woman who thought she had missed a period might insert a sharp object—like whalebone, a corset rib, or a knitting needle—through her cervix to her uterus to cause bleeding (and hopefully not puncture the uterus or cause an infection). In addition, nineteenth-century medical guides recommended lifting heavy objects, horseback riding, vigorous exercise, jumping from a modest height, and having a tooth pulled, on the theory that the shock could jolt the body into restoring menstrual flow.

MARGARET SANGER

1900–World War II

The legacies of Horatio Storer and Anthony Comstock left many women with few resources for controlling child-bearing, especially in the early years of the 1900s. Margaret Sanger was determined to change that.

Born Margaret Higgins in 1879, six years after the Comstock Act was passed, Sanger was headstrong, intelligent, and passionate, with a tendency toward exaggeration. She was driven to escape her family's poverty. Her older sisters helped pay for her to go to boarding school.

Afterward, she studied nursing and found her life's calling while working as a nurse and midwife on the Lower East Side of Manhattan. One summer day in 1912, she was summoned to help care for Sadie Sacks, who was desperately sick from a botched abortion, likely self-inflicted. By then, every state had some kind of law making abortion illegal; usually the only exception was if it was necessary to save a woman's life.

When Sadie was better, she begged her doctor for the secret to preventing another pregnancy. His flippant answer: "Tell Jake to sleep on the roof."

A few months later, Sadie died from another abortion attempt.

Biographers have questioned whether Sadie was a real person or a mix of women Sanger met in her work. Regardless, Sanger was deeply troubled that poor women turned to dangerous abortions. Upper- and middle-class women who couldn't find a regular doctor to help them could afford to pay doctors operating illegally. But poor women like Sadie went to illegal abortionists who charged $5 for questionable procedures or tried to induce a miscarriage themselves, using poisons, buttonhooks, hairpins, or any other pointed object they could find. Thousands of women are believed to have died each year from these procedures in the early part of the 1900s.

Police generally ignored the illegal abortion business unless a woman died. But if a woman showed up at a hospital bleeding heavily or feverish with infection, doctors often refused to treat her until she told police who had performed the procedure. In the days before antibiotics, there was little they could do to help her.

Experts estimated that anywhere from one hundred fifty thousand to a million illegal abortions were performed each year in the early 1900s. The rate climbed to as many as one in four pregnancies during economically tough times immediately after World War I and during the Great Depression.

Sanger understood that abortion was sometimes necessary but believed that having access to preventative methods was a far better option. She was credited with coming up with the phrase *birth control*, which seemed like a more specific and direct term than *voluntary motherhood*.

She began to write articles about female anatomy and birth control, and for several months, she published a magazine called the *Woman Rebel*. In 1914, she was charged with violating the Comstock Act for sending the *Woman Rebel* through the mail. Officials declared the content obscene and lewd.

Margaret Sanger, around 1913.

Rather than face trial, she left her husband, William, and three children in New York and escaped to Europe for nearly a year. Sometime after that, a man visited her husband and asked for a copy of Margaret's pamphlet "Family Limitation," which explained birth control in detail. A month later, Anthony Comstock arrested William for sharing "obscene, lewd, lascivious, filthy, indecent, and disgusting" information.

William Sanger was tried in September 1915. He argued that the law violated free speech and that Comstock had "an incurable sexophobia." But the judge sided with Comstock and sentenced William to thirty days in jail.

Only then did Margaret Sanger return to face the accusations against her.

Ironically, the seventy-one-year-old Comstock fell ill

immediately after William Sanger's trial and died soon after, ending the long reign of a one-man morality police force. His laws, however, endured.

The *Woman Rebel* case against Margaret Sanger was dropped eventually. But she suffered a much more painful loss: Her youngest child, five-year-old Peggy, died of pneumonia soon after she returned from Europe.

Sanger found her focus in redoubling her efforts to make birth control available.

On October 16, 1916, she opened America's first birth control clinic in an immigrant neighborhood in Brooklyn, New York. It was, she knew, a direct violation of state law.

Over the next few days, more than four hundred women, many

Women with babies in carriages wait outside Sanger's new birth control clinic in October 1916.

with babies in carriages, lined up to get information about how to prevent another pregnancy. The cost was ten cents.

"It is wrong to keep these women in ignorance," she told a reporter. "Why should not that poor, worn-out woman possess the knowledge which is common property in the homes of the wealthy?"

The state disagreed. At 2 p.m. on October 26, a female detective and two male officers came to shut down the clinic. Sanger, her sister Ethel Byrne, and an aide were arrested for imparting birth control information, mostly about items available at drugstores, like condoms and pessaries, which were inserted into the vagina to block the opening of the cervix. Sanger, who relished a good fight, lost her temper, yelling at the female officer, "You are not a woman. You are a dog!"

Sanger and Byrne were tried, convicted, and sentenced to thirty days in jail.

World War I would soon dominate American daily life. Realizing the threat of sexually transmitted infections to the military, the United States began to provide condoms to soldiers. Attitudes were shifting.

Sanger appealed her conviction, and in 1918, a New York appeals court judge reached a new conclusion: A doctor could prescribe birth control to cure or prevent disease, though not to prevent pregnancy. He upheld Sanger's conviction because she wasn't a doctor. But his decision opened the door for her to try another clinic.

The Sangers' marriage, long strained, ended in 1921, and in 1922, Margaret married Noah Slee, a wealthy businessman who adored her and helped bankroll her mission. In 1923, she opened a birth control "research clinic." During the 1920s, she founded the American Birth Control League to provide research and information about birth control, edited the *Birth Control Review* magazine, and helped open clinics in almost two dozen cities nationwide.

In 1932, Sanger and her lawyer, Morris Ernst, finally found a way to challenge the federal Comstock Act.

One day, U.S. Customs officials intercepted a package shipped to Sanger for testing; it contained cone-shaped rubber diaphragms, or pessaries. Spotting an opportunity to make a point, she arranged for more of the devices to be shipped to her clinic's doctor, Hannah Stone. When those were confiscated, too, Sanger launched a legal challenge, which became known as *United States v. One Package of Japanese Pessaries*.

In 1936, a federal judge ruled that the devices were legal if they were used for the health of patients. An appeals court upheld the ruling, effectively overturning the federal Comstock ban on sending contraception through the mail.

The next year, the American Medical Association formally recognized birth control as part of the practice of medicine and committed to teach birth control methods in medical schools.

Without question, Sanger was a birth control revolutionary. But she remains controversial because of her affiliation with the eugenics movement, which promoted the idea that society could be improved through better breeding.

The eugenics movement took root around the turn of the century with the notion that personality traits like intelligence, criminal behavior, and "feeblemindedness" were inherited, as were diseases like epilepsy. The theory was promoted as science, though genetics was little understood at the time.

It gained widespread popularity: Prominent philanthropists such as the Rockefellers and Carnegies funded eugenics groups. A range of Americans, including presidents Theodore Roosevelt and Woodrow Wilson, and W. E. B. Du Bois, a notable civil rights leader, embraced some of the ideas.

Some eugenics supporters used the theory to perpetuate white supremacy. Some eugenicists wanted American-born white women to reproduce more, and some wanted immigrants, African Americans, and the poor to have fewer children.

Sanger, however, wanted voluntary birth control for all women. Regardless of one's race or class, she believed all women should be able to control when they had children. She helped open a birth control clinic in New York City's Harlem neighborhood and worked to launch a pilot project, supported by prominent African American leaders, that opened clinics for black women in Tennessee and South Carolina in the late 1930s.

Some critics have charged that her intent was racist because the clinics aimed to reduce black births. The race and gender scholar Dorothy Roberts disagreed. True, Sanger wanted white leaders to run the clinics rather than black managers. But Roberts concluded that Sanger "was motivated by a genuine concern to improve the health of the poor mothers she served rather than a desire to eliminate their stock."

Still, Sanger also believed that women with low intelligence or "inherited" diseases like epilepsy should not have children. Facing fierce opposition from the Catholic Church and others, she also was willing to join forces with more openly racist eugenicists, hoping that they would help birth control become more mainstream.

The broader eugenics movement helped lead a dozen states to adopt laws allowing men and women who were confined to institutions as "mental defectives" to be forcibly sterilized—that is, to undergo surgical procedures that would prevent them from ever having more children.

In Virginia, seventeen-year-old Carrie Buck became a test case. Her foster parents committed her to the state's Colony for Epileptics and Feebleminded after she was raped by a family member and became pregnant. The state asked a court to allow a doctor to sterilize her. An expert witness, a prominent eugenicist, concluded Buck was feebleminded, as was her mother and infant daughter. Her illegitimate pregnancy, he said, typified a "low grade moron."

The U.S. Supreme Court in 1927 upheld the state's right to sterilize her, saying it would be better for society. "Three generations of imbeciles are enough," wrote Justice Oliver Wendell Holmes Jr. in the chilling decision.

By the mid-1940s, more than forty thousand people had been forcibly sterilized under

Carrie Buck and her mother, Emma, in 1924.

state laws, with California and Virginia accounting for half of them.

California's sterilization efforts were so aggressive that Nazis in Germany looked to them in creating laws that justified the sterilization of more than two hundred thousand allegedly feebleminded people. Later, they were used to support the massacre of millions of Jews, gays, and others in the Holocaust. Not surprisingly, eugenics fell out of favor in the run-up to World War II.

But the eugenics movement left a complicated legacy. It helped change the reasons for birth control from increasing women's rights to controlling the population, which was inextricably tied to racial issues.

In North Carolina, for instance, Dr. Clarence Gamble, an heir to the Procter and Gamble fortune, agreed to fund a large, statewide effort to establish birth control clinics for poor black and white women in the late 1930s. Gamble believed in contraception for the less fit and a higher birth rate for college graduates, and he wanted to reduce the number of black people receiving public assistance.

Despite the reasons behind the clinics, black women also wanted access to the same options as white women. Fifty women showed up the day a clinic opened in a cotton-farming area, including a woman who had delivered six children in seven years.

Neither Sanger's programs nor the North Carolina effort forced black women to use birth control or threatened them if they didn't. But the experiences, treatment, and attitudes toward black women and white women were worlds apart.

PREGNANT PAUSE:
When the Rabbit Died

If quickening was no longer proof of pregnancy, how—and when—did a woman know for sure that she was expecting?

That was a tricky question until at least the 1930s. Other than the obvious symptoms of missing monthly menstruation and feeling tired or nauseous, there was no formal confirmation, though for a time several hundred years ago, so-called piss prophets in Europe thought they could tell based on the color of a woman's urine or how it mixed with wine.

Scientists didn't identify the hormones tied to fertility and pregnancy until around the beginning of the twentieth century. The first real pregnancy tests, developed in the late 1920s, called for injecting rodents, then rabbits, and, finally, frogs with a woman's urine to see if pregnancy hormones caused changes in the animal's reproductive system. The tests took days or weeks and weren't always accurate.

Unfortunately, to determine the results of the test, the animal also had to be dissected. ("The rabbit died" was an old-fashioned way of saying someone was pregnant.)

Animal testing was used until the 1960s, when scientists devised biochemical tests. Even then, there were false positives. Finally, in the early 1970s, researchers came up with an accurate test, though a visit to a doctor's office was still required.

In 1977, the first home tests were sold under the name e.p.t, for "early pregnancy test." They required mixing chemicals and waiting two hours, but they allowed women to make the discovery in private. Today, home pregnancy kits require only urine and produce an almost immediate response.

A CRIME

World War II–1960

As they were training to be doctors, both Alan Guttmacher and Edgar Keemer were taught that abortion was wrong, something that good doctors didn't do, except to save a woman's life. Then, as young doctors, they both faced painful abortion decisions that changed their lives.

Guttmacher, who was white, became one of the nation's most highly regarded obstetricians and a prominent spokesman for women's health and abortion reform. But for years, he declined to support abortions that weren't "therapeutic," or approved by a committee of other doctors for health reasons.

Keemer, who was black, chose a different path, agreeing to provide abortions in his Detroit office to the women who came to him—an illegal abortionist in the eyes of society. Other doctors referred patients to him but shunned him both professionally and socially. Though he believed he was helping preserve women's lives, the state saw him differently. He was arrested and convicted and spent time in prison.

What both doctors agreed on was that the official medical establishment's approach to abortion favored white women with connections and pretty much ignored everyone else.

As a new doctor at the Johns Hopkins Hospital in Baltimore in the 1920s, Guttmacher was asked to help a pregnant fourteen-year-old girl whose father had sexually abused her. The Children's Aid Society asked him to end the pregnancy.

Guttmacher was "fired with moral indignation" that a young teen would have to carry and deliver her father's baby. He begged the obstetrics chief to let her have an abortion at the hospital.

But abortion was illegal in Maryland except to save a woman's life. This girl was healthy. The obstetrics chief wouldn't approve an abortion unless the Baltimore district attorney would say in writing that the procedure would be allowed.

The district attorney, however, wasn't about to authorize someone to skirt the law. But he told Guttmacher that he wouldn't investigate if an abortion were performed.

That wasn't enough for Guttmacher's boss. The girl later gave birth to her father's child.

Soon after, Guttmacher said, the wife of one of his fellow doctors was allowed to have a legal, "therapeutic" abortion at the hospital because of her health. The issue? She was underweight, so the reason listed was "severe malnutrition."

The obvious discrimination between how women of different social classes and races were treated made a deep impression on Guttmacher, the son of a rabbi and a mother who became a social worker. The common saying at the time, he recalled, was "the rich get richer and the poor get children."

He came to believe, he wrote later, that "abortion, above all else in American medicine, reeked of class privilege. Money could, and still can, buy a safe abortion, but poverty purchases butchery and death."

From his Baltimore base, Alan Guttmacher became something of a radical. He volunteered his services to the Planned Parenthood Federation of America, the successor to the American Birth Control League. He also treated women who had not been able to get pregnant, becoming an early practitioner of artificial insemination. He believed women should know about their bodies, and he wrote several books explaining fertility, pregnancy, and fetal development, starting with *Life in the Making* in 1933.

Dr. Alan Guttmacher in the 1950s.

In 1942, Guttmacher pushed for a change to abortion laws that would allow doctors to consider cases where pregnancy threatened a woman's health, not just her life. Already, he noted, 100,000 to 250,000 criminal abortions took place every year in New York City alone because of hospitals' rigid rules. The "holier-than-thou attitude of the medical profession in regard to this problem is revolting," he said.

Starting around the same time, many hospitals changed their procedures and created "therapeutic abortion" committees of three or more doctors—nearly always men—who would decide whether an abortion was appropriate under state law and the hospital's standards. Often, the committees allowed women to have abortions but then also required that they be sterilized, especially if they were poor. If they couldn't have more children, they wouldn't ask for an abortion again.

Once the committees were in place, the number of legal abortions the hospitals performed dropped, and then fell further in the 1950s and 1960s, to as few as one a year. "The fewer abortions, the better we look," one Philadelphia hospital administrator said.

Guttmacher supported the change because it formalized the process. But it also meant even fewer women had access to a legal abortion. Each hospital committee had a different standard for what threatened a woman's life, Guttmacher said later. One would consider cases of rape, while another would not. A hospital might allow an abortion if a woman was exposed to rubella (also then called German measles) in the early months of pregnancy, which was linked to birth defects. Others would turn her away.

Overall, the women who did get approved were overwhelmingly white and able to pay. Public hospitals that served the poor performed very few therapeutic procedures.

In response, even more women sought illegal procedures,

which were estimated at perhaps one million or more a year after World War II. That demand encouraged all kinds of people—barbers, salesmen, surgery technicians, and hospital attendants—to perform abortions for a fee and persuaded more women to try to abort themselves, sometimes with horrific results. Los Angeles County Hospital treated more than two thousand women a year with abortion-related complications in the mid-1950s, while Chicago's Cook County Hospital saw more than three thousand women a year. The number of cases was even higher in the 1960s.

When Edgar Bass Keemer Jr. was a young doctor in Indiana, a nineteen-year-old woman came to him, begging for an abortion. Her father was prominent in town, and she didn't want to embarrass him. Keemer, like Guttmacher, had been taught that abortion was a terrible thing. He turned the young woman down and urged her to talk with her father.

Soon after, the woman, an excellent swimmer, died from drowning.

The next time a young woman came to him seeking an abortion, he agreed to do it.

By the 1940s, he had set up his practice in Detroit,

Dr. Edgar B. Keemer Jr., around the time of his graduation from Meharry Medical College, in 1936.

Michigan, mostly serving inner-city black and white women who had few choices. Early on, police ignored such doctors unless a woman died. But after World War II, law enforcement began to crack down on abortion providers, raiding their offices and tracking down their patients to testify. Exactly why isn't clear. It may have been a backlash to a surge in abortion procedures, a response to the increased independence of women during the war, or a law-and-order mind-set in the 1950s.

In August 1956, Keemer was arrested with another doctor and two office assistants and charged with running a lucrative abortion ring. Police said they charged $200 or more per procedure, equivalent to $1,900 or more in today's dollars.

His lawyer urged him not to testify—and if the doctor did take the witness stand, he should deny performing abortions. But Keemer insisted on trying to explain that he performed abortions to preserve women's lives. But unlike hospital doctors, he didn't have the stamp of the medical establishment.

As his lawyer had predicted, a jury found Keemer guilty.

In a statement, the doctors accused the court of asking the jury to "play doctor" and determine whether the women had been properly diagnosed and treated. "We are guilty," they said in a statement, "guilty of conspiring, agreeing to and advising and doing any and everything in our knowledge as doctors to alleviate physical and mental suffering, improve health, and save the lives of every patient that had confidence enough to consult us professionally."

Keemer served fourteen months in prison and lost his medical license. For a time, he moved to New Jersey. But in the early 1960s, he won his license back, returned to Michigan, and began doing abortions again.

In 1952, Guttmacher left his hometown of Baltimore to become director of obstetrics and gynecology at New York's Mount Sinai Hospital. There he tried, only somewhat successfully, to be sure women who didn't have money had the same access as women who did. Still, he wrote in *Redbook* in 1959, "After thirty-odd years of medical practice, I am convinced that the abortion laws in the United States make hypocrites of all of us."

As the gap between state abortion laws and reality grew in the 1950s, doctors and lawyers began to discuss whether the current laws should be changed.

In April 1955, Planned Parenthood Federation of America and its medical director, Dr. Mary Steichen Calderone, convened the nation's first in-depth conference on abortion, bringing forty-three men and women together to discuss legal, medical, and human aspects of "a socially pressing and tragic problem." The gathering provided detailed statistics on legal and illegal abortions and abortion deaths, as well as insights into how white, well-off women had far more options than black and poor women, and how difficult the problem was.

"I know the terrific frustration of a woman who wants a child and cannot have one," said Sophia J. Kleegman, an infertility expert and obstetrics and gynecology professor at New York University's medical school, during one discussion.

But, she said, "it does not compare with the intensity of emotion and determination of the woman who does not want a child, is pregnant, and *won't have it*. I have learned that such a woman, on the private practice level, determined to have an abortion, usually finds some way of getting it."

Often, she said, women pay exorbitant prices, as much as $1,000 or $1,500, to end their pregnancies. "I firmly believe," she told the group, "that you will never be able to prevent illegal abortions by restrictive legislation in the case of women who want them and can afford to pay for them."

One of the star presenters was George Lotrell Timanus, a doctor who performed abortions in Baltimore, Maryland, from the late 1920s until his arrest in 1950.

The tall, thick-haired, blue-eyed doctor of Swedish heritage said he performed thousands of abortions on women desperate to end a pregnancy, mostly married young women but also teens, nurses, and doctors' wives. Initially, Timanus said, he charged as little as $25, which later rose to $200. In the 1940s, he tried to retire. Area doctors urged him to continue, he said, but he increased his price to $400, to make the operation less attractive.

He also taught Johns Hopkins medical students how to do a dilation and curettage procedure, which was used for early abortions as well as to treat other conditions. During a D&C, a woman's cervix is dilated and a spoonlike instrument called a curette is used to carefully remove the contents of the uterus.

As was also true for Dr. Josephine Gabler in Chicago and Dr. Keemer in Detroit, Timanus got many referrals from local doctors; friends shared his name with friends.

In 1950, a dozen police officers raided his office, arresting Timanus, his staff, a woman on the operating table, and everyone in the waiting room, including two small children.

At his trial, his lawyers argued that he was legally performing abortions for the safety of the women, as allowed under Maryland law. The state argued that legal abortions were done only for certain diseases, not mental health reasons.

Over all the years he had performed abortions, Timanus told the conference, he had required that referring doctors send a letter stating that the woman needed the procedure. After his arrest, he wrote to 350 doctors who had referred patients to him, asking them to speak up for him at his trial. Not one responded.

He was found guilty and served four and a half months in prison. In the end, he faulted his colleagues' willingness to look the other way, rather than the legal system. "It was the profession that convicted me," he said, "in spite of the fact that they were the very ones who had used my services."

In 1959, a group of judges, lawyers, and legal scholars at the American Law Institute recommended that states change their laws to allow abortions if the mental or physical health of the woman was in danger, in cases of rape or incest, and if the fetus was likely to have serious birth defects.

In 1962, the institute included those recommendations as part of a major overhaul of the nation's criminal code that addressed issues from obscenity to insanity to abortion.

That same year, Guttmacher left his prominent post at Mount Sinai to become the president of Planned Parenthood and one of the world's chief advocates for access to birth control. He hoped that legal changes would give doctors more options and help reduce illegal abortions. But it would be years before any states adopted them—and even then, they would come up painfully short.

PREGNANT PAUSE:
Another Double Standard

Though women with private doctors or other connections often had more access to birth control and abortion than other women, doctors were reluctant to allow them to be sterilized so that they couldn't have more children.

White middle- and upper-class women who wanted to have their tubes tied—a procedure in which the fallopian tubes are cauterized—couldn't just ask. Typically, they had to get approval from a hospital's committee, presumably reflecting a belief that a woman's main purpose is to reproduce.

Many doctors and hospitals followed the "rule of 120," created by the American College of Obstetricians and Gynecologists. That guideline said a woman should not be sterilized unless her age multiplied by her number of children equaled 120. In other words, a thirty-year-old had to have four children or a twenty-five-year-old had to have five before she could be considered for a permanent fix.

The rule persisted until the early 1970s. (The rule did not apply to vasectomies, or male sterilization.)

The rule of 120 was often ignored, however, for women of color. In many hospitals in the 1950s and 1960s, in the South and elsewhere, doctors might decide on their own that a poor black or Puerto Rican woman had given birth to enough babies or couldn't afford to have more. The doctor might see "unusual bleeding" as a reason to remove a woman's uterus during a cesarean section delivery, leaving her unable to have more children. Or he might ask her during the pain of labor if she would like to have her tubes tied. She might consent but not understand what she had just agreed to until later. Sometimes, the woman was never asked for her permission.

Fannie Lou Hamer, a prominent Mississippi civil rights activist, went to her local hospital in 1961 to have a small uterine tumor removed. She woke up without a uterus. She called her hysterectomy a "Mississippi appendectomy" and said that she believed six of every ten black women who went to that hospital for something else were sterilized without their consent.

No formal statistics were kept. Many doctors performed sterilizations—or denied them—believing they were practicing good medicine.

Fannie Lou Hamer, 1964.

PREGNANT PAUSE:

A Short History of Birth Control: 1870s to 1950s

As people learned more about where babies came from, they also got more sophisticated about birth control.

The first condoms dated back to the ancient Egyptians in 3000 BCE and were probably made from animal skins.

By the time the United States was founded, condoms were made from animal skins or intestines or fabrics, such as linen, and tied on with a ribbon. They were neither comfortable nor dependable. (And if they were washed and reused, they got pretty stinky as well.)

That changed when Charles Goodyear created vulcanized rubber in the mid-1800s. By the later part of the century, thick, sulfur-smelling rubber condoms were widely available, until the Comstock Act made them hard to get. (That's why condoms are sometimes called "rubbers.")

Women had fewer reliable choices. Douches, including a watered-down Lysol disinfectant heavily advertised for "feminine hygiene," were used regularly during the first half of the twentieth century. Margaret Sanger even included diluted Lysol in her "Family Limitation" pamphlet. Women also could buy pessaries, like the Mizpah brand, at drugstores to support a drooping womb. It covered the cervix and could help prevent conception.

By the 1920s, improvements in rubber also led to better diaphragms, rubber domes connected to a round spring. A woman had to be fitted for the proper size and the diaphragms, filled with a spermicide jelly, had to be inserted before sex. They could be messy, but they prevented pregnancy and were popular in the 1940s and 1950s.

Modern-day latex condoms were introduced in the 1930s and were more comfortable and dependable than the rubber ones. After World War II, condoms were likely the most commonly used birth control devices.

As scientists learned more about ovulation in the 1920s and 1930s, they began to think they could predict when a woman was in a safe time for sex without conception. Counting days from a last menstrual period was known as the rhythm method, and the Catholic Church adopted it in the 1950s as a natural birth control method. Unfortunately, the failure rate was high because women don't ovulate on a fixed schedule.

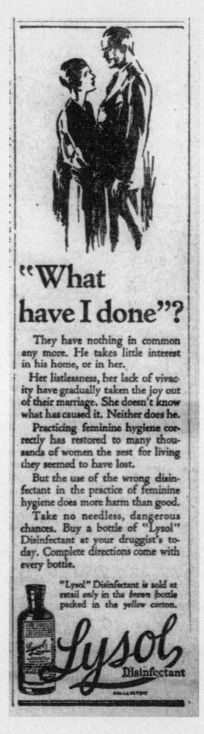

An advertisement for Lysol, 1930.

SHERRI CHESSEN

1962

S herri Chessen was just looking for relief from the wicked nausea of early pregnancy when she went rummaging in the cabinet above the kitchen sink for pills her husband had brought back from a trip to England.

Her decision to take as many as two dozen of those pills in the early summer of 1962 would change the course of her life, thrusting her family into legal, religious, and medical debates, and making her the most public face of the abortion issue in a century.

A British doctor had prescribed the medicine for her husband, Bob Finkbine, a high school history teacher, when he chaperoned a student trip and struggled to sleep. After taking just a few, Bob brought the rest home.

Chessen didn't think twice about taking them for her queasy stomach. At thirty years old, she was a busy working mother with four children, ages eighteen months to seven. Keeping her birth name of Chessen, Sherri was the popular host of Phoenix's *Romper Room*, a television program that, in the days before preschool and *Sesame Street*, introduced children under five to good manners, stories, and games. In fact, she had just won two regional Emmy awards for outstanding female performer in Phoenix television and for best children's program. Now she was looking forward to a fifth child—at least once the morning sickness went away.

In July, however, an article in the local newspaper caught her attention: Thalidomide, a tranquilizer and sleeping pill prescribed in Europe, was resulting in terrible birth defects. Children were being born without arms or legs and with other deformities.

Remembering her husband's pills, she called her doctor. He called London and reported back with bad news: The medicine she had taken was thalidomide.

After much gut-wrenching discussion, she and her husband decided to pursue a legal abortion.

Like nearly every state in the United States, Arizona's law banned abortion except to save the life of the mother. There was no exception for potential profound birth defects or for rape or incest.

To get a legal abortion, Chessen would have to prove her life was at stake. If she didn't have a serious physical problem like heart trouble, cancer, or difficulty delivering a baby, she had to argue she was so emotionally distressed that an abortion was the only solution. Then, a panel of doctors had to recommend the procedure.

Sherri and Bob met with doctors for evaluations and waited. During the weekend before the panel's decision, Sherri realized that another pregnant woman might think about taking the wrong drug and should be warned.

She called the local newspaper and shared her story about discovering the side effects of thalidomide, hoping to alert other women.

Sherri Chessen with three of her children, August 1962.

But the medical writer focused on the possible abortion, not the medication. On Monday, July 23, the front-page headline of the *Arizona Republic* read "Pill May Cost Woman Her Baby."

The couple wasn't identified, but the news story called attention to whether the hospital could legally perform the abortion under the state's strict law. On the same day the doctors' panel approved the procedure, the county attorney warned that he would have to charge the doctor or the hospital with a crime if someone filed a complaint.

With that threat, the hospital refused to schedule the abortion unless it was declared legal first. It filed a lawsuit against the county and the state, citing the request of Mr. and Mrs. Robert Finkbine.

If Sherri and Bob weren't distraught before, they were now. Television and newspaper reporters flooded their home. The *Arizona Republic* ran two stories on the front page and devoted another inside page to their story, describing her as a "small, wide-eyed, doll-faced brunette who is 'as cute as a bug's ear.'"

Their phone began to ring and mail began to pour in, offering advice, doctors' names in other states, and opinions about their decision.

"I'm right on the verge of breaking down," Sherri told reporters. "I don't think I could stand up under another six months of wondering about the baby."

She was about two and a half months pregnant, and she told interviewers that she was desperate to have the abortion before she felt the baby move. While the doctors of a century ago didn't think that was medically important, it mattered dearly to her. "If that happens and they still haven't taken the baby, I'm lost," she said.

To prove her procedure would be for health reasons, her lawyers set up appointments with two psychiatrists, she said in an interview. One wrote that the mother and successful television host was suicidal, though she told him that she would never do such a thing as a mother of young children. The other treated her rudely and concluded she should have an abortion. But he also said she should be sterilized and her children removed from her home because she wasn't fit to be a mother.

On July 30, a week after the first story ran, Judge Yale McFate dismissed the lawsuit; he couldn't rule on something that hadn't happened yet. "As a person," he said, "this judge is impelled to grant a hearing; as a judge, I cannot do it."

With the hospital unwilling to take the risk, Sherri had no legal options in the United States and just a few outside of it. Abortion was legal in Japan, but she was denied a visa because of the publicity. A few other countries had more lenient laws.

Soon after, Sherri donned a blond wig and dark glasses, and she and Bob headed to Sweden; their children stayed with relatives. "We feel it is better to have four children and a normal mother than five children and a disturbed mother," Bob told a reporter.

Bob Finkbine and Sherri Chessen, on a stopover on their way to Sweden.

Once there, Sherri had to run another obstacle course, meeting with Swedish gynecologists, social workers, psychiatrists, and radiologists. Two more weeks passed before they finally got approval and the pregnancy was ended.

The doctor told her the fetus lacked arms and legs. "It was not a baby. It was an abnormal growth," he said.

The international story touched a nerve with those who had strong religious beliefs about whether a fetus was a person or a potential person. Vatican Radio, speaking for the world headquarters of the Roman Catholic Church, condemned the procedure. "Morally and objectively," it said, ending the pregnancy "was a crime, and all the more because it was accomplished legally." It emphasized that the church opposed any abortion, even if the fetus was a danger to the mother, "because it is not its fault."

The Swedish Lutheran State Church took a different moral position, saying that "it is in accordance with the commandment of charity that the realized human value of the mother gets priority over the potential human value of the fetus."

Back in Phoenix, the couple received some ten thousand pieces of mail, many of them angry and accusing them of murder. Some letters threatened harm to their four children, and the Federal Bureau of Investigation provided protection for their first few weeks back home.

Even after the dust settled, Chessen didn't get her old position back at *Romper Room*. Advertisers stopped hiring her to do commercials. The TV station gave her a writing job and then an upbeat afternoon women's talk show, though she couldn't discuss anything controversial. When she got pregnant again, she had to quit and wasn't hired back. She had two more children, healthy ones, giving her the six that she had wanted all along.

She admitted that she made an unusual abortion advocate. Given her many children, a friend had joked, "You don't even look like you're for birth control."

But she continued to speak up for a woman's right to make the decision whether she should have a baby—and years before others were doing so, she called for change. On the way home to Phoenix that September, she called the nation's abortion laws "as archaic and outmoded as an ox cart in the jet age." And she made a daring prediction: "Some day in the future, America will regard abortions as they do in Sweden. There it is not a religious issue or a judicial issue, but a medical issue."

PREGNANT PAUSE:
Illegitimate

From a teenage lover, to an unwed mother
Kept undercover, like some bad dream
While unwed fathers, they can't be bothered
They run like water, through a mountain stream

—"Unwed Fathers" by John Prine and Bobby Braddock

For an unmarried young woman—especially a teenager—a pregnancy was a true crisis in the 1950s and 1960s. She was usually expelled from high school or college. She was nearly always labeled a "bad girl" or a "slut," who brought enormous shame to herself and her parents. Her child was called a bastard.

In the late 1950s, an estimated two hundred thousand

unmarried women got pregnant each year, climbing to more than three hundred thousand annually in the mid-1960s.

Some pregnant women and their boyfriends were pushed into quick marriages to avoid an illegitimate child. Some wealthy young women left the country for an abortion or tried to get an illegal abortion, though many young women didn't know what an abortion was or how to get one. Some had babies who were raised by family members.

African American families were far more likely than white families to support pregnant daughters and welcome their children into the family. At the same time, they were scorned for doing so. Young black mothers were frequently accused of being promiscuous and having children primarily to receive government financial assistance—even if neither was remotely true.

Meanwhile, white, middle-class parents shipped thousands of their pregnant teenage daughters to "maternity homes" or homes for unwed mothers in other towns and states to preserve the family's reputation. Sometimes, out-of-state family members or doctors took in pregnant girls as well until the babies were born and adopted.

Ann Fessler interviewed more than one hundred birth mothers for her 2006 book, *The Girls Who Went Away*. They told her that parents and clergy often insisted that they would be better off if they disappeared for a while, gave up their babies for adoption, and moved on. Between 1945 and 1973, about 1.5 million infants were adopted by those who weren't related.

Lydia Manderson was sixteen when she got pregnant. "My parents made the decision for me to go to a home," she said many years later.

The Salvation Army home an hour from her California home had twenty beds in a long room. Residents were known by a number, not a name. Manderson said that on arrival, she was checked for sexually transmitted diseases "because it was assumed I had them." In truth, she had only been intimate with her boyfriend.

At least two hundred such homes operated around the country, many run by the Salvation Army, the National Florence

Crittenton Mission, and the Catholic Church, and mostly for white women. The residents often had chores and could continue their schoolwork.

One woman, a college graduate, said she came to believe "what we were really doing was producing babies for this home to market."

She tried to see herself as "just breeding babies for someone else" rather than as a mother who was abandoning her child. But the guilt was powerful. "For months after I left the home," she said, "I'd wake up in the night crying and sort of rocking my pillow."

There was no preparation for childbirth, and the mothers often were left alone at the hospital. "The birth was humiliating," said Nancy Horgan, who was seventeen when she got pregnant. After being in labor for hours, she remembered being "taken to a big room and strapped to the delivery table." She could see her child being born in a reflection in the lamp overhead. But when attendants realized she was watching, they tipped it so she couldn't see.

While many young mothers willingly agreed to an adoption, some felt like they were forced or tricked into signing legal papers.

Those who wanted to keep their children were labeled selfish, immature, and sometimes mentally ill. In the mid-1960s, about 40 percent of unwed white mothers gave up their infants for adoption, compared with fewer than 2 percent of unwed African American mothers.

After the adoption, Fessler found that many of the birth mothers ached to know more about the children they delivered. They remembered their birthdays, and for years they searched crowds for a young person who looked like them.

When adoption laws changed years later, many of the women reconnected with their children in tearful reunions and built family bonds. "I lost this relationship so many years ago, and now here it is," Manderson said of reconnecting with her son. "It has come back to me."

ESTELLE GRISWOLD

1960–1965

Sherri Chessen was pushed into the spotlight when she faced a personal crisis. But Estelle Griswold had to intentionally step into the headlines to try to blast away the remains of Comstock's legislative legacy.

Griswold became director of the Planned Parenthood League of Connecticut in 1954, though she was an unusual choice. She was raised in the Catholic Church, which considered birth control a sin. She had trained to become a singer; lived in France, Holland, and Germany; and worked to help resettle refugees after World War II.

Griswold wasn't able to have children and didn't even know what a diaphragm was. But now fifty-three years old and living in New Haven, Griswold's cluelessness about birth control wasn't her biggest challenge. The real problem was that the league wasn't able to do anything.

In many states, Planned Parenthood had long helped married women with what it gently called "family planning"—a more socially appealing name for birth control. But Connecticut still had its "Barnum law," championed in 1879 by P. T. Barnum, the circus promoter who was also a state lawmaker. While the Comstock Act had banned mailing contraception, the Barnum law went much further: It actually banned the use of birth control.

Since 1923, Margaret Sanger and other birth control advocates had fought to get the Connecticut legislature to repeal or at least modify the law. But year after year, Catholics and their church leaders would rally to defend the law, sometimes making far-fetched arguments. "Psychiatrists have noted that the problem child's behavior can be traced to the emotionally unstable and sexually frustrated mother using birth control measures," one Hartford doctor testified in 1955—without citing any proof. The year after Griswold joined Planned Parenthood, lawmakers again refused to change the law.

To bypass the law, Griswold created a contraception referral service that made doctors' appointments and set up transportation for married women at a Planned Parenthood clinic in Port Chester, New York. Later, clinics in Mount Kisco, New York, and Providence, Rhode Island, were added. In keeping with the moral standards of the times, the service wasn't available to single women.

Thousands of women were helped, though having to travel was inconvenient for those who didn't have the money or the contacts to convince a private doctor that they needed birth control for their health.

At the least, the service aided and abetted the use of birth control, but no law enforcement stopped them. Certainly, a violation of the law would be difficult to prove. The state, she said in an interview, was "not going to put a gynecological table at the Greenwich toll station and examine a woman."

But Griswold was also lucky that police never pulled her over: Her car trunk was full of contraceptives that she delivered to the out-of-state clinics.

With the legislature still appearing immovable, Griswold and her colleagues began to search for a lawsuit—again. Back in 1943, a doctor had challenged the law, saying that it interfered with his constitutional right to practice medicine and to prescribe contraception to those who needed it. But the Supreme Court shot down his argument for technical reasons, saying it didn't interfere with his liberty or property rights—though it might limit the rights of his patients.

This time, Griswold and other opponents of the law lined up several patients, using made-up names to hide their identity: Paul and Pauline Poe, Ralph and Rena Roe, Harold and Hanna Hoe, and Jane Doe. Pregnancy was a serious threat to the health of three of the women; each claimed that outlawing birth control denied them their constitutional right to life and liberty.

Like the 1943 case, *Poe v. Ullman* rose through the legal system to the Supreme Court. In 1961, the Supreme Court ruled, on a five-to-four vote, that there wasn't really a case. Rather than considering the Connecticut law itself, the justices said the state had never actually prosecuted women for taking birth control, so neither the doctor nor the patients had grounds to sue.

The decision underscored the difficulty in trying to challenge the constitutionality of a law: Lawyers had to find someone whose circumstances were a perfect fit for the questions at stake. Often, lawsuits appear to rise up organically out of one injustice or another. But, in fact, when lawyers want to challenge a constitutional question, they look carefully for just the right person and right situation that will lead to the outcome they want. As the two Connecticut cases show, however, courts won't rule on events that haven't happened yet.

At the same time, Planned Parenthood still could not dispense birth control there because it was against the law.

Griswold really had only one option: start a clinic to provide birth control and see if the law would be enforced.

Just as Margaret Sanger had done in 1916, the Planned Parenthood League in November 1961 opened the doors to a clinic in New Haven, with plans to see patients three times a week.

During the clinic's fourth session, two police officers showed up while the waiting room was full of women. Griswold was thrilled. She tried to make the most of the officers' visit. While one officer tried to take notes, she rolled out all the difficult medical terminology she could think of. She gave the other one a sample of each contraceptive on hand, a whole bagful, along with some informative and descriptive pamphlets and books.

On November 10, the clinic was shut down. Griswold and Dr. C. Lee Buxton, the clinic's doctor and a Yale Medical School professor of obstetrics and gynecology, were arrested, fingerprinted, and charged with violating the state's law forbidding birth control.

In the days after the shutdown, Griswold and Buxton told reporters that they believed the law was inconsistent and unnecessary. Condoms for men could be purchased at drugstores because

Estelle Griswold and Dr. C. Lee Buxton (in the center) talk with their lawyer, Catherine Roraback (left), during their Connecticut trial for dispensing birth control.

they had a health benefit: They could prevent sexually transmitted diseases. (Even so, they were kept under the counter, putting buyers in the awkward position of having to ask for them.) A private doctor could legally prescribe birth control to a female patient by saying it was for a medical reason. Yet a woman couldn't go to a public clinic to be fitted for a diaphragm.

Buxton pointed out another contradiction: Connecticut allowed a woman to have an abortion if her life was in danger, but it would not allow her to prevent a pregnancy that might kill her.

Further, said a sharp-tongued Griswold, the state couldn't truly enforce the ban on birth control even "if they put a policeman under every bed in Connecticut."

Griswold and Buxton were tried in state court in January 1962. A detective was called first. Griswold recalled that a lawyer asked,

"'Well, what did she explain to you?' And he said, 'She explained plenty.'"

The courtroom buzzed when all the contraceptive devices were displayed.

Griswold's and Buxton's lawyer argued that their free speech had been denied. But after a daylong trial, the two were found guilty and fined $100 each.

As the case moved through the appeals process, both contraception and the role of women in America were undergoing something of a revolution. For years, the most reliable products had been condoms and diaphragms, which were messy but effective if used properly and regularly. But Margaret Sanger always dreamed of the possibility of a pill, and in the 1950s, with the help of a wealthy widow and an independent scientist, she helped launch its development. In 1960, the U.S. Food and Drug Administration approved the sale of Enovid, the first birth control pill and perhaps one of the first daily medicines for prevention rather than a cure.

Early versions called for a pill to be taken daily for twenty days and then stopped for about a week. The birth control pills contained high doses of hormones, which could cause blood clots, headaches,

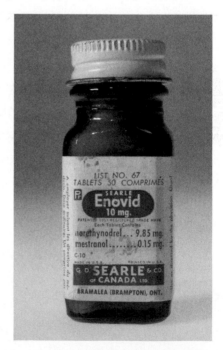

Enovid, introduced in 1960, was the first birth control pill.

and weight gain. The pills—which later became known simply as *the Pill*—were pricey, about $11 a month, the equivalent of almost $100 in today's dollars.

Still, this new drug was far more reliable than any option had ever been and could be taken privately and at a convenient time separate from the heat of romance. There was no relying on a man to put on a condom or pull out during intercourse.

The only catch: Young women had to remember to take it. That was partly solved in 1963, when drugmakers introduced a numbered, circular pill dispenser that helped women better track whether they had taken their medicine that day.

Over time, manufacturers were able to greatly slash the hormone dosages, reducing the side effects and the cost but not the reliability. By 1962, more than 1.2 million American women were taking the Pill, a number that exploded to more than 6.5 million by 1965. By then, the price had dropped to about $2.25 a month, or about $20 today.

The introduction and popularity of the Pill—and the slow pace of Griswold's case—coincided with a sea change in the attitudes and demands of American women. On the heels of the civil rights movement, women began to challenge long-entrenched sex discrimination that allowed companies to pay them less than men and restricted them to a handful of poorly paying jobs, like nursing, teaching, and secretarial work.

After the Equal Pay Act of 1963, which called for equal pay for equal work, and the Civil Rights Act of 1964, which outlawed racial and sex discrimination in the workplace, women demanded the chance to compete for better jobs traditionally reserved for white men.

For too long, they had been treated as second-class citizens who existed to make babies rather than as complete and competent people. Still, many employers forced women to quit or fired them when they became pregnant, practices that weren't outlawed until the 1970s.

The reality of a woman losing her job made an unplanned pregnancy an immediate financial crisis as well as a personal problem. Yet neither married nor single women in Connecticut or Massachusetts could legally get birth control. Vestiges of the Comstock-related laws still sat on the books in more than twenty other states, and later research showed that birth control was harder to get in those states, even if the laws weren't enforced.

After the initial trial, a Connecticut appeals court and the state Supreme Court of Errors both affirmed Griswold's and Buxton's convictions. Finally, in late 1964, the U.S. Supreme Court agreed to hear *Griswold v. Connecticut.*

For a question to come before the Supreme Court once was unusual enough. The nation's highest court was asked to consider more than two thousand cases in its 1964–65 term, but it agreed to hear fewer than 150. With two new justices appointed by President John F. Kennedy since the previous case and changing views about women's rights, the court was willing to review Connecticut's birth control law a third time.

The Supreme Court gallery was packed on March 29, 1965, the first day of the two-day hearing. Estelle Griswold and Lee Buxton were late to arrive and had trouble finding a seat.

In asking the Supreme Court to overturn the Connecticut law, Tom Emerson, a Yale law professor, used something of a novel approach: He argued that several parts of the Constitution gave married couples in Connecticut a right to privacy or a right to expect the state to stay out of their personal business.

The right to privacy wasn't a new idea. Back in 1890, future Supreme Court Justice Louis Brandeis and a colleague, Samuel Warren, wrote an article in the *Harvard Law Review* about such a right, drawing on another legal scholar's premise that individuals have a "right to be let alone." In 1928, then Justice Brandeis wrote in a dissent, disagreeing with a majority ruling, that the right to be let alone was "the most comprehensive of rights and the right most valued by civilized men."

In a general sense, the court had acknowledged a right to privacy in several previous cases as a form of liberty—but it had never actually based a decision on the right to privacy. In 1923, it ruled in a case called *Meyer v. Nebraska* that a state law that prohibited the teaching of foreign languages to elementary school students infringed on the liberty of parents and teachers. Then, in 1925, deciding *Pierce v. Society of Sisters*, the Supreme Court said that parents had a "fundamental liberty" to choose to send their children to private and religious schools instead of public schools.

In this case, Emerson argued, the state shouldn't have the power to tell married couples, in their most private, personal moments, whether they could use birth control. Nor should the moral views of one religion be forced on everyone.

Justices fired so many questions at Emerson during the allotted time for his argument that he hardly had time to make his case. Abortion came up when one justice asked, "Would your argument concerning these things you've been talking about relating to privacy invalidate all laws that punish people for bringing about abortions?"

No, Emerson answered, because an abortion takes place outside the home. "There is no violation of the sanctity of the home," he said.

Joseph Clark, an assistant prosecutor, had the difficult job of defending the state's law. He told the court that he believed the law existed "to reduce the chances of immorality," or the likelihood that using birth control might mean a woman would have sex outside of her marriage. He also noted that a couple could choose birth control that didn't require a doctor, such as the rhythm method, withdrawal, and abstinence.

Outside the Supreme Court, Clark had said he personally thought the law was foolish. But that didn't mean it was also unconstitutional. He added, "Legislatures have the right to enact stupid laws."

This time, the Supreme Court disagreed. On June 7, the last day of its 1964–65 term, the Supreme Court overturned Griswold's and Buxton's convictions. In a seven-to-two vote, the court concluded, for the first time, that the U.S. Constitution grants Americans a right to privacy—in this case, to married couples who wanted to use birth control.

Even so, the justices didn't fully agree on which parts of the Constitution granted this right. Writing for the majority, Justice William O. Douglas saw privacy throughout the Bill of Rights. The First Amendment, which guarantees freedom of speech, religion, and assembly, also implicitly covers a right to associate with one another without government intrusion, he wrote. The Third Amendment, which keeps soldiers from being housed in private

Estelle Griswold (left) and Cornelia Jahncke, president of the Connecticut Planned Parenthood League, celebrate their Supreme Court victory making birth control legal in the state for married couples.

homes without the owner's consent; the Fourth Amendment, which prohibits unreasonable searches and seizures; and the Fifth Amendment, which protects people from incriminating themselves in a criminal case, each encompasses some "zone of privacy." The Ninth Amendment says that people have additional rights beyond the ones specifically spelled out. And the Fourteenth Amendment forbids states from depriving people of liberty without due process of law or fair treatment.

In other words, Douglas wrote, each of these amendments

have "penumbras," or implied rights, that are "formed by emanations from those guarantees that help give them life and sub-
stance."

Douglas's awkward wording—"penumbras, formed by
emanations"—sounded mildly suggestive in a case involving marital sex and generated some snickers among the court's clerks,
new lawyers who assist the justices. But Douglas chose more elegant language in noting, "Marriage is a coming together for better
or worse, hopefully enduring, and intimate to the degree of being
sacred." Within that, he said, is "a right of privacy older than the
Bill of Rights."

Other judges concurred with the majority but waved off the
rights supposedly emanating from other amendments to focus
on the Ninth or Fourteenth Amendments.

Justices Hugo Black and Potter Stewart were the two dissenters. Black called the statute "offensive" and Stewart called it "an
uncommonly silly law." But they said they didn't see anything in
it that violated any part of the U.S. Constitution. Based on their
views, any change would have to come from state lawmakers.

During the long wait, Griswold and the Connecticut Planned
Parenthood League had been confidently preparing a new clinic
to finally provide birth control in the state. It opened in September 1965 in New Haven, and two more clinics followed soon
after.

Now sixty-five years old, Griswold retired from the state's
Planned Parenthood League at the end of 1965. But within a couple of years, she and Buxton were back at it, working together to
change abortion laws.

"I knew that there was another job to be done," she said later.

The debate over abortion was escalating as some doctors saw a need for more flexibility and women demanded more control over childbearing and reasonable access to safe procedures. There is no way to know how many illegal abortions took place across the country in the 1950s to the mid-1960s, especially since many were self-induced. But estimates ranged from 500,000 to as many as 1.2 million a year.

Some experts said 500 to 1,000 women died each year from complications—often women of color. Most of them were unable to pay a skilled abortion provider so they went to cheap, unskilled providers or tried to abort themselves. In the mid-1960s, nearly all of the women who died as a result of illegal abortions in New York City were black or Hispanic.

Buxton, who was in failing health, was even considering performing illegal abortions so he could be arrested again, though Griswold discouraged him from doing so. He passed away before much progress had been made. But the two of them left a substantial legacy, giving women new reproductive rights and helping give birth to a powerful and controversial legal doctrine of privacy rights.

In the aftermath of the Supreme Court decision, *Time* magazine made a spot-on prediction: "Lawyers can now spend years happily fighting over just what else the new right of privacy covers."

PREGNANT PAUSE:
Deaths from Abortions

During the 1960s and up to the present day, some abortion rights advocates said that as many as five thousand or ten thousand women died a year from illegal abortions when the procedure was a crime.

It's a dramatic figure—but it isn't accurate.

Antiabortion advocates have charged that the number was wildly exaggerated for political reasons. But mostly, it was just outdated.

The big number comes from a study of abortion deaths in the 1930s, before antibiotics were widely available. And the researcher may have stretched that number a bit.

By the 1950s and 1960s, tens of thousands of women still showed up at hospitals in need of medical care from botched abortions, but far fewer women died.

Government records showed that a few hundred women a year died from abortion-related complications from 1950 until the mid-1960s. Many researchers believe the real statistic was undercounted because women or their families lied about what happened and so the deaths were attributed to other causes.

Christopher Tietze, a doctor who specialized in abortion data, said in 1967 that the real number of abortion deaths a year was likely closer to 500, and probably no more than 1,000.

This part is certainly true: The numbers fell sharply once abortion became legal.

Government Statistics on Abortion Deaths

	Pregnancy-related deaths	Abortion deaths
1950	2,960	316
1955	1,901	266
1960	1,579	289
1965	1,189	235
1970	803	128
1975	403	27

Source: Centers for Disease Control/National Center for Health Statistics

PART II

REFORM

*In 1970, Assemblywoman Constance Cook sponsored a
bill to make abortion legal in New York. In the state
capital of Albany, she recalled, "I was just getting condemned roundly. I had to face incredible demonstra-
tions, antiabortionists would bring truckloads of kids
with roses in their hands. Nuns would stand in the
halls of the Capitol and cross themselves when I'd go
by . . . You know, it kind of gets to you after a while."*

*But in her home area of Ithaca, two funeral directors
approached her. "Separately and independently, they
came to me and said, 'Don't give up, you're on the
right track.' And one of them said, 'I've buried more
women than I ever want to remember under a false
certificate, who really died from an illegal abortion.'"*

—Ellen Chesler interview with Constance Cook,
January 13, 1976

CLERGY

1965–1970

For decades, many women frantic to end an unwanted pregnancy relied on a whisper network of friends and friends of friends who might know someone who could help. Anyone who had a connection was in great demand.

In the mid-1960s, the process became somewhat more formal. In San Francisco, Patricia Maginnis, an activist who spoke frankly of her three abortions, helped form the Society for Humane Abortion to fight for changes in abortion laws. Before long, women were calling, begging for help in securing a safe abortion. Maginnis compiled a list of doctors in Mexican towns on the U.S. border, like Tijuana and Juarez, who would do abortions. The group made copies with a mimeograph machine and handed out the lists on college campuses, on the streets of San Francisco, and in other communities where they spoke.

In Chicago, a male friend asked Heather Booth in 1965 for help

California abortion activist Patricia Maginnis, left, with supporters, 1970.

finding a doctor to provide an abortion for his sister. Booth, then a nineteen-year-old student at the University of Chicago and a civil rights activist, was able to locate a doctor near the university who would do the procedure.

A few months later, she got another call. Then, another and another—from white students, black women who lived in the neighborhood, and working-class women with families. The first doctor she found would sometimes stop doing abortions out of fear of being caught. Booth found another doctor, who insisted that his patients be blindfolded so they couldn't identify him. The two doctors charged $500 to $600—more than $4,000 in today's dollars—but were willing to do some procedures for free.

Over three years, Booth realized that even police officers were sending wives and girlfriends her way. Eventually, she would gather like-minded women to help her and form the Chicago group that became known as Jane.

Clergy members were also hearing from women who would do anything for an abortion. Many ministers began to see abortion as a medical problem, not a religious or political issue. James Ewing, a United Church of Christ minister at Washington University in St. Louis, Missouri, became distraught over the rumored death of a student who had sought an abortion. In 1965, he contacted a friend and medical school professor to ask about a better way to protect young women; the two began to guide those seeking abortions to safe procedures. A few denominations, including the Unitarian Universalist Association and the American Lutheran Church, already had called for easing abortion laws, and other faith leaders were growing increasingly concerned about the risks women were taking.

In Los Angeles, Huw Anwyl, a native of Wales and a United Church of Christ minister, first learned about abortion from a father who was determined to find one for his pregnant fourteen-year-old daughter. Without knowing the history, Anwyl didn't understand how a medical procedure could be illegal. "I said, how can it not be legal? If somebody has their leg amputated, it's not a legal issue."

Unable to find a doctor in Los Angeles, the father took his daughter to Tijuana, Mexico, and Anwyl accompanied them. They met their contact on the street, and he drove them to a home. Furniture was moved, an examining table was brought in, and the abortion was done in the front room.

"Well, my eyes were like saucers," Anwyl said later. "The girl came out of it fine, but what was going through my mind through all of that was that my little girl Jane, she was the same age. I couldn't get it out of my head: This could be Jane.

"This should not be."

Larry Lader, a journalist, became one of the nation's most visible abortion rights activists after writing a biography of Margaret Sanger. In 1965, his article for *New York Times Magazine*, "The Scandal of Abortion Laws," highlighted the large illegal abortion business and the nation's inconsistently applied laws. The next year, his book *Abortion* offered a clear-eyed study of the widespread underground practice and the pain the rigid laws inflicted.

"Abortion is the dread secret of our society," it began.

Phone calls and letters came in after the article appeared and multiplied as Lader promoted his book on radio and television. Desperate pleas filled Lader's mailbox. Women from out of state appeared at his apartment, asking for help finding a New York doctor right away. His phone rang during the day—and in the middle of the night. Lader committed to helping as many of them as he could, finding a doctor in the Washington, D.C., area, Milan Vuitch, and another who operated out of a New York City apartment.

In September 1966, Lader had lunch with Reverend Howard Moody of Judson Memorial Church in New York, a Baptist/United Church of Christ church in New York City's Greenwich Village neighborhood, and two Episcopal priests, one from New York and another from San Francisco. At some point, one of the ministers asked Lader how they could help.

"Organize the clergy to refer women to qualified doctors," he answered. The seed was planted.

As Lader recalled later, Moody was just the right person to lead the effort. Raised a Southern Baptist in Dallas, Texas, he started preaching from street corners as a five-year-old and was teaching Sunday school by fourteen. Moody attended Baylor University, a Southern Baptist school, with plans to go into the ministry. But he began to question his denomination.

At twenty, he dropped out and enlisted in the Marines just six months before Pearl Harbor. He served in the South Pacific during the war. After-

Howard Moody, inside Judson Memorial Church, 1962.

ward, he finished his degree in California and went to Yale Divinity School. Still sporting a crew cut, the hairstyle he would keep throughout his life, he became pastor at Judson Memorial in 1956. There, he won a reputation for social and political activism, tempered by a streak of realism.

After the meeting with Lader, Moody and a small number of clergy began to discuss the possibility of helping women, eventually expanding their group to a couple of dozen ministers and rabbis.

All of them needed to learn more. They asked women who had undergone abortions to share their experiences and what might have been helpful to them ahead of time. They talked with lawyers about potential legal issues and doctors about medical ones. A lawyer with the New York Civil Liberties Union urged the group to be public about their work so they wouldn't appear to be hiding anything.

At one memorable meeting, a doctor brought a life-size model of a woman's pelvic region and typical medical instruments. As the clergy watched, he demonstrated a dilation and curettage, or D&C. He explained when and why a woman might feel pain and showed how the cervix is dilated and the curved, spoonlike curette is used to gently scrape the uterus.

"The nervous jokes and incredulous questions made it fairly obvious that we had majored in theology and not biology," Moody wrote later. Only the presence of a female Methodist minister kept the demonstration from deteriorating into a bachelor party atmosphere, he said.

Lader attended the meetings and pushed the preachers to get to work. "He used to *shame* us," recalled one pastor. "He was very vocal, very in your face."

When the New York legislature failed to pass a bill that would loosen the state's abortion laws in March 1967, the clergy members realized they needed to act. The last of the decisions, and one of the toughest, was picking a name. They had agreed that they would talk with women about all their options, including adoption, keeping the baby, or abortion. But they disagreed on whether they would be the Clergy Consultation Service "on abortion" or "on problem pregnancies."

They worried that using "problem pregnancy" would leave the impression that they were discouraging abortions. So while abortion was still a word that was typically whispered in private, they finally decided to be direct. They would be the Clergy Consultation Service on Abortion.

On May 22, 1967, the *New York Times* ran a front-page story about a groundbreaking new service: Twenty-one Protestant ministers and Jewish rabbis would begin to refer women who wanted abortions to medical providers.

Moody, the spokesman for the group, said the clergy would "offer compassion" and "increase the freedom of women with problem pregnancies," which could mean helping her find a safe abortion or an adoption agency.

While the clergy weren't encouraging abortions, they also didn't share the Catholic Church's belief that the procedure amounted to murder. "There is a period during gestation," they said in a statement, "when, although there may be *embryo* life in the fetus, there is no living *child* upon whom the crime of murder can be committed."

Moody told the reporter that the ministers and rabbis did not think their actions would be illegal. But they also said that they believed "there are higher laws and moral obligations transcending legal codes," and that they had "a pastoral responsibility and religious duty to give aid and assistance to all women with problem pregnancies."

The initial plan called for two clergy members to be available each week. Women would call a phone number and get a recorded message with the names and phone numbers of clergy they could contact for meetings.

The first day, Rabbi Lewis Bogage of Central Synagogue in New York received thirty-five calls, and the phone kept ringing.

Women called from in and around New York but also from all over the United States, willing to travel to New York to get access to a caring person and a safe abortion.

At the recommendation of their lawyer, the clergy referred women only to abortion providers outside of New York. That way, if law enforcement wanted to prosecute the clergy for making referrals, they would have to cross state lines to do so. In addition, the group had decided to refer only to licensed physicians who used a local anesthetic or none at all, even though it would be more painful for the women; general anesthesia was deemed too dangerous in a doctor's office.

For all their good intentions, the clergy primarily counseled white women with financial means, leaving low-income women, often women of color, to fend for themselves. With no money to help those who could not pay, women had to be able to pay for their travel and abortion expenses. Initially, the procedure cost about $600, or more than $4,500 in today's dollars, though prices were negotiated down over time.

Arlene Carmen, a Jewish woman who was Judson Memorial's administrator, joined a couple of others in personally checking out abortion providers. Carmen rejected offices that were dirty or in neighborhoods where women wouldn't feel safe. The doctor had to be operating out of an office, not a motel, and needed to be pleasant and kind, not abrupt or condescending. If the office was acceptable, she pretended to be pregnant, going through the motions almost up to the time of the abortion, when she would then explain why she was there.

Over three years, Carmen figured she investigated about two dozen providers. During that time, clergy sent women to doctors in

Puerto Rico; Pennsylvania; Washington, D.C.; Montreal, Canada; New Orleans, Louisiana; and occasionally Florida. Some also were referred to Japan, and eventually, women in need of abortions after the first twelve weeks were referred to England.

Carmen witnessed a close call when she agreed to accompany a sixteen-year-old named Donna to Puerto Rico, with plans to visit other doctors while she was there.

The procedure seemed to take an unusually long time, and she heard scurrying in an adjacent room. Eventually, the doctor summoned her, taking her aside.

"Well," he said, "she died."

He paused. Carmen's legs wobbled. She thought she would collapse.

"But we saved her," he added.

The young woman was further along than thought, and the anesthetic caused such a fierce reaction that she had to be revived. The abortion wasn't performed. Instead, Carmen called the teen's father, who came to Puerto Rico to get her.

The experience led the clergy service to require women to get a note from a doctor confirming they were pregnant, with an estimate of how far along they were. But to the surprise of service members, a number of doctors refused to provide a note, fearful that they would be complicit in an abortion. So women had to go to a local clinic for an estimate—another delay and another cost.

At its peak, the clergy counseled about ten thousand women a year in New York. One survey of about six thousand five hundred women who consulted with the clergy found that about a third were Catholic, most were between eighteen and twenty-five years old, and at least half had failed to use birth control. In many cases, they said they had become pregnant the first time they had sex.

Within a year, the Clergy Consultation Service began to spread across the country. In Los Angeles, Reverend Anwyl helped launch a service in May 1968. After an article appeared in the *Los Angeles Times*, more than one thousand calls came in during the first two weeks.

Initially, the Los Angeles ministers sent women to Mexico and Japan, and later, clergy and other activists convinced local hospitals to perform more legal, therapeutic abortions, which qualified for state aid.

Clergy also formed referral services in Chicago, Philadelphia, New Jersey, upstate New York, and elsewhere. By the late 1960s, men and women of faith in twenty states were supporting women in search of safe, though illegal, abortions.

PREGNANT PAUSE:
Robert Douglas Spencer

Dr. Robert D. Spencer hung out his shingle in Ashland, Pennsylvania, in the 1920s, specializing in the diseases of local coal miners. Before long, a miner's wife asked if he could help her end her pregnancy, and he performed his first abortion.

After the first one, there were others. In time, word spread well beyond central Pennsylvania to New York and Washington, D.C., which were less than two hundred miles away.

The writer Susan Brownmiller first told a friend about him in the 1950s. When her friend reported back that his clinic was spotless, his manner was kind, and he charged her only $50,

Brownmiller added him to her address book. Later, she dramatically told another friend, "Really, I think of it as the telephone number of God."

Among East Coast college students, he was sometimes called "the angel of Ashland."

Spencer was a rarity among abortion providers, a regular doctor who charged as little as $5 or $10 at first. His nondescript three-story clinic included overnight beds because in the early years, black patients were turned away from Ashland's hotels. By the 1960s, his top price reached $100, far less than others'.

Women in different parts of the country faced different options. One study of a small Southern city in the later 1960s found five abortionists—a chiropractor, an antiques dealer, a midwife, a mechanic, and a doctor.

Spencer was arrested three times and tried twice, but juries acquitted him. Later, a town official explained, "There aren't too many people in this county he hasn't helped."

Spencer never tried to hide his abortion practice, though he stopped doing procedures for stretches at a time. But he was back in business in his late seventies, just before his death in 1969. He estimated he performed 30,000 abortions over his career, and he never regretted it. "I always figured a doctor is supposed to help people, to help the living," he said.

RIGHT TO LIFE

1965–1968

F ar from New York, change was coming—to the surprise of
nearly everyone.

As New York–area pastors were putting finishing touches on
the Clergy Consultation Service, lawmakers in Colorado, North
Carolina, and California were lining up support for bills that
would loosen the restrictions on state laws that allowed abortion
only to save the life of the mother.

The technical details came from the modest changes that the
American Law Institute had suggested years before. But there
was a powerful new motivation: a major outbreak of rubella, a
highly contagious childhood disease, in the mid-1960s.

Scientists had known since the 1940s that up to half of women
who were exposed to rubella during the first months of pregnancy
risked miscarriage or delivering infants with serious birth defects. The epidemic that spread across the country in 1964 and

1965 was devastating. An estimated 2,100 newborns died before or just after birth and 20,000 babies were born with congenital rubella syndrome, which caused blindness, hearing loss, and heart defects, as well as physical and mental disabilities. More than ten thousand women miscarried early in their pregnancies or sought legal abortions by going through hospital therapeutic abortion committees. (A vaccine wasn't available until 1969.)

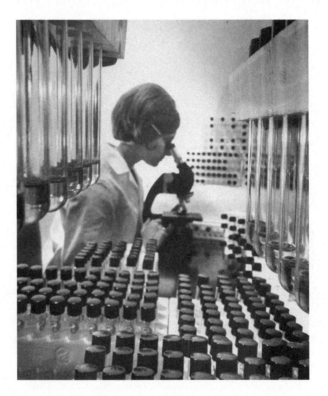

A lab technician at New York University Medical Center works on a vaccine for rubella, 1965.

In Colorado and North Carolina, lawmakers in April and May 1967 were able to fairly quickly adopt less restrictive laws—allowing abortion in cases of incest and rape, in the likelihood that a child would have birth defects, or to preserve the health or life of the mother. But California, where Catholics comprised one out of four residents, became a battleground.

There, many doctors had routinely asked hospital abortion committees for permission to perform abortions on women who had been exposed to rubella. To them, it seemed like good, compassionate medicine. True, the state's law allowed abortion only to save the life of the woman; rubella itself didn't threaten the lives of adults (though the fear of bearing a child with serious disabilities might be emotionally distressing). But the doctors operated under a belief that law enforcement wouldn't go after reputable physicians at reputable hospitals who went through a proper committee process.

That changed after *Life*, a national magazine, ran a cover story in spring 1965 featuring two pregnant women who made the difficult decision to have abortions. Dolores and William Stonebreaker had waited years until their finances improved to have a second child. But Dolores contracted rubella from their son very early in her pregnancy. At her husband's and doctor's urging, she decided to terminate it, though abortion was a sin in her Catholic faith.

The national publicity about rubella-related abortions, as well as stories in local newspapers, grated on Dr. James V. McNulty, a prominent Los Angeles obstetrician who also served on the state's medical board. At one California Medical Association meeting, McNulty insisted that physicians were "performing criminal acts," recalled one doctor. "He more or less shook his fist and implied he was going to get us."

In particular, McNulty believed that considering disabled infants to be a burden disregarded their human value.

After the *Life* article ran, state investigators went into hospitals in Los Angeles and San Francisco and asked for patient records on abortions. They interviewed (and secretly recorded) doctors about performing abortions on women exposed to rubella, even those who did only a few each year. Then, the investigators, using patient records, sought out the women who had abortions and interviewed them. The aggressiveness of the probe prompted many hospitals to completely stop performing rubella-related procedures.

After reviewing the evidence, prosecutors declined to file charges against the doctors. But in the summer of 1966, the State Board of Medical Examiners accused nine prominent San Francisco doctors of violating the state's abortion law. It threatened to revoke their licenses to practice medicine.

If McNulty had hoped to put an end to abortion in the state, he miscalculated. Doctors in California created a legal defense fund. Dozens of medical school deans and medical society leaders signed a legal brief in their defense.

More striking, the skirmish changed public opinion. In 1966, about two of every three Californians and about half the state's Catholics supported reforming abortion laws. A year later, almost three out of four Californians and about two of every three of the state's Catholics favored more liberal rules for abortion.

Reforming the abortion law had come up before the state legislature in the past and failed. But the rubella tragedy had changed the views of doctors, clergy, and citizens, who all supported more flexible policies.

Concerned, the state's Catholic bishops met in the fall of 1966 to debate strategies, in perhaps the first organized effort to challenge changes to abortion laws. One recommendation called for creating a citizens' committee with both Catholic and non-Catholic members to dilute the anger of abortion rights supporters who saw opposition as a Catholic issue.

In December, the bishops released a statement, "Thou Shalt Not Kill," calling abortion "the silent execution of innocent fetal life." Proposals that would allow for more abortions "stand contrary to the law of God as well as the laws of men," the statement said, concluding, "Our hope is that all men will preserve and care for the right to life of the unborn child."

That night, a group of Catholic clergy and lay leaders, along with a representative of a public relations firm, met to create the groundwork for one of the very first active Right to Life Leagues. The antiabortion group took its name from the Declaration of Independence's reference to man's right to life. But it also drew on the Catholic belief that an embryo has a right to live from the moment of conception. (Later, playing off the right-to-life idea, those opposed to abortion began to call themselves "pro-life.")

Soon after, a four-month budget of $12,600 (nearly $100,000 today) was put together, and Catholic leaders were urged to recruit prominent Protestant and Jewish lawyers, clergy, and businessmen to the new league while also organizing parishes to write letters detailing their opposition.

Lawmakers were bombarded with mail, but the overall effort wasn't very well thought out. In fact, Elizabeth Goodwin, vice chair of the league, took the group to task afterward for failing to put forward a cohesive case. Worse, one hundred women traveled to Sacramento to oppose a law intended to help women, but their recommendations were ignored. Not one woman was allowed to speak publicly.

Governor Ronald Reagan, a future president of the United States, had problems with the bill. Eventually, he admitted that he most opposed the clause that allowed the procedure if a child would be deformed. A disabled fetus should be protected, he insisted. But he also believed abortion was appropriate to protect a woman's health and in cases of rape and incest.

Newly elected California governor Ronald Reagan, his wife, Nancy, and their two children check out the governor's mansion in early 1967.

In a compromise, the exception for fetal disability was removed, and an abortion reform bill passed in June 1967. Reagan signed it soon after. (Later, as more and more abortions were performed for the mother's mental health, Reagan regretted signing the bill.)

Two years after they were charged, eight of the nine San Francisco doctors were reprimanded and their licenses were suspended for ninety days—although the suspensions were to be waived while they served a year of probation. Ultimately, courts overturned the penalties.

McNulty also softened his stance. "I don't think we should impose the Catholic view on the majority," he said in a 1967 interview. "I was just interested from a legal standpoint . . .

"Even though I'm Catholic—they always point that out—the law is the law."

For abortion reform advocates, it was a mixed victory. The attack on reputable doctors initially left many hospitals unwilling to approve abortions that would have been allowed before. To qualify for an abortion, a woman who had been exposed to rubella had to be considered suicidal by doctors. In addition, with more hurdles to jump, the cost of an abortion climbed. Illegal abortions in California continued for a time at an estimated rate of one hundred thousand a year.

Those opposed to abortion lost in the legislature. But a Right to Life group run largely—but not entirely—of Catholics had found a voice.

The swift progress in easing restrictive abortion laws rattled the U.S. leadership of the Catholic Church.

In April 1967, as new laws were being debated in Colorado, North Carolina, and California, the National Conference of Catholic Bishops voted to spend $50,000 (about $400,000 in today's dollars) on a nationwide education campaign aimed at halting any kind of abortion reform.

But the reform efforts already had momentum. In the weeks after that vote, all three states adopted their liberalized laws; similar campaigns were underway in more than two dozen other states. In addition, in June, the American Medical Association, which had helped make abortion a crime in the previous century, joined the call for easing the restrictions.

The leaders of the Catholic Church felt their long-held political clout slipping just as they were losing ground on a human rights issue they considered to be life-and-death. Perhaps just as disturbing to them, polls showed that more than half of the nation's Catholics disagreed with the church's position that all abortion was wrong. In church doctrine, abortion wasn't ever acceptable—not even in cases of incest or rape, since that meant taking an innocent life that had no say in its creation. If the mother's life was in danger because of cancer or heart disease, the church taught that it was best to try to save both lives.

Responsibility for the church's new education program opposing abortion fell to Father James McHugh, the thirty-five-year-old head of the U.S. Catholic Conference's Family Life Bureau. McHugh had some progressive ideas, including the belief that the church's stance against abortion should be tackled separately from the church's rigid opposition to birth control. After all, less than a decade after the introduction of the Pill, most Catholic couples were using contraception and ignoring the church's teaching. Further, challenging both birth control and abortion would likely alienate people of other faiths who might oppose abortion but supported contraception.

Though it wasn't said specifically, the Catholic Church's be-

lief that sex should occur only in marriage and only with the possibility of producing children was also becoming a tough sell. Young people were openly rejecting what they saw as outdated moral positions, such as waiting until marriage to have sex.

McHugh concluded that the more meaningful and productive argument was that human life from conception on had to be protected.

Father James McHugh in the late 1980s, around the time he became a bishop.

Through that lens, fighting abortion was a battle for human rights and the civil rights of the embryo.

As McHugh watched state legislatures wrestle with whether to change their abortion laws, he came to believe that the most effective way to stop changes to abortion laws was through local groups like California's Right to Life League, which was made up of bishops and laypeople, including some who weren't Catholic.

In 1968, two more states, Maryland and Georgia, relaxed their laws.

That June, in a letter to American bishops marked "Special Abortion Report," McHugh suggested revving up some tactics that had been successful in turning back changes in other states, including forming statewide committees and recruiting lawyers, doctors, and informed laypeople. Given the times, those doctors and lawyers were almost always men.

He encouraged the bishops to "educate our people of the moral evil of abortion as a private act, and of the threat to human dignity and the sanctity of life that is a consequence of liberalizing the law." He added that the bishops should focus on "the threat to public order" rather than focusing on the church's moral opposition to abortion.

He also urged them to form their own state Right to Life committees by the fall of 1968 so that they would be prepared for the next legislative session. In other letters, he added that the committees shouldn't appear to be a Catholic organization. Rather, he said, they should seek out "non-Catholics and other concerned citizens," even if the others wanted some exceptions, for instance, in cases of rape.

"It's best," he added, "if this group has no structural link" with the local diocese or the state bishops' conference.

To support the state and local groups and provide materials, a National Right to Life Committee was quietly created. McHugh based the new group in Alexandria, Virginia, separate from the Catholic Conference's offices in Washington, D.C., "so as to shift attention away from the so-called exclusively Catholic opposition."

In reality, though, the small, volunteer national committee was run from his Washington office. His personal assistant took on the additional role of executive secretary of the National Right to Life Committee. Beyond some internal documents, it isn't clear if outsiders even knew there was a national organization. There doesn't appear to have been any formal announcement or news coverage. When McHugh was quoted on a related issue, it was as the head of the Family Life Bureau.

Meanwhile, individual Right to Life groups popped up in a few states, like New York and Minnesota, usually started by devoted locals without initial help from the Catholic Church.

Amid growing public discussions and debate about birth control, abortion, and sexual morals, Pope Paul VI, on July 25, 1968, issued the encyclical *Humanae Vitae*, a formal declaration to Catholic bishops that translated to "Of Human Life."

Pope Paul VI.

Many Catholics had been hoping for a relaxation of the church's position, especially after the pope put together a commission in 1964 to study population issues, the family, and birth. Commission members, including bishops, theologians, doctors, and laymen—and even a few women—studied the subject for two years. They came to a surprising conclusion: The Catholic Church should allow the use of birth control.

But the seven-thousand-word *Humanae Vitae* declared that God's natural law teaches "that each and every marital act [of sexual intercourse] must of necessity retain its intrinsic relationship to the procreation of human life."

The encyclical conceded that there might be moral reasons to limit a family's size. But it reaffirmed that the rhythm method and abstinence were the only acceptable forms of contraception for Catholics. Anything else was prohibited.

In addition, he declared, abortions, "even for therapeutic reasons, are to be absolutely excluded," along with sterilization, permanent or temporary, for men or women.

The pope acknowledged that "perhaps not everyone will easily accept this particular teaching." That was true. The decision disappointed many Catholics, including some priests and bishops.

In the more than fifty years since, the Catholic Church has not changed this position. It continues to consider the use of medical birth control a moral wrong and opposes family planning efforts around the globe.

PREGNANT PAUSE:
Images

Around the time of the rubella story, *Life* magazine also published a photographic breakthrough: stunning images of embryos and fetuses.

The April 1965 issue featured enlarged embryos in development, titled "Drama of Life Before Birth." Swedish photographer Lennart Nilsson spent a dozen years creating the vibrant photo essay, which started with blown-up photos of a woman's microscopic, ripe egg and hundreds of racing sperm. The beginnings of human life were shown in various stages of development over twenty-eight weeks, until a fetus weighed a couple of pounds and was more than ten inches long.

Over the first eight weeks shown, an embryo became a fetus,

Antiabortion protestors hold up copies of *Life* magazine's photo essay during a demonstration at St. Patrick's Cathedral in New York, 1971.

growing cartilage and then developing a bone skeleton with defined fingers and toes. *Life* sold eight million copies of the issue with Nilsson's images, which later became a book, *A Child Is Born*.

A baby reaches full term, with working lungs, a developed brain, and a complete digestive system, at about forty weeks from a woman's last menstrual period. Or, put another way, roughly thirty-eight weeks from the day the sperm and egg combined—two weeks longer than a typical school year.

Nilsson took one photo of a fetal face using a tiny endoscope—a medical instrument that was inserted into the uterus—with an electronic flash. But most of the photos were of embryos and fetuses that "had been surgically removed for a variety of medical reasons." The reasons weren't disclosed.

Some embryos were separated from their amniotic sacs for the photos; sometimes fluid was added, or the placenta, which provides nourishment, was peeled back to make better, clearer images. A University of Cambridge exhibit suggested that Nilsson posed the images, for instance, putting a fetus's thumb into its mouth in one particularly poignant photo.

When pressed for his opinion, Nilsson avoided the question of when human life begins. "It depends on yourself," he said. "I'm a journalist telling you things. It's my mission in life."

Within a few years, Right to Life groups and others opposed to abortion would embrace these oversized images and other photos—sometimes staged or edited for dramatic effect—to underscore their belief that the embryos and fetuses are human life and to protest that abortion is murder. More than sermons and proclamations, what really convinced many to oppose abortion were photographs, not words.

There was, however, an omission in Nilsson's work and the other images. Nowhere in the photos of an embryo's development was the presence, or even the existence, of the living woman who carried it and who, in most cases, would have been responsible for caring for it after birth.

REPEAL

1966–1970

The late 1960s were some of the most tumultuous and unsettling years in modern American history. Protests against the unpopular Vietnam War turned angry and violent. Assassins' bullets ended the lives of civil rights leader Martin Luther King Jr. and Democratic presidential candidate Robert F. Kennedy in 1968. Women organized in large numbers for the first time since the 1920s to demand fairer treatment. And some African American men, impatient with what seemed like glacial progress of the nonviolent civil rights movement, called for more aggressive and pointed action.

Amid the upheaval, more women and their male allies began to fight for a more radical approach to abortion restrictions. They were done tinkering. Instead, they demanded that women have control over their own bodies and that abortion laws be eliminated altogether. As the decade progressed, they demanded to be heard over the traditional establishment of mostly white, mostly male lawyers, doctors, church leaders, and legislators.

In California, the Society for Humane Abortion, run by the outspoken Pat Maginnis, had seen its mailing list explode from fifty in 1964 to fifteen thousand by the end of the decade. As an early believer that a woman has a right to choose whether to continue a pregnancy, Maginnis had never supported modest changes to the law.

Most women who wanted an abortion still were seeking out illegal providers. Those who had the money and time to work through the hospital committee system discovered other, unexpected penalties: Women who were declared suicidal to qualify for an abortion might see their life insurance canceled. Their health insurance costs might spike or their driver's licenses might be revoked because of their mental health records, Maginnis said.

In Chicago, Caroline "Lonny" Myers, an anesthesiologist and mother of five, joined with Don Shaw, an Episcopal priest; Spencer Parsons, a Baptist minister who was dean of the Rockefeller Chapel at the University of Chicago; and others to form a new group aimed at repealing the Illinois law. Thinking the word *repeal* was too radical, they called themselves Illinois Citizens for the Medical Control of Abortion. (Among their donors was the Playboy Foundation, which supported reproductive rights and First Amendment freedoms, even though it was created with funds from the men's magazine famous for its photos of mostly nude women.)

Myers similarly had no patience for the timid reform laws that allowed abortions only under certain circumstances. With those, she said, the result still was "a bunch of men deciding for a woman" whether she should have a baby.

In fact, the new laws that had been adopted in several states were not working very well. In Colorado, lawmakers had fretted that the legal changes would turn the state into an abortion mill. Instead, the reforms mostly allowed doctors to legally do what they had been doing before. Close to half the state's hospitals declined to do any abortions because of religious reasons. When one of the Clergy Consultation Service's rabbis moved to Colorado from New York, he was stunned to find "the problem here was the same as in New York," despite the new law. So he set up an abortion counseling service there as well.

The number of legal abortions climbed to about four hundred a year after the law was changed, up significantly from fifty-one before. But most abortions performed there were still illegal.

"We tried to change a cruel, outmoded, inhuman law—and what we got was a cruel, outmoded, inhuman law," lamented Richard Lamm, a Colorado state representative at the time and later the state's governor. "We still force women either to have a baby or to have an illegal abortion."

The slow pace of change even changed the mind of Alan Guttmacher, the president of Planned Parenthood. For decades, Guttmacher had argued for modest changes like the ones that California and Colorado adopted. But as more and more women continued to seek out illegal abortions, he, too, became convinced that the old abortion laws should be abolished altogether.

The repeal movement also gained new support with the birth and growth of the feminist movement. In 1966, a group of women who were angry that good jobs and decent pay were closed to most women—despite the 1964 Civil Rights Act—gathered over lunch to talk about forming a women's organization like the long-running National Association for the Advancement of Colored People, or NAACP. Women from unions and government joined lawyer Pauli Murray and author Betty Friedan to brainstorm. Each kicked in a dollar as seed money.

Founders of the National Organization for Women gather at a 1966 Washington, D.C., organizing conference.

Friedan wrote *NOW* on a napkin, for the National Organization for Women. She added a mission: to "take action to bring women into full participation in the mainstream of American society now."

That fall, at the founding convention, Friedan was elected as the first president. Aileen Hernandez, who had fought sex discrimination as a commissioner of the new Equal Employment Opportunity Commission, was executive vice president.

Initially, the mix of older, conservative women and younger participants focused on economic issues—access to education and advanced degrees, an end to classifying low-end jobs as "female" and management jobs as "male," maternity leave without having to quit a job, and the passage of an Equal Rights Amendment to the U.S. Constitution. Murray dubbed the system that relegated women to low-paying jobs as "Jane Crow," a play on the Jim Crow laws that enforced racial segregation in the South.

Though reproductive issues impacted a woman's ability to support herself, Friedan was reluctant to push for abortion rights that might alienate Catholics and more conservative members.

But in late 1967, the younger people at NOW's national convention insisted on calling for abortion laws to be repealed. "It was the kids, and not just the New York bloc, who led the fight," remembered one woman who was there. "Kids from Michigan, Ohio, and Texas kept standing up and shouting, 'We've got to have an abortion plank!'"

The plank, adopted as part of a NOW "Bill of Rights" ahead of the 1968 election year, affirmed "the right of women to control their own reproductive lives," by removing laws limiting access to contraception and abortion. It also caused a permanent rift; some members quit NOW to form a new organization focused just on education and workplace issues.

At a major conference on abortion rights in 1969, Friedan passionately defended the right of women to control their childbearing as "a basic and valuable human civil right not to be denied or abridged by the state." Too often, she said, lawmakers passively regulated women by insisting that some of their reasons for abortions were more acceptable than others.

"What right have they to say," she asked. "What right has any man to say to any woman: 'You must bear this child'?"

At that conference, Friedan, Larry Lader, Lonny Myers, and wealthy donors Stewart Mott (a General Motors heir) and Beatrice Kellogg McClintock (the wife of an investment banker) took the first steps to beginning the National Association for the Repeal of Abortion Laws, or NARAL, the first national organization aimed at securing a woman's right to an abortion.

Though black women like Pauli Murray and Aileen Hernandez were NOW founders, the group wasn't as inclusive or responsive as it should have been. Black women faced additional racial and economic discrimination. Among other things, some new mothers who received public assistance payments were threatened with losing those funds if they didn't agree to be sterilized. Many black women lacked access to affordable birth control. Wealthy white women could get safe abortions and they could not.

Black women wanted the white middle- and upper-class women of the new feminist movement to fight for racial equality as well as women's rights, understanding that both black women and black men needed access to better jobs and higher wages.

At the same time, black women were under pressure from the more radical side of the civil rights movement. At the first national conference of Black Power in 1967, a majority of the 1,100 delegates voted for a resolution rejecting birth control programs because they believed such programs sought to exterminate black people, a conviction that had its roots in slavery, lynching, and other crimes against African Americans. Others, including the Black Muslim movement, also argued that black women should forego birth control and have more children.

Dick Gregory, a comedian and civil rights activist, considered birth control a form of black genocide. "I guess it is just the 'slave master' complex white folks have," he told *Ebony* magazine. "For years they told us where to sit, where to eat, and where to live. Now they want to dictate our bedroom habits." His response: He and his wife, Lillian, had eleven children, including one who died as an infant.

But many black women, who were also often struggling to work and care for children, didn't want to be told that they should reproduce. They wanted the right to make their own decisions, "to determine when it is in *her own best interests* to have children, how many she will have, and how far apart," wrote Frances M. Beal, a founder of the black women's liberation committee within the Student Nonviolent Coordinating Committee.

Shirley Chisholm, first a member of the New York State Assembly and then the first black woman elected to the U.S. Congress, understood that some black men thought birth control clinics represented a white-power plot. But, she said, "I do not know any black or Puerto Rican *women* who feel that way. To label family planning and legal abortion programs 'genocide' is male rhetoric, for male ears."

Instead, she said, "Women know, and so do many men, that two or three children who are wanted, prepared for, reared amid love and stability, and educated to the limit of their ability will mean more for the future of the black and brown races from which

Shirley Chisholm speaks at a New York abortion rights demonstration in 1972.

they come than any number of neglected, hungry, ill-housed and ill-clothed youngsters."

She personally knew young women who had suffered permanent injuries from botched abortions. She knew women regularly risked injury and even death to end a pregnancy, and she supported changing abortion laws. When NARAL called in 1969, asking her to take a leadership role, she agreed to be an honorary president.

In March 1970, reflecting the surging feminist wave, Hawaii became the first state to truly legalize abortion, leaving the decision solely to a woman and her doctor. The new law required that a woman be a resident of Hawaii for at least ninety days, however, making it unlikely that women would travel there for the procedure. Alaska's legislature also moved to repeal its law. And the powerful New York legislature headed for a showdown on the contentious issue in a state where four out of ten residents were Catholic.

Three times, New York lawmakers had dismissed efforts to modify the state law that originally took effect in 1830. But the first clue that 1970 might be different came early in the year, when the powerful senate majority leader, Earl W. Brydges, indicated he *might* ease his opposition a little bit. He made clear, however, that he wasn't interested in anything dramatic. "Perhaps I should accept the position of the militant women who say they should be able to do anything they want to with their bodies, but I just can't accept that view of society," he said.

To change the law, the state senate and the state assembly in Albany, New York, would have to approve a bill, and the governor, Republican Nelson Rockefeller, would have to sign it. Rockefeller was on the record saying he would support a change. And the speaker of the assembly, also a Republican, said that if the measure came to a tie, he would vote in favor of repealing the old law.

At the time, views on abortion were more likely to split along religious lines than between Republicans and Democrats. Many Republicans supported changing the laws, while many Democrats, often Catholic ones, did not.

To the surprise of many, Brydges allowed the bill to come to a vote in the state senate—the first time abortion had ever been debated in that chamber.

On March 18, 1970, the senate galleries were jammed with

spectators. Female senate staff members lined the perimeter of the senate floor, peering through puffs of cigarette smoke. Rules were suspended so that television cameras could record the historic debate.

Senator Clinton Dominick, a reserved, quiet Republican and father of five, addressed his all-male colleagues with a deeply personal story. His wife had recently discussed the subject with him, he said. At forty-eight years old, she told him, she would seek an abortion if she became pregnant again.

"And you know," he added, "I would have helped her."

The emotional debate continued for five hours. One senator showed color slides of fetal development, as evidence that it represented human life. Another spoke of the special joys of his disabled child.

At 5 p.m., a black senator from Brooklyn, Waldaba H. Stewart, cast the deciding vote. "I cannot agree with those whose morality allows them to support wholesale extermination in wars or who support a welfare system that brings slow death to those who are poor," he said.

The measure passed the senate by a vote of thirty-one to twenty-six, with Republicans and Democrats on both sides.

The bill, which would make abortion solely a decision between a woman and her doctor up to the twenty-fourth week of pregnancy, came up in the state assembly in late March.

Republican Constance Cook—the bill's key sponsor in the assembly and one of only four women in the legislature—had worked for years to get to this point. A seasoned politician, she believed repealing the law was the only way to go. The previous bills, which called only for modest changes to the law, appalled her. "It's incredible how those men make the whole decision as to what women's lives shall be," she said of the reform proposals. "It is strictly up to them, sitting there in Albany, a couple hundred miles away . . . deciding about so personal a matter as having a child for someone else."

Assemblywoman Constance Cook introduces a bill to legalize abortion in New York, March 1970.

She worked with doctors, clergy, and funeral directors. She lined up support from NOW, NARAL, and dozens of women's groups, professional groups, and labor unions. She even got support from an unlikely place: "Some of the most dramatic anti-abortion speeches were made by men who told me privately that of course, I was right, that they were very glad when they could get their daughter or their lover an abortion," she said later.

"They admitted that I was right, but no way would they ever vote with me."

A rare female lawyer who worked while raising two children, Cook made a measured appeal during the debate, making clear that their votes weren't about whether abortions would be done—only what kinds of abortions there would be.

"There are many who say that this bill is abortion on demand," she told the assembly. "I submit that we have abortion on demand in the state of New York right now. Any woman that wants an abortion can get one. And the real difference is how much money she has to spend."

A woman with $2,500 could travel for a safe abortion, she continued. A woman with $25 "has it done here under the most abominable circumstances. And if she doesn't have the $25, she can abort herself. And regretfully, this is happening more often than you or I like to admit."

The lower assembly was split, but she had counted and re-counted and felt certain she had just enough votes. As the debate went on late into the night, two lawmakers departed after leaving behind instructions to vote "yes" on their behalf, as others had done in the past. Inexplicably, the speaker of the assembly refused to count the two absentee ballots. The vote appeared to fail.

Cook made plans to bring the bill back up for reconsideration.

In the meantime, abortion opponents ramped up their pressure on lawmakers. The state medical society pushed for restrictions. A small Right to Life group, led by Ed Golden, a construction company owner and father of five from nearby Troy, New York, wrote letters and contacted lawmakers. But the most visible pushback came from the Catholic Church.

One lawmaker said he was in church with his young daughter when his priest called those assemblymen who supported the bill "murderers." Another said his "monsignor raised Cain with me."

"My church saw fit to have my name called as one who acted improperly—and had it printed in the parish newspaper," said Charles Rangel, an assemblyman from Harlem who became a powerful U.S. representative.

But while others changed their votes in response to the pressure, Rangel would not. "I am hurt and disappointed that the clergy did not so act when we tried to stop the welfare cutbacks, or get decent housing, or get basic health care and hot water for our people," he said.

The bill got a second chance on April 9.

Yet again, Cook thought she had the votes. In particular, she had two pledges in her pocket: the speaker's promise and that of an assemblyman from the district next to hers, who had confided that he would change his vote, if need be. But at least three "yeses" had turned to "noes," and it wasn't clear if "noes" would turn to "yeses."

Four hours of wrenching debate followed, with some men passionately arguing that anyone who approved the bill would be killing innocent children. At one point, a woman in the gallery shouted out "Murderer!

"You are murderers, that's what you are. God will punish you," she said, before capitol police stopped her.

Finally, a roll call began. When all the votes had been cast, the bill appeared to fail by one vote. As the clerk moved to close the vote, George M. Michaels, a popular Democrat from the conservative Auburn area, rose to speak.

Nervously, with his face drained of color, he told his colleagues that one of his sons had chastised him for voting against the bill. Another son, who was studying to become a rabbi, begged him not to cast the vote that doomed the bill. But the Jewish five-term representative also knew his solidly Catholic district.

"I fully appreciate that this is the termination of my political career," Michaels said as television cameras swiveled to find

Assemblyman George Michaels, immediately after changing his vote and allowing an abortion legalization bill to pass.

him. "But what's the use of getting elected, or reelected, if you don't stand for something?"

Trembling, his eyes filling with tears, he went on, "I cannot in good conscience stand here and thwart the obvious majority of this house. I therefore request you, Mr. Speaker, to change my negative vote to an affirmative vote."

Michaels slumped into his chair and then buried his head in his hands as the chamber erupted in applause.

Speaker Perry Duryea Jr. had to call out to be recognized, so he could cast the necessary seventy-sixth affirmative vote needed, as he had promised.

The senate had to approve the slightly different bill, which it did, and Governor Rockefeller signed it into law, following through on his commitment.

George Michaels was defeated in the next Democratic primary.

On July 1, 1970, abortion became legal in New York State for the first time in 140 years.

Changing the law had seemed simple when it happened. But in reality, addressing whether abortions would be performed in doctors' offices, clinics, or hospitals; who would do them; how much they would cost; and how many women would want one was both daunting and emotionally complex.

"A few years from July 1, when presumably other states will have repealed their abortion laws, efficient clinics will be operating and emotions will have cooled, it may look easy again," wrote Linda Greenhouse in the *New York Times*. "But the day when an abortion carries with it no more bureaucratic or emotional baggage than a tonsillectomy will be a long time coming."

PREGNANT PAUSE:

A Short History of Birth Control: 1960s to 1990s

The introduction of the Pill in 1960 was revolutionary, allowing women to truly control when they would have children. But the Pill wasn't great for everyone: Some women experienced nausea, headaches, bloating, and weight gain. More troubling, a small number of women suffered from blood clots and even strokes—especially older women and those who smoked.

At the time, doctors didn't detail the side effects and the packages didn't come with inserts listing them. In 1969, Barbara Seaman, a women's health activist, published *The Doctor's Case Against the Pill*, warning of serious potential dangers, from blood clots to cancer fears.

The disclosures frightened some women and prompted Senator Gaylord Nelson, a Wisconsin Democrat, to hold hearings about the Pill's safety. Some feminists worried that male doctors were experimenting with women's bodies, while birth control opponents saw a chance to question contraception methods.

Medical professionals and others saw the hearings as political, aimed at reducing women's options. Ultimately, the U.S. Food and Drug Administration agreed to require inserts in Pill packages explaining the possible side effects.

Concerns about the Pill were followed by an even greater birth control crisis. The Lippes Loop, introduced in the 1960s, was the first successful intrauterine device, or IUD. A new one, the Dalkon Shield, was heavily promoted in the early 1970s. Soon, however, women began reporting serious pelvic infections, some of which led to sterility and a few deaths. Sales of the Dalkon Shield were halted in 1974, but many women continued to use the device, and lawsuits over it continued until well into the 1980s.

The one-two punch of worries about the Pill and the Dalkon Shield led many women to abandon both the Pill and all IUDs, even safe ones. Many young women instead returned to older, less reliable methods, like condoms and diaphragms. Unintended pregnancies remained high.

By the late 1980s, American women had far fewer contraceptive choices than women around the world. Nearly every pharmaceutical manufacturer had stopped researching new birth control methods, deciding that the risk of public outcry wasn't worth the small profits from new products.

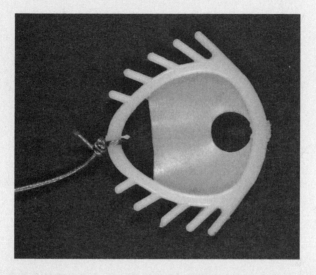

Serious infections related to the Dalkon Shield intrauterine device in the 1970s led to lawsuits and discouraged many women from using IUDs.

COURTS

1969–1970

In the fall of 1969, a young Dallas lawyer named Linda Coffee was doing legal research when she ran across a surprising new court decision out of California.

In a groundbreaking four-to-three vote, the California Supreme Court ruled in September of that year that the state's old abortion law—which outlawed abortion except to save the life of the mother—was so vague that it was unconstitutional. In short, the ruling said, determining when a woman's life was in danger was hard to define, especially since a hospital abortion during the first twelve weeks of pregnancy was safer than actually giving birth to a child.

In addition, the court said, the law infringed on a woman's right to privacy.

The case was huge news in California but got little attention nationally. It was filed by Dr. Leon Belous, an obstetrician who was convicted of illegally referring a young woman to an abortion provider before the state's law was changed in 1967.

For Coffee, the ruling was an aha moment. Like most states, Texas outlawed abortions except to save the life of the mother. Maybe, she thought, the Texas law could be challenged as unconstitutional, too. But she wasn't exactly sure where to start.

For a recent law school graduate, just twenty-six years old, she had plenty of smarts to guide her. As a Dallas high school student, she had been active in her Baptist church and had gone to New Zealand as an exchange student. She attended Rice University, majoring in German and studying for a summer in West Germany. Wanting a professional career, she applied to the University of Texas law school and was admitted.

Coffee entered law school in the summer of 1965, one of just five women in her class of more than one hundred. It was a good fit for her, and she excelled. She was admitted to Order of the Coif, an honor society, and when she took the state's bar exam, she tied for the second-highest score in the state.

One of her classmates was Sarah Ragle, the daughter of a Methodist minister, whose family had moved from dusty town to dusty town in West Texas when she was growing up. In high school, she had been a drum major and president of the Future Homemakers of America. Ragle skipped two grades along the way, and she entered McMurry College, a Methodist school in Abilene, at sixteen, expecting to become an English and speech teacher. But as a student teacher, she realized that teaching "Beowulf" to teenagers wasn't as fun as she thought it would be. So she chose law school instead.

The few women at the University of Texas law school at the time hung out in the Ladies' Lounge, a small room off the women's bathroom that had some couches and chairs. There, Coffee and Ragle studied together and sometimes chatted. Ragle, an excellent typist, made extra money typing other students' papers for twenty cents a page.

Coffee and Ragle each had a secret. While many of the women were focused on marrying men, Coffee was gay, something she wouldn't acknowledge publicly for many years. In 1967, Ragle found herself pregnant. She was serious about her boyfriend, Ron Weddington, but he had served in the army and was still working on his undergraduate degree. Neither was ready to start a family.

Ragle wanted an abortion and Weddington offered to consult some friends. "It took me about three phone calls" to get a referral to a doctor in Piedras Negras, Mexico, he said later. To pay the $400 cost, Sarah cleaned out her savings and Ron came up with the rest. They drove to Eagle Pass, Texas, on a Friday, crossed the border, and returned home that weekend, after a scary but uneventful procedure.

Ragle finished law school in the fall of 1967, and Coffee graduated a few months later. Texas law firms made clear that they had no interest in hiring any females as lawyers, even those who had been outstanding students. Both women struggled to find jobs, sharpening their awareness of the way women were dismissed in the professional world. Ragle finally was hired to do legal research for a special committee of the American Bar Association that was reevaluating ethical standards for lawyers.

Coffee at first landed at a state agency that helped legislators draft bills. But her mother, who worked as a secretary at the

Baptist General Convention of Texas, heard that Sarah T. Hughes, an ardently feminist federal judge, was looking for a clerk to help with the court's work. Coffee applied and was hired for a year, starting in June of 1968.

Linda Coffee and Judge Sarah T. Hughes.

Ragle married Weddington that August, becoming Sarah Weddington. Her husband was by far the more laid back and outgoing of the two, and also more liberal. Through him, they became close friends with several other politically active couples.

In 1969, a few of the Weddingtons' female friends, upset that birth control and information about abortions were hard to get— especially if you weren't married—began work on a referral service that would help women find contraception and safe abortions. At the time, even the local Planned Parenthood refused to provide birth control to University of Texas students.

The women reached out to Sarah for research and advice about whether they were taking legal risks. Then, one proposed something almost outlandish: Weddington should file a federal lawsuit challenging the state's abortion law. After all, the Texas legislature wasn't showing any interest in reforming its nineteenth-century law. And Weddington had a couple of major advantages: She was a woman—and she would do it for free. That was crucial, since the project was a shoestring effort. The referral service could be the plaintiff, the party filing the lawsuit.

Weddington, now twenty-four years old, saw the need but didn't see herself doing it. "No, you need someone older and with more experience," she told her friend. "You need somebody in a firm, with research and secretarial backup."

Still, she agreed to think about it.

Around the country, it was becoming apparent that legal challenges to abortion laws might bring about faster—and more permanent—change than convincing roomfuls of white male politicians in every state, one by one. Legislatures can change with every election, meaning laws could potentially change that often, too. Legal decisions, however, are often based on previous decisions. A single big ruling could influence future decisions for many years.

In November 1969, two months after the California Supreme Court ruling, a federal judge in Washington, D.C., concluded that the District of Columbia's law was also unconstitutionally vague in saying abortions were allowed to preserve the health or life of the mother. Milan Vuitch, an abortion doctor who had been arrested and was facing five years in prison for providing illegal abortions, had challenged the law.

In addition, many activists thought that a group of four lawsuits filed in New York late in 1969 would eventually be the ones to set a new precedent for the rest of the country. But they became irrelevant after the state's legislature changed the New York laws in 1970.

Coffee was inspired by the feminist movement and, on her own, was researching the possibility of filing a lawsuit challenging the Texas law. When Weddington visited Dallas in 1969, they chatted about the abortion law and their shared interest in overturning it. The two former classmates were a study in contrasts. Coffee, nearly twenty-seven years old, had unruly brown hair and little appetite for chitchat. Weddington, almost twenty-five, was blond-haired and blue-eyed, well-coiffed, well-spoken, and outgoing.

In December, Weddington called Coffee, who had more court experience, to ask if she would be interested in filing the lawsuit. Coffee had learned a lot about the federal judicial system during her clerkship and now was working for a small bankruptcy firm.

Coffee sent Weddington an upbeat letter the next day. "I am very enthusiastic about the possibility of your organization in Austin (I can't remember what name you told me yesterday) bringing an action to challenge the Texas Abortion Statute," she wrote. Her law firm already had given her permission to work on such a case.

"Would you consider being co-counsel in the event that a suit is actually filed?" she wrote. "I have always found that it is a great deal more fun to work with someone on a law suit of this nature."

Weddington said yes, and the two quickly realized the suit should be filed in Dallas, where Judge Hughes would likely be ap-

pointed to a panel of three federal judges to consider the constitutional issue. They decided that the Austin group probably couldn't
file the suit, since no one had been arrested. Instead, they concluded that they needed to find a pregnant woman and others who
would make the best case for throwing out the old abortion laws.
They both began to ask around.

As Coffee was quietly researching abortion laws, groups of
women in Dallas were also growing more disenchanted with the
Texas law. In late 1969, the First Unitarian Church's Women's Alliance began to study abortion laws and rights in Texas. "With each
presentation, the collective blood pressure of the group began to
rise," wrote one participant.

In January 1970, the Women's Alliance invited Planned Parenthood to send a speaker. Virginia "Ginny" Whitehill volunteered.

Whitehill knew little about abortion at the time, but the forty-
one-year-old mother of two teenage daughters had long been an
outspoken advocate for birth control. In the early 1960s, as a new-
comer to Dallas, she had joined the Junior League, then known as
an organization of society ladies; she chose Planned Parenthood
for her volunteer work. For a time, Whitehill brought a portable
typewriter to the county hospital every month and compiled a
list of the women who had given birth there that month and their
addresses—several hundred of them. Then, she and other volunteers would mail the women letters with information on how they
could space out their children, knowing that many of them did not
have access to information about birth control.

Whitehill didn't really enjoy public speaking, but she was
good at it. Speaking to the Unitarian women, she and a Planned

Parenthood friend were especially persuasive. They cited statistics about illegal abortions and their consequences, and emphasized why the law needed to change. Whitehill also was a participant in a trendy new movement called zero population growth, based on the belief that the world's population was growing too fast and that the birth rate needed to slow to roughly two children per couple to avoid economic and environmental disasters.

Virginia "Ginny" Whitehill and Dr. Hugh Savage, a Fort Worth obstetrician, in 1971. Both worked to change the restrictive Texas abortion laws.

Worries about a population explosion had been around for a while. But the idea gained new followers with the 1968 publication of *The Population Bomb* by Paul R. Ehrlich, a Stanford University professor. Though not as overt as the eugenics movement, the zero population growth movement had class and racial overtones. Some blamed the poor and minorities for having too many children and increasing the number of people receiving public assistance. Before long, the zero population growth theory would also fan fears of famine, uncontrollable pollution, and overcrowding. That led some countries, like India and China, to adopt forced sterilization and mandatory contraception.

In the same way that a broad belief in eugenics helped make

the idea of birth control more than solely a women's issue in the early part of the 1900s, the zero population growth movement also helped make the idea of abortion more mainstream.

At the Dallas women's gathering, Whitehill made the case that population challenges were a problem of the middle class. "The middle-class child uses eleven times more of the earth's natural resources than the poor child," she said.

After hearing the presentations, one participant wrote later: "It was abundantly clear to a majority in the group that there were gross inequities that must be addressed and corrected in women's reproductive rights in this nation. We were eager for the challenge!"

Inspired, the women formed a committee to study abortion, agreeing to produce pamphlets, send letters, and lobby the state legislature to change the law. To provide seed money, the First Unitarian Church and the local National Council of Jewish Women each kicked in $50. The group's first leader soon moved for her husband's job, and Whitehill took over.

Whitehill, perhaps the only woman in Dallas who was a member of both the feminist NOW and the Junior League, volunteered to call her Planned Parenthood contacts for funding. To her surprise, prominent oil heir Everett DeGolyer Jr. agreed to donate $500. So did Jane Murchison, then the wife of the owner of the Dallas Cowboys football team—although Murchison called Whitehill back about an hour later with a serious concern: "Ginny, I just want to ask you," she said, "is this anything about that women's lib stuff?" referring to the nickname for the women's liberation movement.

Whitehill told her, "Well, Jane, this is just about family planning, and how women sometimes need more than just the traditional, and sometimes they need help if they have an accidental pregnancy. We're not focusing on anything else." That satisfied Murchison, who added, "I just don't know if I like any of that women's lib stuff."

Over the next few months, other prominent locals would donate money as well, including an heir to the Hunt oil fortune, business leaders, and the wife of Stanley Marcus, of the Neiman Marcus stores.

As the women were getting organized, Reverend Claude Evans, the chaplain at Southern Methodist University, and Reverend Robert Cooper, the associate chaplain, were starting the city's first Clergy Consultation Service. For years, Evans had counseled pregnant female students, sometimes helping them go to homes for unwed mothers. Those with money found ways to have an abortion. But after one young woman insisted on getting a cheap abortion and then ended up in the hospital, he decided that helping find safe abortions should be part of his work.

Claude Evans, chaplain at Southern Methodist University, led the Dallas Clergy Consultation Service.

In April 1970, he announced his position in a Sunday sermon, saying that the church must seek "a morally responsible position on unwanted pregnancies." The decision was personal as well as professional. As the father of three sons and a daughter, he imagined his daughter in the same position as the students.

"Had my daughter found herself pregnant, had she concluded a marriage was not indicated, that there was not enough mature love between the two to support the demands of parenthood . . . I would have moved heaven and earth to find a respectable physician," he said in his sermon.

The chaplains recruited about two dozen other ministers to join them and worked closely with Howard Moody and Arlene Carmen to model their Clergy Consultation Service on Problem Pregnancies after the New York one. By then, the New York law had changed and Moody was focused on starting a low-cost abortion clinic that attracted women from all over the United States.

In Dallas, most clients of the Clergy Consultation Service were young women. But, Cooper said, one woman was in her fifties, and his wife, Shirley, once helped out a developmentally disabled preteen girl and her mother, who had traveled to Dallas from Austin after the girl was raped at her school.

Nationwide, the rebellion was growing. Soon after Evans's sermon, both the United Methodist's general conference and the general assembly of the Presbyterian Church of the United States adopted resolutions saying that abortion laws should be removed and the decision should be up to a woman and her doctor, and perhaps her minister.

Along with individual referral groups like the women in Austin, as many as three thousand clergy members across the country ultimately joined a Clergy Consultation Service, providing coun-seling services to more than one hundred thousand women a year. In Dallas, a police detective whose daughter wanted an abortion told Evans that officers would leave him alone as long as there weren't problems. Clergy in others cities told similar stories. But they weren't all so lucky.

Police raided Rabbi Max Ticktin's Chicago home in January 1970, while he was traveling in Israel. Ticktin was accused along with a Detroit abortion doctor as being part of "an international abortion ring." (What made it international? Ticktin had told the woman that she could go to London or Puerto Rico for a legal abortion.)

Ticktin, a rabbi to Jewish students at the University of Chicago, had unknowingly counseled a woman working undercover for the Michigan State Police. But the outcry was so great that Detroit authorities backed off within a few weeks.

Similarly, Reverend Robert Hare, a Presbyterian minister and member of the Cleveland, Ohio, Clergy Consultation Service, was indicted in 1969 for referring a Cleveland woman to an abortion doctor in Cambridge, Massachusetts.

The thirty-five-year-old pastor had never met the doctor. But Hare took his first trip to Massachusetts to plead innocent. Sup-porters raised $16,000 for a defense fund.

Twice, judges threw out charges against him. Both times, the state got his case reinstated. It was still pending as numerous lawsuits challenging abortion laws began to move through the legal system.

PREGNANT PAUSE:
Curtis Boyd

When Dr. Curtis Boyd was training at a county hospital in Fort Worth, Texas, in the early 1960s, he was told that he should call police if he believed a patient had had an illegal abortion. Early on, he reported a woman.

The police came and "they were really, I thought, disrespectful of her. They gave her a hard time, threatened her," he said in an interview. Finally, in tears, she gave them information about her abortion.

"After that," Boyd said, "I never found a woman I thought had had an illegal abortion."

Boyd had grown up in rural East Texas, drawing water from a well and studying the Bible with his grandfather. In high school, he was called to preach in rural churches. But as he grew older, he began to question his evangelical upbringing and joined the Unitarian Universalist Church.

When his medical training ended, he returned to Athens, Texas, to open a family practice. In the later 1960s, while he was serving on the school board in Athens, the Unitarian Church asked for his help, first as a consultant on abortions and then to perform them in conjunction with the Clergy Consultation Service.

Once he started, he couldn't keep up with the demand. The clergy made the appointments, and women "came in droves," he said later. He charged $100,

A young Dr. Curtis Boyd.

about $700 in today's dollars, but never turned away anyone who couldn't pay.

As the father of three young children, he risked losing his medical license or going to prison. His wife supported abortion rights but didn't want him doing illegal procedures. They talked about what would happen to the family and the children if he went to prison. "And the only answer I knew," he said, was "it was going to be hard."

Ultimately, too many women and their hippie-looking friends were coming to his Athens office, often in Volkswagen buses. Police began to park outside. "They thought I was dealing drugs," he remembered.

He moved his office in Dallas for a while and then moved his practice again to Santa Fe, New Mexico, which was more liberal.

"I never thought of [abortion] as being wrong," he said. "That was one thing that carried me: It was the right thing to do."

JANE ROE

1969–1970

The Dallas Clergy Consultation Service was formed too late to help Norma McCorvey—and she was probably too poor to be able to take advantage of it. But in late 1969, she would have welcomed the chance to know more about getting a safe abortion in Dallas.

The petite woman with a head of thick, curly hair was twenty-two years old but looked and acted younger. In the summer of 1969, she had a brief relationship with a man she liked. That fall, she realized she was pregnant.

Youthful as she was, she had already done a lot of living. Born Norma Leah Nelson in Louisiana in 1947, she moved with her family to Houston, Texas, as a toddler and then to Dallas in the late 1950s. Her parents divorced before her teen years and her dad wasn't around often. Her mother whipped her and called her names. Norma, for her part, was rebellious. She spent time in a Catholic boarding school and also in a state reform school for some minor legal troubles.

At fifteen, she was working as a carhop serving burgers and fries on roller skates when she met her first boyfriend, Elwood "Woody" McCorvey, a sheet-metal worker in his early twenties. They began to date, and when she was sixteen, she dropped out of school and got her mother's permission to marry him.

Before long, Norma discovered she was pregnant. Woody, she said later, cheated on her—though, like many of her stories, that may not have been true. What was true, as she would say later, was that she was her "own worst enemy."

She divorced Woody, but kept his name, and began to raise her child with her mother's help.

McCorvey found she preferred dating women to men and began working and hanging out at lesbian bars, though no one actually called them that in those days. Her friends nicknamed her "Pixie."

At some point, McCorvey signed over her legal rights to raise her baby to her mother. She said later that her mother tricked her into doing it because her mom disapproved of her lesbian relationships. But her mother, who was a drinker herself, said she sought custody of the baby because her daughter was abusing alcohol and drugs.

As McCorvey hopped from job to job, she had occasional relationships with men. She wasn't aware of the growing birth control options available in the 1960s, nor could she have afforded something like the Pill. Publicly funded birth control clinics in Dallas were still a few years away. At nineteen, she got pregnant again. This time, she gave the baby up for adoption.

Norma McCorvey, 1982.

McCorvey became pregnant for the third time in 1969. "I only ever slept with four or five men, but I got pregnant with three of them," she said later. "With women it wasn't so easy to get pregnant."

A friend suggested she try to get an abortion. McCorvey had no idea how to do that, and her doctor couldn't help her—abortion was illegal in Texas, he explained. Her friends at the mostly lesbian bars she frequented weren't much help, either. She didn't have the money to travel to a state where abortion was legal. She became increasingly despondent. Bearing a child and giving it up had been painful the last time. She didn't want to do it again.

Eventually, a doctor referred her to Henry McCluskey, a lawyer who handled adoptions. He listened to her story and her frustrations. He couldn't help her with an abortion. But he knew a lawyer who might be interested in speaking with her.

Linda Coffee and Henry McCluskey had been friends since they attended the same Baptist church as children. Earlier in 1969, Coffee had helped McCluskey compile a brief on a case he was working on. He was aware she was looking for the right person to challenge the state's abortion law. So when Norma McCorvey appeared in his office wanting an abortion but unable to get one, he let his pal Coffee know.

Despite McCorvey's complicated and troubled past, she was exactly the kind of person Coffee was seeking to be the plaintiff. "It had to be a pregnant woman wanting to get an abortion," Coffee said. "She couldn't have the funds to travel to California" or elsewhere for a legal abortion because then she wouldn't have a legitimate complaint. Nor could she self-abort because that wasn't a crime under Texas law. And if she were able to get an illegal abortion, she almost certainly would want to move on with her life and not fight the state.

Around January 1970, McCorvey and Coffee met at the recently opened Colombo's Pizza Parlor. Whether others were at the meeting isn't clear. Weddington recalled being there, though she was living in Austin at the time. Coffee's memory is fuzzy and McCorvey's was unreliable.

McCorvey said later that she still held out some hope for an abortion, but it was apparent that she was in her fourth or even fifth month of pregnancy. An abortion at the time, legal or illegal, would have carried more risk than an early-term procedure.

Weddington recalled that she did offer to try to find an abortion provider at some point, but McCorvey declined. Later, though, McCorvey would allege that her lawyers wanted her to remain pregnant.

McCorvey told Coffee that she had a child that her mother was raising, but she didn't mention her second pregnancy. In her memoirs, McCorvey also said that she told her lawyers that she was pregnant because of a rape—but they didn't think that was important. (Weddington, in her memoirs, also recalled McCorvey saying this.)

McCorvey's story of being raped has long been part of the narrative around the lawsuit. Beginning in 1973, McCorvey told many interviewers about a sexual assault, sometimes in elaborate detail. (In 1987, however, she would confess in a television interview that she had made up the rape story.)

But in an interview, Linda Coffee

Linda Coffee doing research, 1972.

said that McCorvey "never brought it up to me." If McCorvey had said so, Coffee said she would have mentioned it in the lawsuit. There was no exception in the Texas law for rape, so McCorvey still wouldn't have been able to get a legal abortion.

At the same time, if McCorvey had mentioned being raped, that would have given Coffee pause because "that would make her less of an everywoman." Coffee said she first read about the rape allegation in a magazine when the lawsuit was over.

McCorvey was assured that being a plaintiff wouldn't cost her a penny. She would probably not have to testify and a made-up name would be used to protect her identity. But the lawyers could not guarantee her anonymity, Coffee said, so "we had to have someone who could take the publicity."

McCorvey seemed up to the task. Weddington thought she was "street smart and likeable." Coffee found her to be "a sympathetic figure."

Around the time she met McCorvey, Coffee was getting to know Marsha King, who was also in her twenties. Married to David, King had become pregnant the previous year and gone to Mexico for an abortion alone. She suffered from a medical condition, and her doctor recommended that she avoid getting pregnant for the time being. But she couldn't tolerate the Pill's side effects.

A pregnancy wouldn't threaten her life. So if other birth control failed, she wouldn't be a candidate for a legal abortion. Coffee and Weddington thought King and her husband also might make good plaintiffs because the law interfered with their "marital happiness."

In early 1970, Coffee and King spoke at a meeting of Dallas women interested in changing the abortion laws and shared their plans to file a lawsuit. The word got around and a local reporter called Coffee, intending to write a story. The call motivated her to get the lawsuits filed.

Over the next few days, she put together two short lawsuits. One, not quite three pages long, was on behalf of Jane Roe, "an unmarried pregnant woman" who wished to end her pregnancy with an abortion because of the "economic hardships and social stigmas involved." The other, roughly four pages, was on behalf of John and Mary Doe, a married couple who didn't want to have to face the risks and "extreme humiliation" of seeking an illegal abortion.

In both lawsuits, Coffee asked for a panel of three federal judges to hear the cases because they challenged state laws that were believed to be illegal under the U.S. Constitution. Both suits, drawing on the California and D.C. decisions, called the Texas law "unconstitutionally vague." They argued that the state's statutes interfered with the patient-doctor relationship and denied the plaintiffs "the fundamental right of all women to choose whether to bear children."

Linda Coffee's name was the only one listed. She filed the complaints on March 3, 1970, against Henry Wade, the Dallas County district attorney. To pay the filing fee, she wrote two $15 checks from her personal account.

Coffee had been practicing law just ten months. Weddington had less legal experience than that. Neither thought that really mattered. The U.S. Supreme Court would probably consider the issue eventually if there were several cases around the country. Their lawsuit became one of a growing number challenging abortion laws. "Linda and I saw our roles as adding to the mountain of litigation. We thought it would help push some other case up there," Weddington said later. "We were not thinking of it as a U.S. Supreme Court case."

Linda Coffee's original receipt from the filing of *Roe v. Wade*.

PREGNANT PAUSE:
The Texas Abortion Law

The Texas law that Linda Coffee and Sarah Weddington challenged was as notable for what was *not* in it as for its strict limits on abortion.

The law permitted a medical abortion only "for the purpose of saving the life of the mother." But it didn't address abortions that were self-induced. It did not restrict women from leaving the state to get an abortion elsewhere or punish them if they did so. And it did not assess any special value to potential human life or portray a fetus as a person under the law.

The penalty for performing an abortion was two to five years in prison. A failed abortion was punishable only by a modest fine. However, if the woman died, her death was treated as a murder.

Here is the law as it appeared in *Roe v. Wade* documents:

> **2A Texas Penal Code art. 1191, at 429 (1961):**
> "If any person shall designedly administer to a pregnant woman or knowingly procure to be administered with her consent any drug or medicine, or shall use towards her any violence or means whatever externally or internally applied, and thereby procure an abortion, he shall be confined in the penitentiary not less than two nor more than five years; if it be done without her consent, the punishment shall be doubled. By 'abortion' is meant that the life of the fetus or embryo shall be destroyed in the woman's womb or that a premature birth thereof be caused."

> **2A Texas Penal Code art. 1192, at 433 (1961):**
> "Whoever furnishes the means for procuring an abortion knowing the purpose intended is an accomplice."

> **2A Texas Penal Code art. 1193, at 434 (1961):**
> "If the means used shall fail to produce an abortion, the offender is nevertheless guilty of an attempt to produce

abortion, provided it be shown that such means were cal-
culated to produce that result, and shall be fined not less
than one hundred nor more than one thousand dollars."

2A Texas Penal Code art. 1194, at 435 (1961):
"If the death of the mother is occasioned by an abortion so
produced or by an attempt to effect the same it is murder."

2A Texas Penal Code art. 1196, at 436 (1961):
"Nothing in this chapter applies to an abortion procured or
attempted by medical advice for the purpose of saving the
life of the mother."

JANE HODGSON

1970

For years, Dr. Jane Hodgson was a pillar of the Saint Paul, Minnesota, obstetrics community. As a young doctor, she developed a faster pregnancy test, keeping a supply of frogs in her office refrigerator so that she could tell women more quickly if they were pregnant. As a specialist in helping women who had trouble getting pregnant, she had delivered thousands of babies. She served as president of the Minnesota Obstetrical and Gynecological Society.

She was, an old friend once said, "the straightest of the straight."

But around the same time that Linda Coffee was working on her Texas lawsuit in late 1969 and early 1970, Jane Hodgson was running out of patience.

Like so many doctors, she had been taught during medical school in the 1930s that abortions were both wrong and dangerous. But time and again, women who didn't want to be pregnant sobbed in her office and begged for help. Young teenagers were forced to carry babies to term. Desperate college students turned to illegal abortionists and then returned with infections. Hospital committee members who reviewed the cases hesitated to allow even a woman with breast cancer to have a therapeutic abortion; at the same time, doctors' wives and daughters were cleared for legal hospital abortions.

Story by story, her attitude changed. She had done a few legal abortions without concern. But, she said, "It's the ones I've refused to perform that haunt me."

Rather than abortion being immoral, "I came to feel that the law was immoral," she said. She began to think about how she could challenge it. When her patient Nancy Widmyer came to her after having rubella in the first weeks of her fourth pregnancy, Hodgson saw an opportunity.

Widmyer, twenty-three years old and with three young children, didn't want to risk having a disabled child; she wanted to terminate the pregnancy. Hodgson explained her options and asked whether Widmyer would be willing to be a test case. There was some reason to hope that Minnesota's restrictive law might be overturned: In previous weeks, judges had struck down South Dakota's similar abortion law and part of the Wisconsin law.

In mid-April 1970, Hodgson, three other doctors, and "Jane Doe"—later identified as Widmyer—filed a lawsuit asking a panel of three federal judges to rule before May 1 that the Minnesota law was unconstitutional. A quick decision was needed to be sure Widmyer's pregnancy was still in an early stage.

When no ruling was forthcoming, Hodgson performed Wid-

Jane Hodgson at a Dallas gathering, 1971.

myer's abortion at a local hospital. She knew she might lose her license to practice medicine. But at fifty-five years old, she felt like she could handle the criticism. Her husband, a cardiac surgeon, could support the family.

Police came to her office and took Hodgson to the police station, making her the first doctor to ever be arrested for an abortion performed in a hospital. "It makes me very unhappy to break the law," she told a local newspaper. "But the present law is a handicap to good medicine."

Some of the responses surprised her. A longtime nurse in her office, Hodgson's favorite, quit. Local colleagues refused to speak up on her behalf—or in some cases even talk to her. At the same time, many doctors at the private Mayo Clinic in Rochester, Minnesota, where she had previously trained, supported her decision.

In November, Hodgson went on trial in Minnesota state court for violating state law. The state's prosecutor challenged her on the issues that were central to the abortion debate at the time: Did she support "abortion on demand"?

Patients cannot demand a doctor perform an operation, she

told him. "Abortion on demand is name-calling used by the opposition. It's inflammatory."

"Would you deny an abortion to an unmarried girl if the law were repealed?" the prosecutor asked, apparently concerned about unmarried women having sex.

"It depends on the circumstances," she said.

And, he asked, did she consider the fetus to be the "equivalent of human life"?

"I do not," she told him. Each sperm and each ovum is potential human life, she said, "part of the wonderful human cycle to which there's no beginning and no end." Faced with a choice between potential human life and a living woman, she added, "I'm concerned with the living generation."

Still, Judge J. Jerome Plunkett found her guilty of performing an illegal abortion. She faced a felony conviction—and up to four years in prison. But the judge, praising her "very courageous" decision, sentenced her to only thirty days in jail and a year of probation, a misdemeanor.

The sentence was suspended while she appealed her conviction to the Minnesota Supreme Court.

As Dr. Hodgson was protesting the Minnesota law, the lawsuit challenging the Texas abortion law was moving forward. As Coffee and Weddington hoped, a three-judge panel was named that included federal district judges Sarah T. Hughes and William "Mac" Taylor Jr. as well as a judge from the Fifth Circuit Court of Appeals, Irving Goldberg.

In addition to Jane Roe and the Does, Dr. James Hubert Hallford, who was facing state criminal charges for performing illegal abortions, joined the lawsuit. Hallford's attorney heard about the *Roe* filing on the radio and realized that his client would benefit from overturning the state law. The lawyers asked the court to allow Hallford to be an intervenor, and the court agreed.

Dallas County District Attorney Henry Wade had assigned the case to John Tolle, an assistant district attorney who happened to have the office next to Wade. Tolle filed a response to Coffee's lawsuit, arguing that Jane Roe didn't have the right to sue because the Texas law was concerned only with those who performed abortions, not with pregnant women. In addition, he wrote, if Roe "is in fact an unmarried pregnant woman she has assumed the risk attendant upon such condition."

In other words, pregnancy was a risk she took when she had sex.

More threatening to the case, the district attorney's office wanted to interview Jane Roe, hoping that maybe she was too far along in her pregnancy to have an abortion, which might make the case irrelevant. Or maybe the assistant district attorney could uncover details about her life or her situation that might make the court uncomfortable about her. If she could be questioned, she might not be able to remain anonymous, which might persuade her to back out of the lawsuit.

The request went before Judge Hughes, who was reluctant to force Jane Roe to reveal herself. In a compromise, Coffee agreed to provide an affidavit, or statement, in which Roe gave facts about herself under oath.

First, however, the lawyers had to find McCorvey. Sometimes she stayed with her father, sometimes with friends. Marsha King

IN THE UNITED STATES DISTRICT COURT
FOR THE NORTHERN DISTRICT OF TEXAS
DALLAS DIVISION

JANE ROE, PLAINTIFF   X   CIVIL ACTION

                        X

VS.   X

                        X   NO. CA03-3690

HENRY WADE, DEFENDANT   X   CA-3-3691

AFFIDAVIT OF JANE ROE IN SUPPORT
<u>OF MOTION FOR SUMMARY JUDGMENT</u>

STATE   OF   TEXAS   (

                            (

COUNTY OF DALLAS   (

BEFORE ME, the undersigned authority, on this day personally appeared NORMA McCORVEY, to me well known, who after being by me first duly sworn, did depose and say as follows:

(1)   My name is NORMA McCORVEY, I am over the age of twenty-one and am fully competent to testify. I presently reside at 4706 San Jacinto in Dallas, Texas.

(2)   On March 3, 1970 I filed a lawsuit in the United States District Court for the Northern District of Texas, Dallas Division, which cause is presently pending under cause no. CA 3-3690.

I filed this suit under the fictitious name of Jane Roe for the following reasons:

      (a)   I am not married at the present time and have not been at any time in the past six years.

      (b)   Because of my pregnancy I have experienced extreme difficulty in securing employment of any kind. I feared the notoriety occasioned by the lawsuit would make it impossible for me to secure any employment in the near future and would severely limit my advancement in any employment which I might secure at some later date.

      (c)   I consider the decision of whether to bear a child a highly personal one and feel that the notoriety occasioned by the lawsuit would result in a gross invasion of my personal privacy.

A page from Jane Roe's short affidavit.

finally located her shortly before the case was to be heard. What was obvious to everyone was how very pregnant she now was.

McCorvey signed a three-page affidavit confirming that she was single and pregnant, without any mention of the circumstances of how she got pregnant. (Linda Coffee kept the original, with McCorvey's real name and address; it would be available only if the judges or opposing attorneys asked to see it.) The statement said she had wanted an abortion because of the economic hardship of a pregnancy and because "of the social stigma attached to the bearing of illegitimate children in our society."

She had only a tenth-grade education, she said, and her pregnancy made it extremely difficult to find a job. She didn't have the money to go out of state for an abortion, and she feared her life would be endangered if she had the kind of abortion she could afford.

electing whether to bear an unwanted child or to risk my life by submitting to an abortion at the hands of unquallified personnel outside of clinical settings.

Norma L. McCorvey
alias Jane Roe

STATE OF TEXAS   (
COUNTY OF DALLAS   (

SWORN TO AND SUBSCRIBED TO before me on this the *21st* day of May, 1970.

Peggy J. Clewis
Notary Public in and for
Dallas County, Texas

Linda Coffee held on to Norma McCorvey's original affidavit, with McCorvey's signature and the embossed seal of a Texas notary. A copy without her name and signature was filed with the court.

That short document turned out to be Norma McCorvey's total contribution to the lawsuit. She was never questioned. She never appeared in court, and she was never asked to testify.

Before long, she would deliver her baby and give it up for adoption. Her future contact with Coffee and Weddington would be sporadic, in part because no one really knew how or where to find her.

FEDERAL COURT

May–June 1970

On May 22, 1970, *Roe v. Wade* and its companion case faced their first test: a hearing before the three federal judges.

Each side was given only thirty minutes to make its case.

Ahead of the hearing, both sides had prepared briefs, outlining how the U.S. Constitution and previous legal decisions supported either abolishing or keeping the Texas law.

Coffee's inexperience showed. The fourteen-page brief filed under her and Weddington's names included several embarrassing typos—"discussed" was spelled "disgussed" and "Xerox" as "zerox," for instance—as though no one had taken the time to proofread it. By contrast, Hallford's lawyers filed a thorough and detailed fifty-four-page response arguing why the Texas laws were misguided.

Dallas County and the state, for their part, didn't take the lawsuit challenging a decades-old law very seriously. The district attorney's office didn't much care for prosecuting doctors for doing abortions unless there was a significant injury or death, because they had more serious crimes to handle. At the same time, no one thought the law was in jeopardy. "It looked very routine," Tolle said later.

Tolle had met Linda Coffee when she was working for Judge Hughes. She had been very helpful to him and he respected her abilities. Still, the Dallas County attorney and the state's assistant attorney general didn't even bother to meet and coordinate their strategy ahead of the court date.

After all, Texas had a long history of denying rights to women, especially married women. Females had not been allowed to serve on juries until 1954. Until 1967, a married woman couldn't own property or get a bank loan without her husband's permission. Even as the abortion law was being challenged, many married women couldn't get a credit card without their husband's signature. So it wasn't surprising that the state's position gave little weight to a woman's right to decide whether she would become a parent.

The brief Tolle filed was truly brief—all of three pages—and to the point. While Roe and the Does claimed a woman's right to privacy in deciding whether to have children, the state, he wrote, believed "that the right of the unborn child to life is greater than the Plaintiff's right to privacy."

All the lawyers had decided in advance that no witnesses would be called and no testimony would be entered. The presentations would be purely legal.

At 2 p.m., Judge Hughes's courtroom was filled with supporters of Weddington and Coffee, including Ginny Whitehill and

The Dallas courtroom where three judges heard *Roe v. Wade* as it looks today, after restoration.

women from the Unitarian Church. A handful of protestors outside held signs calling for abortion rights.

Coffee led off, arguing more technical legal issues, though the judges quickly began to interrupt her. She called on the court to find the whole law unconstitutional. "I think the statute is so bad the Court is just really going to have to strike it all down. I don't think it's really worth salvaging," she said.

Weddington followed, appearing in her very first contested legal case. She was nervous until Judge Hughes offered her a smile and quick wink.

Intending to argue specifically for Roe and the Does, she

quickly found herself answering questions about the most controversial issues around abortion.

"Does the state have any compelling interest that could regulate or modify" a right to privacy? Judge Goldberg asked. Would it matter who performed the procedure? Or how far along the pregnancy was?

Weddington acknowledged that she could see a need for an abortion law to require that procedures be done only by licensed medical professionals. And she wrestled with how developed the fetus must be before the state might have an interest in protecting it over a woman's privacy rights. Perhaps, she said, "you could recognize life when the fetus is able to live outside the body of the mother."

Lawyers for Dr. Hallford then argued that the statute was too vague and broad, so much so that doctors and hospitals couldn't agree on what "saving the life of the mother" means.

Time was up quickly, and the state began its case. Jay Floyd, an assistant attorney general for the state of Texas, tried to argue that Roe and the Does didn't have a right to sue—Roe because she was too far along to have an abortion and Mary Doe because she wasn't pregnant. The judges questioned that argument. The lawsuit had been amended to be a class action, representing not just Roe but any women who were pregnant and wanted an abortion, now and in the future. In addition, Judge Goldberg noted, children who sued because their schools were segregated sometimes grew up before their cases were resolved.

Tolle, representing the Dallas County district attorney, tried to argue that the issue of an unborn child's rights belonged to the state legislature and not the courts. Regardless, he said, "I think the State's position will be and it is, that the right of that child to life is superior to that woman's right to privacy."

But, Goldberg noted, nothing in the state statute addressed the life of the embryo—just that abortion was legal only to save the life of the mother.

When the state's time was up, Judge Goldberg had one more question for Weddington and Coffee: If the judges struck down the law, would it affect more than Dallas County?

Weddington was surprised. The state attorney general's office was involved, so weren't they part of the lawsuit?

"No," said the assistant attorney general, emphatically.

"Do you have any response to the question?" Goldberg asked.

"We goofed," Weddington replied.

It wasn't a stellar debut, or a strong ending. But Weddington and Coffee's supporters felt like they had presented a convincing case for why the law was vague and violated a woman's right to privacy. Lawyers on both sides left feeling like their side would win.

The judges didn't need much time to decide the case. They reached their decision in just a few minutes of conferring.

Personally, Hughes told an interviewer later, "I was in favor of permitting abortion." In addition, she said, the Texas law "was just unconstitutional, that's all."

From Goldberg's view, "It was actually an easy case for us," he said. "The statute we had before us was clearly bad," because it made almost any abortion criminal, even if a woman had been raped.

But, he said, he didn't expect the case to have much of an impact—or that the Supreme Court would consider it.

The judges didn't wait long to release a decision, either. Hughes quickly composed a relatively short opinion, which was handed down on June 17, less than a month after the hearing.

The ruling: The state's abortion laws were unconstitutional because they were too broad and too vague, and they "deprive single women and married couples of their right, secured by the Ninth Amendment, to choose whether to have children."

The burden was on the state, the court said, to show that any interference with that right to choose reflects "a compelling state interest," such as whether a competent person performs the procedure. In forbidding all abortions, except to save the life of the mother, the state law was "overbroad."

Further, the law was too vague because it didn't define what "saving the life of the mother" meant. It wasn't clear, the court said, whether the woman's death had to be certain or if shortening a woman's life was enough. That vagueness violated the due process clause of the Fourteenth Amendment, which says the state can't deny a person life, liberty, or property without due process of law.

The judges found that Roe and Hallford had standing to sue, but the married couple, the Does, did not because they weren't actually facing an unwanted pregnancy.

While emphatically declaring the state's laws unconstitutional, the court declined to issue an injunction that would ban the state from enforcing the laws, saying the circumstances didn't require it. It looked to the state legislature to come up with new laws.

The *Dallas Morning News* wrote cheekily: "The controversy

over abortion really boils down to a single question: Which comes first, the woman or the egg?"

Linda Coffee applauded the decision and said that Jane Roe was pleased, although the decision was too late to help her. Henry Wade, the district attorney, had a reputation for being tough on crime, and he promised to appeal. Then, he went further.

Even though the judges found the law unconstitutional, they didn't bar him from enforcing the old abortion laws. "Apparently, we're free to try them, so we'll still do that," Wade told a local newspaper.

Dallas County District Attorney Henry Wade, 1970.

In making that statement, he gave Coffee and Weddington an opening. Normally, the judges' decision would be appealed to the next level, the federal Fifth Circuit Court of Appeals. The state of

Texas was already planning to appeal the decision there. But if Wade was going to continue to prosecute cases, they could appeal directly to the U.S. Supreme Court for an injunction to stop him from doing so.

Soon, *Roe v. Wade* would join a growing number of abortion cases seeking a decision from the nation's highest court, including appeals from Minnesota, Wisconsin, and Georgia, among others.

Surely the U.S. Supreme Court would agree to hear one of them.

JANE

1968–1972

By the time *Roe v. Wade* was filed in Dallas in 1970, the women running the Jane abortion service in Chicago were arranging about two dozen abortions a week.

The Jane service had started with Heather Booth's personal referrals from her University of Chicago dorm room in the mid-1960s. But after Booth married and then had her first child in 1968, she recruited other women to continue her work.

Two leaders emerged. Ruth Surgal was a social worker who had been active in the Chicago Women's Liberation Union. Jody Howard Parsons had a frustrating personal experience. She was diagnosed with a cancer called Hodgkin's lymphoma in her twenties, while she was pregnant with her second child. She waited until after the child was born to start extensive radiation and chemotherapy treatment. She also begged her doctor to tie her tubes. He initially refused, prescribing varying strengths of birth control pills.

When she became distraught over the possibility of becoming pregnant again, he agreed to her request to be sterilized. But during the procedure, he discovered she was eight weeks pregnant. Despite her cancer, a hospital committee turned down her request for an abortion, saying her life wasn't in imminent danger. She had to threaten suicide to two psychiatrists to finally get a legal abortion. The experience angered and embittered her, and drove her to help other women who wanted an abortion.

The new leaders quickly ran into challenges. Their short list of local abortion doctors charged $500 and up, way more than many women could afford. Some of them had dubious practices. One was often drunk and demanded sexual favors from women. Another charged white women twice the price he charged black women. Yet another sent an associate to meet the patient, blind-folding her so she wouldn't know where she was going. Eventually, the two women convinced a few providers to do some free or reduced-price abortions in exchange for a steady stream of clients who paid full price.

Women needing abortions would call a hotline and leave a message. A volunteer known as "call-back Jane" would phone them back to get basic information, recording on an index card their age and how far

An ad for the Jane service.

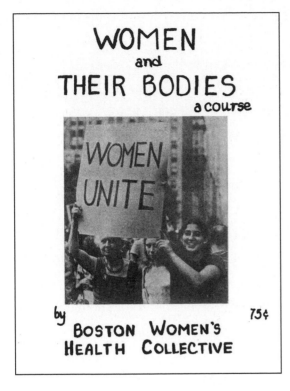

The original cover for what became *Our Bodies, Ourselves.*

along their pregnancy was.

Then, "Big Jane" would assign the woman to a volunteer counselor, who would meet with the client to explain the risks, the cramping and pain she might feel, and whether an abortion was really what she wanted. Jane members also shared copies of a radical new guide to women's health, *Our Bodies, Ourselves.* Created by a small group of women in Boston, calling themselves the Boston Women's Health Collective, the guide was often the first time women learned about female anatomy, menstruation, masturbation, birth control, and abortion.

By 1970, Parsons and Surgal were mostly working with one abortion provider, Mike, who was doing up to fifteen abortions a day on Fridays and Saturdays. By promising Mike regular business, Jane's leaders were able to gradually reduce the price for abortions in the first ten weeks or so of pregnancy to $350, with some free procedures included.

Jane members bought their equipment at medical supply stores.

A friendly pharmacist provided them with numbing medicine, antibiotics, and a drug called Ergotrate to reduce bleeding.

Initially, Mike worked in clients' homes or motel rooms. But after an angry husband chased him through a motel lobby shouting "baby killer," Jane members offered their apartments instead. That allowed volunteers who were willing to be present to help prepare instruments and hold the hands of patients.

Jane's business changed dramatically when abortion became legal in New York State on July 1, 1970, just two weeks after the Dallas ruling in *Roe v. Wade*. Within months, anyone who could cobble together about $400 (or about $2,600 today) could fly to New York and pay for a legal abortion. Before long, New York was inundated with pregnant women seeking procedures. More than one hundred thousand abortions were performed there in the first nine months after the law was repealed, about half of those on women who came from out of state.

Over the next few months, Jane's clients changed from many who could afford to pay to mostly poor and mostly African American women who couldn't get to New York. To serve them, the group pressured Mike to reduce the price further.

Though tens of thousands of women traveled to New York for abortions, the experience wasn't always easy or smooth.

One eighteen-year-old later told authorities that she had come from the Boston area with her husband and brother and had just enough money to pay a doctor. But the doctor's office failed to tell her that she would have to pay a hospital as well. She was more than $200 short.

The three sold their return bus tickets and donated blood to raise money. They spent three nights sleeping on the street and in parks, trying to hustle up a little more. The doctor refused to lower his price. Finally, a woman loaned her the final $25.

Meanwhile, Howard Moody and the Clergy Consultation Service helped support a new clinic to provide abortions at a low cost, and a New Orleans doctor offered to staff it. More than seven hundred patients were treated a week—until the state health department discovered the doctor had lost his license the year before for performing illegal abortions in Louisiana. The doctor resigned and a new doctor had to be hired and trust rebuilt.

A seventeen-year-old from the Midwest took her first airplane flight alone in the fall of 1970, hoping to have an abortion over a long weekend. But the doctor who examined her discovered she was sixteen weeks pregnant, not nine. She was too late for an early-term abortion.

For abortions after about thirteen weeks, doctors in New York injected a saline solution into the amniotic sac, which caused labor and a miscarriage within a couple of days. But the teen's chosen doctor couldn't get her into a hospital for the procedure for weeks.

She returned to a reporter's apartment and made more than three dozen calls all over the state. Some places were cheaper but could not help her for weeks. Others were well beyond her budget. Finally, a Planned Parenthood referral service directed her to a Brooklyn doctor who worked to get her into a local hospital.

Once admitted, however, the hospital needed a notarized letter from her father because she was a minor. When that finally arrived, a saline solution was injected and she went into labor.

But she needed an additional procedure to remove the placenta—and even after that, she ran a high fever for a couple of days. She finally returned home a week later than expected, still owing the doctor almost $300.

Not long after abortion became legal in New York, a handful of Jane volunteers also began performing second-trimester abortions, which had a higher risk for infection and bleeding than early-term procedures. The women who wanted them were often emotional and frantic. Sometimes they were teenagers who had hoped for too long that the pregnancy would go away. Or they were older women who had tried numerous other ways to end the pregnancy first. "Women needed abortions just as much at four months as they did at eight weeks," explained Laura Kaplan, a Jane member.

But later-term abortions required more counseling and preparation. At regular meetings, Jane volunteers passed around the index cards to choose the women they wanted to counsel. Time and again, the later abortions were the ones that were left, until someone finally gave in and said, "Oh, all right, I'll take that one."

Initially, an abortion provider from Detroit taught the Jane volunteers how to inject a special paste into the uterus to induce a miscarriage, a procedure they used for several months. Mike, however, preferred to puncture the amniotic sac with forceps and push out the amniotic fluid; he taught the women how to do that as well.

In both procedures, the clients went into painful labor in the next few days. Those with insurance were encouraged to go to a hospital and say they were miscarrying. Those who gritted their teeth through labor at home had to come back for a regular D&C to be sure no tissue remained that could cause a deadly infection.

Sometimes, Jane volunteers stayed with the women until the miscarriage was complete. While the women were relieved when the pregnancy ended, the counselors were often rattled by the intensity of the labor and the appearance of a more developed fetus, which looked fully formed down to the fingernails. Nurses in New York, who were expected to examine the placenta and fetus from later-term abortions to be sure everything had been expelled, reported that the work sometimes gave them nightmares.

As the Jane volunteers began to assist Mike more and more with preparing women for their procedures, they also began to take on other tasks, like giving antibiotic shots, injecting numbing medicine, and cleaning the cervix with Betadine. Jody Parsons began to push Mike to teach her and others how to do that procedure. Gradually, he began to do so.

At some point, it also became known to Jane members that their longtime provider, Mike, wasn't actually a medical doctor. Several Jane members quit over the disclosure. Some of the remaining women began to believe that if he could do it, they could do it.

Martha Scott was a twenty-eight-year-old mother of four when she joined Jane. Initially, she worked as a counselor, meeting with clients at her house one or two evenings a week after her children were in bed.

During that time, she became pregnant with her fifth child. She already had a houseful, including an infant and a twin who was disabled, and she wasn't prepared to have another. She told her doctor she intended to have an abortion. To her amusement, his office provided her with a phone number for Jane.

Martha Scott in the 1970s.

Mike performed the abortion.

Eventually, Scott moved into other roles, including helping out at the Front, the apartment where clients, their friends, and family gathered before their surgery, and driving clients from the Front to the Place, where the abortion happened. Then, she was asked to assist with abortions, and over time, Mike trained her to do them. At his urging, she also learned to do Pap smears to check for cervical cancer.

"Now, when I look back on it, I think, boy, what did we think we were doing?" she said in an interview. But women needed the service and the process wasn't really all that complex. "I kind of looked at it like being a garage mechanic and maybe we were the people who fixed the brakes," she said.

Even so, it was emotional work. "One would have to be very hard-hearted not to think that it's too bad this has to happen," Scott said. Some of the Jane members ultimately found it too heart-wrenching and had to take breaks. But "once you have set your head to say 'what I am doing here is protecting a woman, protecting this adult,' the other thing is not so significant," Scott said.

By summer 1971, Parsons, Scott, and a few other women were doing most of Jane's abortions, and Mike eventually stopped traveling to Chicago every week. Without a need to pay Mike's fee, the asking price fell sharply, eventually down to $100. But Jane often accepted $40 or $50, and sometimes, nothing.

Eventually, Jane rented places for the Front and the Place, decorating them to feel homey. At the Place, fun quilts on the beds were covered in plastic sheeting. Wads of facial tissue were used to clean up.

Jeanne Galatzer (now Galatzer-Levy) joined Jane in 1971, shortly after dropping out of college. The year before, she had asked her doctor for birth control and he refused because he didn't believe in giving it to unmarried women. (Friends suggested a less opinionated doctor.) Even so, she was naive about women's bodies and the group was an eye-opener. "I don't think

Jeanne Galatzer-Levy in the 1970s.

I had heard the word *vagina* until I got involved in the service," she said in an interview.

She learned to be an assistant and also helped at the Front, which required playing host to the many people who came in and out during the three (and sometimes four) days a week that Jane operated.

She was working at the Front on the day the police showed up in May 1972. A petite five-foot-two, she remembered opening the door and seeing unusually tall men from the homicide squad. Immediately, she told everyone in the room that they didn't have to talk. At the Place, Jane workers told women the same thing.

Though police had been watching the group, they were confused by what they found. They kept asking where "the guy" was, expecting to find a male abortionist. There were no huge wads of cash usually found in other abortion busts. In fact, they couldn't even figure out what Jane was charging; the clients gave different amounts. So everyone was taken to the police station.

Seven Jane women, including Galatzer-Levy and Scott, were fingerprinted and booked into jail. One of the women, a nursing mother, was released that evening, but the others spent the night in cells. "It was the moment in my life when I discovered actions have consequences," said Galatzer-Levy.

Galatzer-Levy's parents were upset that she had been arrested, but Scott's husband was supportive. He asked a friend to watch the children while he bailed her out and reassured her that it would all be okay.

Following up on the raid, the *Chicago Tribune* reported that all the women arrested "appear to be active in feminist groups and women's liberation movements, according to the police"—as if that made them unusually radical.

"Feminists," the newspaper continued, "believe women have the right to control their own bodies, which includes the right to abortions."

As a group, the seven women interviewed several defense attorneys before finally choosing a female lawyer to represent them. Their lawyer, knowing that abortion cases were pending before the U.S. Supreme Court, worked to delay a trial.

The charges hung over the women for months. Though the women arrested faced decades in prison, Galatzer-Levy, Scott, and some others returned to Jane after a few months, again helping with and performing abortions. The demand was too great, and their experience was needed. During the years Jane operated, organizers estimated that it provided perhaps eleven thousand abortions without a single death.

"We were very ordinary women," Galatzer-Levy said. But "we did extraordinary things."

PART III

ROE V. WADE

The abortion issue, of course, is a most sensitive, emotional, and controversial one, perhaps one of the most emotional that has reached the [U.S. Supreme] Court for some time. The issue is a matter of great public interest. . . . We are aware of this, and we are fully aware that, however the Court decides these cases, the controversy will continue. Our task, however, is to decide them on constitutional principles as we perceive those principles to be.

—Justice Harry Blackmun, statement from the bench in announcing a decision in *Roe v. Wade*

APPEAL

1970–1971

The U.S. Supreme Court had never heard an abortion case.

In fact, none of the nine male justices of the court had ever individually ruled on the legal aspects of abortion. The constitutional challenges to the decades-old state laws were so fresh that it was almost impossible to guess where the men on the nation's highest court would come down.

To get the Supreme Court to consider hearing the Texas case, Coffee and Weddington needed to file a formal appeal by mid-October. But both were busy getting their working lives going— Coffee at the bankruptcy firm and Weddington at a new job as the first female assistant city attorney for Fort Worth. Unexpectedly, Roy Lucas, a New York City lawyer, offered to help them out.

Lucas first heard the word *abortion* when his girlfriend became pregnant during his second year at New York University law school. A friend of a professor directed them to Puerto Rico.

The demeaning experience of seeking an illegal abortion ended the relationship. But it piqued Lucas's interest in the subject. Intrigued by the Supreme Court's 1965 decision in *Griswold*, which said that married couples had the right to use birth control because of a constitutional right to privacy, Lucas decided to spend much of his third year of law school working on a senior essay on whether the right to privacy could be the basis of a challenge to abortion laws.

The paper received an A+, and after law school, Lucas revised it into an article that was published in the *North Carolina Law Review*. In the late 1960s, he also began searching for test cases in New York and elsewhere, including Texas. Like Coffee and Weddington, he thought Judge Hughes would be sympathetic. He

corresponded with a Fort Worth doctor who was involved in the Texas Medical Association about a case there and at one point reached out to Coffee to discuss his idea. But Coffee pulled together *Roe v. Wade* first.

By the summer of 1970, Lucas had lined up a wealthy backer and formed the James Madison Constitutional Law Institute to focus on constitutional challenges, including abortion. Lucas's offer to handle the appeal was welcomed—though at twenty-eight years old, he was just a year

New York lawyer Roy Lucas at a Dallas gathering, 1971.

older than Coffee and only a bit more experienced. In early October, Lucas delivered a filing, arguing that the federal court should have blocked the state from enforcing its abortion laws and contending that the right to an abortion was a constitutional question. None of the three young lawyers, however, thought to spell out who would take the lead if the appeal were accepted.

While a growing number of Americans were demanding an end to race and sex discrimination and protesting the Vietnam War, the Supreme Court was growing more conservative. President Richard M. Nixon, a Republican, pledged during his 1968 campaign to shift the court toward a stricter interpretation of the Constitution and away from the recent "liberal" approach that had expanded rights for poor people, African Americans, and those who had been questioned or arrested by police. In mid-1969, Nixon had appointed a new chief justice, Warren Burger, who supported a law-and-order approach for criminals. The following year, after the U.S. Senate rejected two of his nominees, Nixon nominated Burger's old friend Harry Blackmun to the bench. (Acknowledging that he was a third choice, Blackmun jokingly referred to himself as "old number three.")

Burger and Blackmun had met in kindergarten in Saint Paul, Minnesota, and grown up just a few blocks apart, becoming close friends and golf and tennis buddies. Though they attended different high schools, they worked together in the summer as camp counselors. Blackmun was the best man at Burger's wedding.

Career-wise, however, they had chosen different directions: Blackmun went to Harvard and practiced law in Minneapolis, while Burger went to a local college, started out in Saint Paul, and then moved to Washington, D.C., to join the U.S. Department of Justice. Blackmun spent about a decade as in-house counsel at the Mayo Clinic in Rochester, Minnesota, and then became a federal judge.

The two remained in touch over the years, and when Blackmun was named to the Supreme Court, some dubbed them the "Minnesota Twins." (And, in fact, the two frequently voted the same in Blackmun's early years.)

With the two Nixon appointees in place, the justices began to question whether so many civil rights cases challenging state laws should come quickly to the Supreme Court rather than working through state courts first. Initially, the court looked at the *Roe v. Wade* appeal as a case not about abortion but about jurisdiction— that is, whether it belonged before the Supreme Court rather than before a lower court or state court, or even before an elected legislature. The justices set the appeal aside while they considered another case about jurisdiction issues.

In the term that began the first Monday in October 1970, they also had accepted the court's first abortion case—that of abortion doctor Milan Vuitch.

Since 1964, Vuitch had been arrested more than a dozen times for performing abortions in the District of Columbia, Maryland, and Virginia, though he had never served time. After one District of Columbia arrest, Vuitch sued, questioning the validity of the D.C. law.

Unlike most state laws, the District of Columbia law allowed abortions to preserve not only the life of the woman but also her health. A federal judge, Gerhard A. Gesell, had sided with Vuitch, ruling that the law was unconstitutional because the definition of "health" was unnecessarily vague. A doctor's "professional

After several arrests for providing abortions in the Washington, D.C., area, Dr. Milan Vuitch challenged the D.C. law.

judgment made in good faith should not be challenged," Gesell wrote. "There is no clear standard to guide either the doctor, the jury, or the Court."

The Supreme Court heard arguments in January 1971. The justices knew it was a growing issue; Blackmun started a personal memo summarizing his thoughts on the case with, "Here we go in the abortion field."

The justices struggled to come up with a majority ruling. There was disagreement on whether the criminal case against Vuitch belonged before the court and on whether the D.C. law was constitutional.

Finally, after much back-and-forth, the court reached a decision. By a five-to-four vote, the court ruled that the District of Columbia law was constitutional—but only if the law was viewed in a different way than it had been interpreted in the past.

For instance, the law allowed doctors to perform abortions to preserve a woman's life and health, but doctors performing abortions outside of hospitals were automatically assumed to be breaking the law. That was a wrong interpretation, wrote Justice Hugo Black, in the court's majority opinion. "We are unable to believe that Congress intended that a physician be required to prove his innocence." Instead, he said, prosecutors have the burden of proving that the abortion wasn't necessary to preserve a woman's health or life.

In addition, Black wrote, the common understanding of health included both a patient's psychological and physical health, a general definition that wasn't overly vague.

While the court ruled against Vuitch in concluding that the D.C. law was constitutional, the new, expansive definition of health made abortion more available in the District—so much so that some considered it essentially legal.

Still, the decision didn't resolve the increasing number of cases rolling in seeking the Supreme Court's guidance on disputed state abortion laws. While federal judges in Texas, Wisconsin, Georgia, and Illinois had shot down existing state laws, judges in Minnesota, Louisiana, Missouri, North Carolina, and Ohio had upheld them.

Judge Don J. Young, writing the Ohio opinion, for example, took a dim view of a woman's right to address an unwanted pregnancy. "If it is known generally that an act has possible consequences that the actor does not desire to incur, he has always the choice between refraining from the act or taking his chance of incurring the undesirable consequences," he wrote. "This is peculiarly true with respect to the bearing of children." (His decision to use "he" rather than "she" was also notable, given that only women get pregnant, and men share none of the physical consequences and, sometimes, few of the emotional or financial ones.)

It was up to the Supreme Court to sort out and provide guidance on the constitutional questions that were bedeviling courts from coast to coast.

The day after the Vuitch case was decided, the justices turned their attention to the other abortion cases that had requested a court review. They zeroed in on two cases: *Roe v. Wade* from Texas and *Doe v. Bolton* from Georgia.

The Texas case challenged a law that was common in more than half the states, forbidding abortion except to save the life of the woman. Georgia, by contrast, was one of almost a dozen states that had adopted reforms, allowing an abortion if the pregnancy threatened a woman's life or health, if she had been raped, or if the fetus might have serious defects. Georgia required several additional hurdles: The woman had to be a state resident and her doctor and two other doctors had to conclude that an abortion was appropriate. Then, a hospital committee had to approve the procedure, which had to be performed in a hospital.

Sandra Bensing of Atlanta—known as Mary Doe in the lawsuit—had a background at least as complicated as Norma McCorvey's. In 1965, at age seventeen, she had married Joel Lee Bensing, who sometimes worked in construction. She gave birth in the spring of 1966 and had a second child in November 1967. She became pregnant again in 1969, and the couple put that baby up for adoption. Her husband worked on and off and also was in jail on and off for molesting young girls. Bensing's mother tried to have her committed to a mental hospital, but she didn't stay long.

In early 1970, the two older children were removed from the

family and placed in foster care. Not long after, Sandra left Joel—
and then realized she was pregnant again. She went to a local
hospital seeking an abortion. Three mental health professionals
and an obstetrician examined her. But her application was turned
down because she didn't fit neatly into any of the exceptions allowed under the law. (And, it turned out, the hospital had an in-
formal quota on how many abortions it would allow each month.)

Sandra's case came to the attention of lawyers because she was
also hoping to divorce Joel. In April 1970, she gave a formal statement about her frustrating efforts to get an abortion, saying she
wasn't able to care for another child. She gave her permission for
a lawsuit. The challenge to the Georgia law was filed in federal
court the same day, about a month after the *Roe v. Wade* filing.

In June, a three-judge panel heard arguments, and, as with
Roe, no witnesses were called. In a late-July decision, the judges
ruled that a woman's right to privacy meant that the state couldn't
restrict the reasons why a woman should have an abortion. That
is, abortions couldn't be limited solely because of health reasons
or a rape.

But at the same time, the three male judges said that the decision was too important to leave to a woman and her doctor, and
said the state had the power to regulate whether other doctors or
counselors should also have to give their approval.

As with *Roe*, the judges refused to block the state from enforcing its current law.

Five of the U.S. Supreme Court justices voted to accept both
cases. On May 3, 1971, after a long wait, the court announced that
both cases would be heard sometime in the fall.

For Weddington, Coffee, and Lucas, there was much to do. An

extensive brief outlining the legal issues was due in late summer. Supportive filings from those with a strong interest in the outcome of a case, like health providers, feminists, and abortion rights advocates—known as *amicus curiae* or friend-of-the-court briefs—would be needed. And then one of them would have to prepare oral arguments and handle the volley of questions the Supreme Court justices were likely to ask.

Weddington was still working as an assistant city attorney for the city of Fort Worth but spent much of her free time that spring working with Ginny Whitehill and other women statewide to convince the Texas legislature to repeal the state's abortion law. They lined up speakers to testify before legislative panels and lobbied lawmakers. But no bill ever came to a vote.

After the Supreme Court accepted the case, her boss, the Fort Worth city attorney, asked Weddington if she planned to remain involved.

"Of course," she answered.

The next day, he called her in. He handed her a piece of yellow legal paper, with a note penned in blue ink: "No more women's lib. No more abortion," it read.

PREGNANT PAUSE:
Sally's Story

Blackmun was the rookie on the Supreme Court, but he may have been more familiar with abortion issues than most of the justices. He had seen the impact of botched illegal abortions during his time at the famous Mayo Clinic and had almost certainly heard doctors discuss the issue.

In addition, his own daughter had experienced an unwanted pregnancy.

In the fall of 1966, Blackmun's middle child, Sally, a nineteen-year-old college sophomore, discovered she was pregnant. She knew the news would hurt and disappoint her parents. But she couldn't seriously consider an abortion; it was illegal, and she didn't want to risk her health or embarrass her father, then a federal judge.

She consulted her sister and a chaplain and concluded the best solution was to marry her boyfriend. Her parents weren't thrilled about it but supported her decision.

She and her twenty-year-old boyfriend had a small wedding over the Christmas break. Like many women of her generation, she quit school and moved to live with her husband while he finished college.

Less than three weeks later, she miscarried.

Sally eventually went back to college and then to law school, but it took her a decade to finish both degrees. The marriage ended after six years.

BRIEFS

May–December, 1971

The pointed message from the Fort Worth city attorney was the push Sarah Weddington needed to make a change. She wasn't about to walk away from the abortion case. Plus, she and Ron missed Austin and their friends.

Roy Lucas also needed her help. Extensive legal briefs were due to the Supreme Court in a matter of weeks. Lucas offered to put her on the James Madison Institute payroll as the part-time "southwest" office. She and Ron rented a two-story house near downtown Austin, living upstairs while setting up a legal practice downstairs.

May came and went, and Lucas didn't seem to be making any progress on the brief. In June, Weddington decided she needed to go to New York for a few weeks to help out. It was her first foray into the big city—and her first taxi ride. Lucas had lined up housing for institute employees in a former abortion clinic; part of the building was now used as a counseling and referral center during the day. Weddington's room used to house the switchboard for handling phone calls; her bed was a floral chaise lounge where women once recovered from abortions. There was no air-conditioning. "It was free and that is what it was worth," she said later.

As dreary as the accommodations were, the situation at the institute was worse. At 4 Patchin Place, a three-story townhouse in Greenwich Village that was once the home of poet e. e. Cummings, Lucas and his wife lived upstairs and the institute was housed downstairs. Weddington was shocked at how far behind Lucas and his small staff of law students were.

"Just don't know how all the work piled up here will ever get done," Weddington wrote Ginny Whitehill after her arrival. The secretary had just quit. A filing in a North Carolina case was due in a few days. "Dr. Hodgson's brief to the Minnesota Supreme Court was promised 4 months ago and is hardly begun," she went on, and Hodgson was growing frantic about it. An *amicus curiae* brief that Lucas had promised in support of the *Doe v. Bolton* case "is due August 1 & nothing has been drafted— plus everything for the Texas case. Roy just takes on entirely too much!"

Lucas was able to get an extension on the *Roe* deadline until mid-August. Without a secretary, Weddington took on the role of typist. She tried to help with the North Carolina and Hodgson cases. Quickly, she realized, "that strategy now appears hopeless & I'm planning to just start on the Texas brief. But there's a long way to go before August."

Ron was in Austin painting their new house. In July, "I got this frantic call," he remembered. Sarah explained the situation and asked him to come help. "I locked up the house," he said, and got on a plane.

At the old abortion clinic, Ron slept in a beanbag chair until they figured out how to create makeshift bedding on the floor. At the institute during the day, one of them worked on the first floor while the other set up a desk in the second floor coffee room.

They divided up duties. Working twelve-hour days, she took on women's rights and he focused on federal procedure. He also helped put together a section on how neither government nor laws had ever treated fetuses as people or granted them full legal rights. A fetus could not inherit property or collect damages for an injury. In fact, they pointed out in footnote ninety-six that the Fourteenth Amendment applied only to "all persons born or naturalized in the United States."

While writing the sections, Sarah also sought advice and editing help from abortion rights experts, including Alan Guttmacher, a lawyer for Planned Parenthood, and constitutional law specialists who had worked on the *Griswold* case.

Lucas was in and out that summer, but as the due date neared, he pitched in to help stitch the 145-page brief together, plus several appendices. They argued that the court should have blocked the state from enforcing the law. They also contended that the decades-old Texas law had been created to protect women at a time when many surgeries were fatal. And, they argued, women had a constitutional right to health care and to marital and personal privacy.

Lucas was constantly concerned about raising money for the institute. Morris Dees, an Alabama lawyer, originally agreed to fund the liberal litigation group with proceeds he received from selling a successful business. He started the group with about $150,000 (about $1 million in today's dollars), but then the cash payments declined. In 1970 and the first half of 1971, a maker of vaginal contraceptive foam provided the largest contributions, with help from John D. Rockefeller III and smaller donations from Planned Parenthood and a social concerns fund of the United Methodist Church.

Lucas personally had other income, collecting legal fees for his private practice representing doctors and New York abortion referral companies. But as the *Roe* case was ramping up, the institute's funds were dwindling, so much so that there was worry about paying the printing bills for all the cases Lucas was working on. Lawyers needed to submit numerous copies of every Supreme Court filing. Each had to be professionally printed, with very strict specifications about the paper used, the type size, and the page length.

One institute employee was able to bring in $15,000 from a wealthy connection.

Meanwhile, a key supporter emerged specifically to support *Roe v. Wade*. Ruth McLean Bowers of San Antonio had inherited a fortune from her oilman father. She married, had six children, and then divorced, remarrying in 1970.

A year later, the fifty-year-old was sitting near Ginny Whitehill during the Texas legislative session and they began chatting. Whitehill worried aloud about how their abortion rights group would pay a large bill for printing and mailing information. On the spot, Whitehill recalled, Bowers offered to cover the cost— "and more, if it will help."

A new friendship flourished, and Bowers became a staunch

Ruth McLean Bowers, right, a San Antonio, Texas, philanthropist, in 1987. She provided crucial funding for the *Roe v. Wade* case.

abortion rights supporter. Around the time Sarah Weddington went to New York, Bowers sent the institute $10,000 and convinced a friend to send $500 more. "It appears that Ruth will be THE angel of the Texas case," Weddington wrote Whitehill. "Wasn't that great of her—can't get over it."

Later, friends said Bowers ultimately underwrote all of *Roe*'s expenses. She also was an early supporter of the growing National Association for the Repeal of Abortion Laws.

With Bowers's financial support, and with research from some University of Texas law students and other friends, Lucas and the Weddingtons managed to deliver the brief by the deadline.

Like Roe's lawyers, Jay Floyd, the assistant attorney general responsible for Texas's side in the case, had a lot on his plate. He and his colleagues each juggled dozens of state cases at one time, limiting how much attention each one got. Floyd, who was partial to color-coded files and always-sharp pencils, was considered especially efficient. But he hadn't yet begun the state's *Roe* brief by early September. He asked the Supreme Court for an extension and was given until mid-October.

Lawyers for the expanding right-to-life movement reached out to help Floyd with advice and *amicus curiae* briefs. Many states, including Texas, still didn't have a right-to-life chapter in the early 1970s. But New York's legalization of abortion had brought more people and more passion to the cause, including people who weren't Catholic. The National Right to Life Committee held its first national convention in 1970, attracting 140 people. More local organizations were forming, like a Houston group calling itself the Solid Rock League of Women.

As a volunteer with the National Right to Life Committee, Martin McKernan Jr. became something of a point man for the Texas lawyers, sharing information with and helping coordinate anti-abortion lawyers. McKernan first delved into the issue during his second year at Georgetown University law school, when he set out to write a paper for an ethics class arguing that abortion should be legal. His research led him to images of developing fetuses. Those changed his mind.

"I came to the conclusion that the preborn child was a being separate and distinct from its host," he said in an interview. He changed the focus of his paper.

He also began to track legal cases as a volunteer for the National Right to Life Committee, which was based in the U.S. Catholic Conference headquarters in Washington. When the state of Texas told the National Right to Life group that it intended to appeal the 1970 three-judge decision, McKernan added the Texas attorney general's office to his list for regular legal updates.

Just after he graduated from law school in 1971, McKernan flew to Austin with fetal development photos, hoping to convince the state's lawyers that such medical evidence "should be brought to the attention of the Supreme Court." The day after he returned, he reported to U.S. Army basic training.

McKernan also helped coordinate amicus briefs supporting the state's position. Joseph P. Witherspoon, a former law professor of Weddington's, filed a friend-of-the-court brief on behalf of Texas diocesan attorneys, arguing that an unborn fetus should be considered a person under the Constitution and other laws.

A lawyer for the U.S. Catholic Conference wrote the state to say it planned to file a brief, too. But in July 1971, a month after the second convention of the National Right to Life Committee drew two hundred people in Saint Paul, Minnesota, the Catholic Conference notified Floyd that the National Right to Life Committee would file the amicus brief instead. Despite its close ties to the Catholic Church, the committee said in its brief that it was unaffiliated with any religion. With the National Right to Life name yet to appear in national newspapers, the filing likely was the antiabortion group's most public act to date.

To help out the overworked Floyd, Dennis Horan, a Chicago lawyer, and his law partner, Jerry Frazel, both active antiabortion lawyers, offered to do some of Floyd's work for him. They sent him lengthy medical sections for inclusion in the Texas brief. They also told him they would use those sections in an amicus brief they were filing for a group of obstetricians and medical school professors.

Because the Supreme Court judges probably wouldn't be able to go over everything submitted, they wrote Floyd, "The material will be read in your brief, whereas it will just be part of the record in our Amicus brief." The sections, the lawyers wrote him, were tailored to the Texas case.

Floyd made good use of it: More than twenty-four pages of the fifty-eight-page brief that Texas filed with the Supreme Court repeated word-for-word descriptions of fetal development that appeared in the amicus brief that Horan and Frazel put together. The rest of the Texas brief argued that a pregnant woman did not have a constitutional right to abortion and that any rights she has must be "balanced against the personal right of the unborn child to live."

Later, Floyd said that those descriptions of fetal development changed his view about abortion. When he was assigned the case, Floyd said, "I was noncommittal about abortion." But once he put the brief together, he considered himself pro-life, the term anti-abortion supporters had adopted. Even so, he could understand the other side's view as well. "I'm opposed to abortion," he said later. "But I also feel women ought to have a choice."

After the brief was submitted, McKernan wrote Floyd that he was "very pleased" that some of the medical evidence he had suggested was included, adding, "It greatly adds to the presentation of the total picture to the Court. Please accept my humble congratulations on what I feel is a fine piece of legal writing both in organization and content."

Ahead of the hearings, Floyd wrote out a detailed, thirteen-page outline of the points he wanted most to make.

A few weeks before its 1971–72 term, the U.S. Supreme Court took a surprising turn: Two justices fell terribly ill. Hugo Black, who joined the court in the late 1930s, and John Harlan II, who had served since 1955, both were hospitalized in August 1971.

Black, eighty-five years old, had lost a substantial amount of weight and realized his health was failing. In mid-September, he resigned from the court. He died just a few days later.

Harlan, seventy-two years old, had already lost much of his eyesight but tried to keep working from his hospital bed, where he was being treated for back pain. Soon after, he was diagnosed with cancer. He, too, resigned in September and died at the end of 1971.

The court would start its legal term with just seven members.

At the request of Chief Justice Warren Burger, Harry Blackmun served on a small committee of justices, chaired by Justice Potter Stewart, "to select those cases that could (it was assumed) be adequately heard by a Court of seven."

Stewart, Blackmun wrote later, "pressed for *Roe v. Wade* and *Doe v. Bolton* to be heard," assuming that they were about whether the cases belonged in federal courts, not about abortion law.

"How wrong we were," he added.

In mid-November, the Supreme Court announced that arguments in both *Roe v. Wade* and *Doe v. Bolton* would be heard on Monday, December 13, before the seven sitting justices.

Weddington already had been admitted to the Supreme Court bar—a necessary requirement if she wanted to argue the

The 1971 Supreme Court, before Justices Black and Harlan fell ill and resigned: seated, from left, are John W. Harlan II, Hugo Black, Chief Justice Warren Burger, William O. Douglas, and William J. Brennan Jr. Standing, from left, are Thurgood Marshall, Potter Stewart, Byron R. White, and Harry A. Blackmun.

case—and visited the court in early October to "get a feel of the Court's way of doing things." She also had been practicing what she might say to the court.

At the same time, Roy Lucas was determined to be the one to present their side of the case. He had been researching and challenging abortion laws for about five years and saw himself as more experienced and knowledgeable than Weddington. In the summer, he had written the court to say he planned to argue *Roe*, and he sent another letter saying so just after the court date was set. On the verge of his thirtieth birthday, the ambitious lawyer desperately wanted to be the one to convince the court to change abortion laws.

But others involved in the case had growing concerns about Lucas taking the lead. Several women lawyers and abortion rights advocates felt strongly that a woman should argue such an important case for women. Marsha King—the plaintiff Mary Doe who was so worried about getting pregnant—especially wanted Weddington to handle the oral arguments; King even sent Lucas a telegram saying so.

"I have very conflicting emotions about it," Weddington wrote Ginny Whitehill in a typed letter dated November 23. "I would really like to do the oral argument and I am tremendously pleased that Marsha wants me to do it so much—but I really dislike the hassle." Still, she wrote, "It appears I may do it."

Then, Weddington added in her neat cursive, "*My stomach is already in knots.*"

Coffee and Weddington decided that their clients, the plaintiffs, should have the final say. The Kings and McCorvey wanted Weddington to do it. Coffee preferred her, too, and sent the Supreme Court a letter explaining that Weddington would handle the arguments. "She was younger than I was," Coffee said later, though both were still in their twenties. "She was blond, blue-eyed." Weddington was also the more polished of the two and more comfortable in the spotlight.

The court confirmed the change at the end of November, two weeks before the hearing date.

While Weddington and Lucas wrestled over the oral arguments, Texas assistant attorney general Jay Floyd, on the advice of Dennis Horan, asked the court to postpone the hearing. The state argued that the case should wait until after President Nixon appointed two more justices. Presumably, two more conservative justices would be more supportive of the state's position. To Weddington's and Coffee's relief, the request was denied.

Just before *Roe* was to be heard, the U.S. Senate approved two new justices: Lewis Powell, a highly regarded Richmond, Virginia, lawyer who had led the American Bar Association, and William Rehnquist, a staunchly conservative deputy U.S. attorney general. But the two would not be sworn in until January and could not participate in the case.

Weddington also hurried to find room for the many supporters who wanted to attend the hearing. Her mother was coming, as were Marsha and David King, and Marsha's parents. Weddington also invited abortion rights advocates who had supported the case. Jay Floyd graciously agreed to share some extra state-allocated seats so that Ginny Whitehill and Ruth Bowers could attend.

In the days leading up to the arguments, Weddington drafted an introductory statement and held several practice sessions. While lawyers' briefs are considered more important than their oral arguments, she wanted to do well. Law students, law professors, volunteers with the abortion referral service, and other interested friends peppered her with questions that court justices might ask and critiqued her answers. She tried to keep up with current cases and collected new statistics. She read and reread the state's brief so she could take apart the arguments.

She and Ron headed to Washington, D.C., a few days early to continue her preparation. The day before the hearing, a group of abortion rights lawyers from around the country ran a last practice session with her. That night, she tried to sleep, but questions kept popping into her head; she had to get up to check the answers. Just twenty-six years old, she wanted to be ready for the biggest challenge of her life.

OYEZ, OYEZ, OYEZ

December 13, 1971

There is hardly a more formal place in America than the U.S. Supreme Court. An imposing set of stairs leads up to a landing dotted with marble columns, which sit below the phrase "Equal Justice Under Law." The massive bronze front doors, weighing thirteen tons, feature panels depicting legal history. A Great Hall leads to the court's chamber, where the justices sit in order of seniority at a raised bench.

For many years, as a matter of custom, male lawyers wore fancy attire—gray pinstriped trousers, an ascot, a gray vest, and a black morning coat, which was short at the waist in front and dropped to tails in the back. Later, men appearing before the court traditionally wore dark suits and white shirts. (The court's marshal and the court's clerk, as well as male Justice Department attorneys, still wear morning coats to the court.)

Here, in a room with high ceilings, marble columns, and

elaborate friezes, the seven current justices would hear more about legal theory than the gritty reality of illegal abortions. They would consider the personal and life-changing question of whether women should be forced to continue pregnancies while hearing only the barest facts about Jane Roe's and Mary Doe's personal circumstances.

In the Supreme Court courtroom, lawyers present their arguments from a podium directly in front of the justices; the clock is a constant reminder of their time limits.

In keeping with the court's conservative dress, Weddington chose a dark blue suit with a high neck and a string of pearls. She arrived more than an hour before the hearing was to start, so she could check in and have one more chance to go over her plans.

Weddington, Coffee, and Margie Pitts Hames, the Atlanta lawyer who filed the Georgia case, huddled in the court's lawyers' lounge to review their notes one more time. At the last minute, they discovered that there was only a men's restroom in the lounge. The women's room was in the basement, requiring an extra trip before they could go to the courtroom. (The court finally added a women's restroom in the lawyers' area in the 1990s, two decades after Weddington's experience.)

Weddington, Coffee, and Roy Lucas sat at a counsel's table in the front, with lawyers for the next case behind them. A number of supporters were in the audience, including the law students who had helped with the brief over the summer and Jane Hodgson, the Minnesota doctor who happened to be in town. Ginny Whitehill overheard two women discussing the people in the court. When they saw Weddington and Coffee approach the counsel's table, one of the women said to the other, "I wonder whose secretaries they are?"

Norma McCorvey wasn't there, however. "We were unable to find her and let her know," Marsha King said later.

Jay Floyd had a smaller cheering section: Texas attorney general Crawford Martin, Dennis Horan from Chicago, Father James McHugh of the U.S. Catholic Conference, and a National Right to Life lawyer were in attendance.

At 10 a.m. the court's marshal announced, "The Honorable, the Chief Justice and the Associate Justices of the Supreme Court of the United States!" Velvet curtains parted and the justices entered as the marshal continued the traditional chant: *Oyez! Oyez! Oyez! All persons having business before the Honorable, the Supreme Court of the United States, are admonished to draw near and give their attention, for the Court is now sitting. God save the United States and this Honorable Court!*

A few minutes later, Chief Justice Warren Burger called on

Weddington to begin. She had been nervous as she waited, but as she began her argument with "Mr. Chief Justice and may it please the court," she fell into her element. Her voice was strong, her pace measured, and her Texas accent in gear. She explained the facts of the case, how the federal court had found that the Texas law was too vague and that it violated a woman's right to end a pregnancy, but that the court had refused to block the state from enforcing the law. She was detailing Jane Roe's desire for an abortion when the chief justice cut in: Hadn't the recent *Vuitch* case settled some of the questions?

Weddington had practiced for this and was ready: The two laws were not comparable, she answered. The Texas law allowed for abortions only to save a woman's life, while the Washington, D.C., law was much broader, allowing abortion to preserve the woman's health.

"A doctor in our state does not know whether he can perform an abortion only when death is imminent or when the woman's life would be shortened," she said. "He does not know if the death must be certain, or if it could be an increase in the probability of her death."

Just recently, she told the court, the state's highest criminal court, the Texas

Sarah Weddington, 1971.

Court of Criminal Appeals, upheld a doctor's conviction for performing an abortion. The state court, citing *Vuitch*, had ruled that the state's law wasn't vague at all. It completely ignored the three-judge federal court's ruling in *Roe*. Despite that *Roe* ruling, doctors weren't performing abortions, and hundreds of women were traveling to New York and other places to end pregnancies.

As the justices asked more about the Texas law, she made another point: Because Texas women aren't charged with a crime for seeking an abortion, they had no grounds to ask a state court to hear their plea for an abortion, even in cases of rape or incest or danger to their health, irreparably injuring them. Instead, their only option was to ask a federal court to find the law unconstitutional.

Weddington was on a roll now, and she quickly pivoted into an important point she wanted to make—the painful impact of an unwanted pregnancy. Students who are pregnant, she said, must drop out. Pregnant women are often forced to quit their jobs. They aren't eligible for unemployment compensation, and they aren't required to be rehired. Single moms may be unable to provide for their existing children.

Thus, she said, pregnancy is one of the most significant factors in a woman's life. "It disrupts her body, it disrupts her education, it disrupts her employment, and it often disrupts her entire family life," she went on. And because of that impact, "she should be allowed to make the choice as to whether to continue or to terminate her pregnancy."

As she continued, Justice Potter Stewart, one of the more senior justices, interrupted her to gently urge her to get to the legal issues. "You've told us about the important impact of this law, and you made a very eloquent policy argument against it," he said. "And I trust you are going to get to what provisions of the Constitution you rely on."

Quickly, she cited the 1965 *Griswold* decision and its reliance on a right to privacy. She argued that women had a right to choose whether to bear a child under the Ninth Amendment, two clauses of the Fourteenth Amendment, "and a variety of others."

"And anything else that might have been . . .?" Justice Stewart asked.

"Right," she responded, laughing at her effort to try any legal possibilities.

Weddington struggled, however, to answer questions about how far along into a pregnancy an abortion could be performed. She tried to say that question wasn't before the court, but Justice Byron White wasn't accepting that. He asked about her constitutional position on that, and she again avoided an answer. Late pregnancy might be an issue, she said, but she attributed that to an emotional response rather than a constitutional reason.

"Emotional response by whom?" White queried.

Pushed, she said a woman's constitutional right exists until a child is born, since the Constitution gives rights only after someone is born.

Stewart returned to that subject again later, asking if Texas or other states gave any rights to the fetus. "No, Your Honor," she answered, "only if they are born alive."

On that line of questioning, her time ran out.

Jay Floyd was up next to present the Texas case, and he tried to lead off with a little humor.

"It's an old joke," he began, "but when a man argues against two beautiful ladies like this, they are going to have the last word."

The sexist comment might have drawn chuckles in a Texas courtroom, but in the nation's capital, in a room full of women, the response was dead silence.

Texas assistant attorney general Jay Floyd made a detailed outline of the points he wanted to cover before the Supreme Court. This is page ten.

After a short pause, Floyd turned to an argument that the three judges in Dallas had quickly rejected—that none of the plaintiffs had the legal right to sue. Floyd argued that the married woman's concern that she might get pregnant was speculative. The unmarried Jane Roe couldn't possibly still be pregnant, he said, so there was no case here.

Justice Stewart interrupted him to point out that the case was a class action lawsuit, covering all women in similar situations, not just Jane Roe. Surely, the justice said, "there are at any given time, unmarried pregnant females in the state of Texas."

Yes, Floyd agreed. But he pressed on, trying to argue that at least one named person in the case should be pregnant for the case to continue—even though pregnancies are shorter than many lawsuits.

Justice Stewart interrupted again. If that was so, he asked, "What procedure would you suggest for any pregnant female in the state of Texas ever to get any judicial consideration of this constitutional claim?"

Floyd was direct. "I do not believe it can be done," he replied. "There are situations in which, of course as the Court knows, no remedy is provided. Now I think she makes her choice prior to the time she becomes pregnant.

"That is the time of the choice."

Justice Stewart offered a sarcastic comeback: "Maybe she makes her choice when she decides to live in Texas." The courtroom filled with a round of loud laughter.

Floyd pushed ahead. But he struggled when the justices quizzed him on why Texas was defending its law. He couldn't say why Texas had originally passed the statute in the mid-1850s. He could only suggest an opinion: "I speak personally, if I may—I would think that even when this statute was first passed, there was some concern for the unborn fetus."

But even that statement tangled him up, as he then admitted that a fetus didn't have legal rights.

Justice Thurgood Marshall pressed him on when fetal life exists. "In the first few weeks of pregnancy?" he asked.

"We say there is life from the moment of impregnation," Floyd replied.

"And do you have any scientific data to support that?" Justice Marshall asked.

"Well we begin, Mr. Justice, in our brief, with the development of the human embryo, carrying it through to the development of the fetus from about seven to nine days after conception," Floyd said.

"Well, what about six days?" the justice asked.

"We don't know," Floyd said.

"But the statute goes all the way back to one hour?" Marshall said.

"I don't, uh . . . Mr. Justice, uh, there are unanswerable questions in this field," Floyd stammered, to another round of laughter in the room.

"I appreciate it, I appreciate it," the justice said.

"This is an artless statement on my part," Floyd said, chuckling nervously.

"I withdraw the question," Justice Marshall said.

"Thank you," a relieved Floyd responded.

Floyd finally did find some momentum in arguing that people don't have absolute rights. A right to marital privacy doesn't extend to polygamy, he said, and a right to make decisions about one's body doesn't allow for the use of illegal drugs.

Finally, he argued, abortion laws should be a matter of policy "that should be properly addressed by the state legislature."

Weddington may have sounded more like a politician than a lawyer in her presentation, neglecting to cite many legal cases or convincingly make a constitutional argument. But Floyd came across as ill prepared. He was unable to cite facts or details, and he seemed confused about the state's position.

Harry Blackmun, the newest justice, was dismayed by both of them. As was his habit, he took notes during the arguments, assigning grades to the lawyers. By Weddington's name, he wrote, "large blond hair, rather pretty, plump" and assigned her a C+. (Later that day, her own husband gave her a B+, which she considered an excellent grade in law school.)

Her opponent fared better. Blackmun noted Floyd was "nice looking" and gave him a grade of B.

Immediately after Floyd, Margie Pitts Hames, the attorney challenging Georgia's more liberal law, began her arguments. *Doe v. Bolton* was more complex because the federal court there said a woman could seek an abortion for any reason, but left in place many hurdles that made getting an abortion difficult.

Hames argued that requiring women to seek the approval of two other doctors and a hospital committee was expensive, cumbersome, and time-consuming, and denied women of their rights. For instance, she said, the women's own doctors didn't get to present their cases to the committee, women could not appeal, and they were never told why their cases were denied.

Margie Pitts Hames, in 1982.

"It permits the committee to substitute their judgment, their religious or personal views" for the doctor's, infringing on a doctor's right to practice medicine, she said.

She also took on the most controversial part of the abortion debate. The state was arguing that its law protected fetal rights, she said. But how could it do that if it allowed exceptions for rape, fetal disability, or the health of the mother? Instead, she said, the statute and the state's interest were about the health of women.

Blackmun, noting she was middle-aged and wearing light blue, gave her a C grade.

The most dynamic speaker of the four was Dorothy Beasley, who was in her mid-thirties and Georgia's only female assistant attorney general. She was appearing before the court for the second time in 1971, and she would return in a month to argue another emotional and controversial case, that Georgia's death penalty wasn't cruel and unusual punishment.

In a clear presentation, delivered with conviction (and split in two by a lunch break), she got right to the point. The state "takes the position that fetal life is to be protected," she said.

In addition, she argued, the state didn't believe a woman had a constitutional right to abortion, and it didn't believe the privacy rights of the *Griswold* case applied. "A person has a right to be let alone, certainly," she said, "but not when another person is involved or another human entity is involved."

She defended the state's law, which had allowed abortions in cases of rape or fetal deformities, because sometimes the woman's interest "is superior."

Blackmun, noting she was "thin" with short hair, gave her a B.

When the arguments were done, Weddington and the other *Roe* supporters lingered outside, trying to assess the result. They were unsure how the court's justices would vote.

Even the newspapers were divided. The *Washington Post* focused on the Texas argument that a pregnant woman couldn't challenge the state's abortion laws and that women didn't have a constitutional right once they were pregnant. The *New York Times*, by contrast, reported that the court was asked "to virtually sweep away the states' anti-abortion laws" and rule that "it is unconstitutional for the government to interfere with women's control over their own bodies."

Really, all the lawyers and advocates for both sides could do was wait—and, it turned out, wait some more—until the court came to a decision.

PREGNANT PAUSE:
The Supremes

The Supreme Court for the 1972–73 session: seated, from left, are Potter Stewart, William O. Douglas, Chief Justice Warren Burger, William J. Brennan Jr., and Byron R. White. Standing, from left, are Lewis F. Powell Jr., Thurgood Marshall, Harry A. Blackmun, and William H. Rehnquist.

The U.S. Supreme Court, the nation's highest court, was created as the third branch of government in the U.S. Constitution, for the purpose of resolving cases and disagreements under the Constitution or U.S. laws. It has the power to tell the president or the U.S. Congress that their actions or laws are unconstitutional.

The court initially had six members, but since 1869, it has had nine—a chief justice and eight associate justices. Though all the justices to date have been lawyers, there are no specific age, training, or citizenship requirements for becoming a justice. Justices are appointed for life.

Court justices are nominated by the president and must be approved by the U.S. Senate. Until 2017, senators could filibuster, or delay a vote, on a Supreme Court nominee with unlimited debate until at least sixty senators voted to end the debate. In that situation, at least sixty votes were effectively needed to approve a justice. A Republican majority during the Trump administration, however, eliminated the filibuster for Supreme Court nominees, allowing justices to be approved with a simple majority of fifty-one votes.

The court started its 1971–72 term with seven members, after two members resigned, and returned to full strength at the beginning of 1972.

Here's a scorecard for keeping track of the justices who heard *Roe v. Wade*:

Chief Justice: Warren Burger. Appointed by Richard Nixon (R), 1969.
Age in December 1971: 64
Born and raised in Saint Paul, Minnesota. A lifelong Republican, Burger served in the U.S. Department of Justice and as a federal appeals court judge, where he earned a reputation as a law-and-order advocate.

Associate Justices, by seniority:
William O. Douglas. Appointed by Franklin D. Roosevelt (D), 1939.
Age in December 1971: 73
Born in the town of Maine, Minnesota, and raised in Yakima, Washington. Douglas was a law professor when he joined the Roosevelt administration to work on the New Deal. At forty, he was the second-youngest justice ever named to the court. He was a staunch supporter of civil rights and free speech. He also had an active personal life, marrying four times, the last time in 1966 to a woman who was twenty-three years old.

William J. Brennan Jr. Appointed by Dwight D. Eisenhower (R), 1956.

Age in December 1971: 65

Born and raised in Newark, New Jersey. Brennan served as a New Jersey judge and on the Supreme Court of New Jersey before joining the U.S. Supreme Court. A strong supporter of individual freedoms, he is considered one of the most influential judges of his era. He was the only Catholic member of the court in 1971.

Potter Stewart. Appointed by Dwight D. Eisenhower (R), 1958.

Age in December 1971: 56

Born in Jackson, Michigan, and raised in Cincinnati, Ohio. Stewart practiced law and served on the Cincinnati City Council before joining the Sixth Circuit Court of Appeals. A member of a wealthy Republican family, he was considered a centrist on the court and was often the swing vote.

Byron R. White. Appointed by John F. Kennedy (D), 1962.

Age in December 1971: 54

Born and raised in Fort Collins, Colorado. A star running back at the University of Colorado, nicknamed "Whizzer," White also played professional football and was a Rhodes Scholar before earning a law degree. He practiced law in Denver before serving as deputy attorney general in the Kennedy administration.

Thurgood Marshall. Appointed by Lyndon B. Johnson (D), 1967.

Age in December 1971: 63

Born and raised in Baltimore, Maryland. Marshall was a noted civil rights lawyer for the NAACP and a federal appeals judge before becoming the first African American to serve on the U.S. Supreme Court.

Harry Blackmun. Appointed by Richard Nixon (R), 1970.

Age in December 1971: 63

Born in Nashville, Illinois, and raised in Saint Paul, Minnesota. Blackmun was the in-house lawyer for the Mayo Clinic for almost a decade before becoming an appeals court judge. Considered a conservative when he was appointed, he became more liberal as time went on.

Lewis F. Powell Jr. Appointed by Richard Nixon (R), 1972.
Age in January 1972: 64
Born in Suffolk, Virginia, and raised in Richmond, Virginia. Powell was a longtime corporate lawyer and civic leader in Richmond. He served as president of the American Bar Association but had not been a judge or worked for the Department of Justice before joining the court.

William H. Rehnquist. Appointed by Richard Nixon (R), 1972.
Age in January 1972: 47
Born and raised in Milwaukee, Wisconsin. A staunch conservative, he practiced law in Phoenix, Arizona, before becoming a deputy attorney general under Nixon. In 1986, President Ronald Reagan named him to succeed Burger as chief justice.

DELIBERATIONS

December 1971–July 1972

Three days after the December 1971 oral arguments, the members of the Supreme Court gathered for their weekly conference to discuss and vote on the week's cases.

The justices quickly agreed that Jane Roe in Dallas and Mary Doe in Atlanta did indeed have the right to bring their lawsuits before the court. With the technical issues out of the way, the seven now had to grapple with whether the Texas and Georgia abortion laws were constitutional.

Often at these regular conferences, the justices fell easily into one camp or another. But this time, their views on the complex questions were less clear. Some were ready to throw out the Texas law but leave the Georgia one. Others wanted to toss both—or leave both alone.

After listening to each of their colleagues speak, the justices couldn't even agree on what they had heard. Some came up with a vote of five to two, and another, four to three. Yet another recorded a three-to-three vote, with one abstaining. Blackmun said he thought the Texas law denied Jane Roe her rights and was too restrictive for doctors, but some wrote down that he voted to keep the Texas law. Among all the justices, Chief Justice Burger seemed the most uncertain, though he leaned toward leaving both state laws in place.

The tallies on *Doe v. Bolton* were even more confusing, with perhaps three in favor of overturning the restrictions, two opposed, and two more wanting to send it back to the lower court for a fuller hearing.

The next day, Chief Justice Warren Burger asked Justice Blackmun to draft the court's opinion. While all the justices vote, one justice is asked to write an opinion for the majority and the others decide whether to join that decision. Sometimes justices write their own concurrences, agreeing with the majority but for different reasons. Those who oppose write a dissent.

The move infuriated Justice William O. Douglas. Both the chief justice and Blackmun were in the minority, Douglas believed, and Burger had broken an unwritten tradition. If the chief justice wasn't in the majority, then the most senior justice in the majority—Douglas—should have decided who would write the opinion. Douglas, one of the court's liberal members, also saw something underhanded in the assignment: He feared Blackmun, Burger's friend and a notoriously slow writer, would water down this important decision.

Douglas fired off a succinct note to the chief justice, saying, "to save future time and trouble," a justice in the majority should write the opinion.

The chief justice stood his ground. In a note back, he told Douglas that the positions were too unclear to record an actual vote; the cases "would have to stand or fall on the writing, when it was done." The cases were sensitive, he said, "and quite probably candidates for reargument" once the two new justices were in place.

Douglas stewed.

Blackmun, for his part, wasn't especially enthusiastic about the assignment. Later, he recalled that he was asked to write a memorandum, a dreaded request because memos took time and effort but didn't always become opinions. He even suggested that the cases be held and reargued before the full bench.

Still, Blackmun also asked the Mayo Clinic library for a list of references on the history of abortion and began to wrestle with his approach.

Not long after, he brought up his new assignment one night when his wife and three daughters were together for dinner. "What are your views on abortion?" he asked.

His daughter Susan recalled that her mom, Dottie, and sister Sally both gave middle-of-the-road responses. The oldest, Nancy, a Harvard graduate, had an opinion to the left of that. And Susan, the youngest, remembered offering a "far-to-the-left, shake-the-old-man-up response."

At that, she said, her dad put down his fork. "I think I'll go lie down," he told them. "I'm getting a headache."

While Blackmun worked—or dawdled (depending on which justice was asked)—on the writing of his opinion, Justice William Brennan circulated an opinion on a contraception case that the court had heard in November, just a few weeks before *Roe* and *Doe*.

Surprisingly, seven years after the *Griswold* case in Connecticut, up to half the states still had laws limiting the sale of birth control to unmarried people. This particular case, *Eisenstadt v. Baird*, challenged an 1879 Massachusetts law that allowed only a doctor or a pharmacist with a doctor's prescription to provide contraception—and then only to married couples. Bill Baird, an outspoken and somewhat flamboyant birth control crusader, had given a packet of vaginal contraceptive foam to a Boston University student after a talk at the school in 1967.

Bill Baird at a New York City rally, 1973.

Baird made the appearance so that he could test the law, which carried a penalty of up to five years in prison. He was convicted in 1970 and sentenced to three months in jail. He served thirty-six days before being released while the case was on appeal.

The state had argued that its law discouraged premarital sex and protected the public's health. But in March 1972, the Supreme Court shot down that logic on a six-to-one vote. In the opinion, Brennan wrote that the statute wasn't a deterrent to premarital sex and prescription drugs were already regulated in other ways. Further, he said, if married couples have a constitutional right to birth control, so do unmarried people.

Then, fully aware that the court was considering the Texas and Georgia laws, Brennan slipped in a sentence that could provide guidance on the pending abortion cases as well: "If the right of privacy means anything," he wrote, "it is the right of the individual, married or single, to be free from unwarranted governmental intrusion into matters so fundamentally affecting a person as the decision whether to bear or beget a child."

While members of the court waited for Blackmun to provide a draft, everyone else waited, too.

Jane Hodgson had been waiting months for the Minnesota Supreme Court to rule on her criminal conviction for performing an abortion on a woman exposed to rubella. She was unable to practice medicine at home so in March 1972, she took a job as medical director of Preterm, an abortion and family planning clinic in Washington, D.C. On the weekends, she went home to Minnesota, where her youngest daughter was still in high school.

After charges were thrown out against Reverend Robert Hare for his clergy consultation referral, he took a new job as a church minister in Natick, Massachusetts. Then, in March 1972, during his first week on the job, his congregation learned that he had been indicted again in Massachusetts on the same charge of aiding and abetting an abortion. Fortunately, church members were supportive. But the case dragged on.

Every day, women in Texas and around the country continued to reckon with unwanted pregnancies and to request abortions.

The county hospital in Dallas said the number of botched abortions it treated—about 130 a year—had remained the same for more than a decade, and women still died sometimes from complications. While more options were available to the rich and middle class, one doctor said, the poor had to make do with "quacks" who would accept as little as $75.

Meanwhile, those with money could buy a prepackaged abortion trip. One service charged about $300 to $400 (or about $2,000 to $2,500 in today's dollars) to take women from Dallas to New York, Albuquerque, or Los Angeles for a legal abortion. The cost covered everything, including airfare, motel, medical care, and medicines.

On a Saturday in February 1972, dozens of Texas women, ranging in age from fifteen to a grandmother in her forties, boarded a flight from Dallas to Los Angeles. One woman jokingly called it the "non-family plan."

After spending a night in a motel, the women each had an abortion on Sunday. They returned to Dallas that evening and quickly went their separate ways. "After all," one of the women said, "it's not the kind of thing one uses to form an alumnae group."

After the December 1971 arguments, Sarah Weddington returned to Austin feeling like her work was unfinished. If the Supreme Court didn't strike down the Texas abortion law, Texas legislators could still change it. Plus, the state's rape laws and its credit and employment laws still discriminated against women.

Weddington's women friends decided a woman should run for an open seat in the state House of Representatives. Weddington volunteered to be the long-shot candidate and to pay the $100 filing fee, launching her run two days after her twenty-seventh birthday.

Her campaign was short of money, but her work on the *Roe* case had raised her profile, and her friends were energetic and effective organizers. She got an extra boost when Ann Richards, an experienced political hand, signed on to help. (Richards later became governor of Texas.)

In the May Democratic primary, Weddington came in first of four, but didn't win a majority. To everyone's surprise, she beat her better-financed challenger in a June runoff. She would face a Republican in the November election, presumably with the hope that *Roe v. Wade* would be resolved by then.

In the meantime, the abortion debate was growing increasingly political across the country. Right to Life groups in the Midwest and East had mobilized after New York legalized abortion in 1970 and helped quash changes to abortion laws in numerous state legislatures in 1971 and 1972.

In New York, the Catholic Church, along with Right to Life

and antiabortion groups across the state, rallied supporters and recruited new ones, distributing thousands of photographs of fetuses at various stages of development and filmstrips to make their case. They successfully unseated some of the state lawmakers who had supported abortion rights.

In the spring of 1972, they pushed for repeal of legal abortion in the state, bringing busloads of constituents to lobby legislators. Cardinal Terence Cooke, the Catholic archbishop of New York, declared April 16 "Right to Life Sunday," and an estimated ten thousand marchers worked their way down Fifth Avenue to hear speakers call abortion "murder" and compare it to Hitler's slaughter in World War II.

This time, abortion rights groups were caught by surprise; feeling complacent, they were slow to respond to protect the law they had worked so hard to win.

By May, however, the *New York Times* reported, both sides had "laid siege to the Legislature," with "rallies, impassioned speeches, angry political threats, and a flood of telegrams." Still, Governor Nelson Rockefeller, a Republican, pledged to veto any vote to repeal the current law.

Then, to the surprise of New York politicians, President Nixon waded into the debate. In a letter to Cardinal Cooke that was released just ahead of the scheduled vote, the president criticized the state's abortion law and the destruction of "the right to life of literally hundreds of thousands of unborn children." He expressed his "admiration, sympathy, and support" for Cooke's and others' work as "defenders of the right to life of the unborn." (He also added that the law was the state's decision, not a federal one.)

Rockefeller, who was chair of Nixon's New York reelection

committee, could hardly contain his anger over the president's interference in a state issue during an election year.

Constance Cook, the statehouse Republican who had led the fight for legal abortion, argued back. "The issue is not whether we do or don't have abortions," she said. "The issue is where—in some dirty hotel room or some dingy back room of a doctor's office, or in a hospital under proper medical care."

Nixon's letter, she said, was "a patent pitch for the Catholic vote" and "a political move." And cynical though that sounded, she was right: The year before, some of Nixon's advisers saw an opportunity for him to draw conservative Catholic Democrats to the Republican Party if he took a stand opposing abortion. In response, the president made abortions harder to get on military bases. He then issued a statement saying that he opposed abortion on demand, a term abortion foes used to imply the procedures were a matter of convenience, not need.

Shortly after Nixon's letter, the state assembly and the state senate voted to repeal the law, allowing abortions only if necessary to save a woman's life.

As promised, Rockefeller killed the bill with a veto in mid-May. In a statement, he said, "I can see no justification now for repealing this reform and thus condemning hundreds of thousands of women to the dark age once again."

Nixon declined to comment. In truth, the president didn't have strong feelings about abortion. But he made statements opposing abortion during his campaign to win over Catholics while also trying to appease women and Protestants who supported abortion rights. It was a strong position for a president to take while two cases were awaiting a Supreme Court decision.

PREGNANT PAUSE:
What Religions Say

Along with the Catholic Church, several religious denominations took a position on abortion between the early 1960s and 1970s. More often than not, their statements reflected concerns about women risking their health, and even their lives, to end a pregnancy.

Since then, many faith communities have wrestled with the moral challenges of abortion. Generally, evangelical and Pentecostal churches oppose abortion, while other religious denominations focus on a woman's right to make personal decisions or seek to find a balance between a woman's needs and that of the fetus she carries. The United Methodist Church, for instance, recognizes that there may be "tragic conflicts of life with life."

Even within some religions, there is room for debate and disagreement. The National Baptist Convention, a historically black denomination, allows each congregation to determine its position on abortion.

Below is a look at the original stance of some large religious organizations and their current stances on abortion.

	THEN	NOW
Catholic Church	1968: Opposed to abortion in all cases.	Opposed to abortion in all cases.
Evangelical Lutheran	1966: "There are times and circumstances when interruption of the pregnancy is necessary for therapeutic reasons."	Supports access to safe and affordable services for "morally justifiable" abortions and seeks to reduce the need for abortion.

Islam	While Islam has no single governing authority, the Yaqeen Institute for Islamic Research says the religion believes ensoulment occurs at 120 days from conception and abortion is forbidden after that, except to save a woman's life. Many believe abortion is permissible only up to forty days after conception, and after that, only for specific circumstances, such as rape or extreme fetal deformity.	
Presbyterian Church (USA)	1970: Supports legalizing abortion.	"Affirms the ability and responsibility of women, guided by the Scriptures and the Holy Spirit . . . to make good moral choices."
Reform Jews	1967: Supports humane legislation permitting abortion in cases of rape, incest, fetal deformity, threats to a woman's mental or physical health, and "social, economic and psychological factors."	"Unwavering commitment" to protecting and preserving a woman's right to choose abortion.
Southern Baptist Convention	1971: In favor of allowing abortion in cases of rape, incest, fetal deformity, or threat to physical or mental health of the woman.	Opposed to abortion except to save the life of the woman. In 2019, it urged the Supreme Court to overturn Roe.
Unitarian Universalist Association	1963: Supports legalization of abortion in cases of rape, incest, threat to the mother, physical/mental defect of the child, or compelling reasons.	Supports freedom of reproductive choice.

United Church of Christ	1971: In favor of legalizing abortion.	Supports a full range of reproductive options for all women.
United Methodist Church	1972: Recommended abortion be removed from the criminal code and treated as a medical procedure.	Supports access to safe and legal abortion, but "cannot affirm abortion as an acceptable means of birth control."

Five months after the oral arguments and a few days after the New York repeal rebellion, Harry Blackmun finally circulated "a first and tentative" memorandum in the *Roe* case.

Several justices and their law clerks were terribly disappointed.

The arguments presented were, at best, thin. Most of the opinion focused on whether Jane Roe, the married Does, and Dr. Hallford had standing to sue. (Only Roe did, Blackmun wrote.) He found the wording of the Texas law so vague as to be unconstitutional. That's as far as he went, dismissing the need to address whether women have a constitutional right to decide to have a child. He had hoped this approach might lead to a unanimous opinion.

In a note with the draft, he asked his fellow justices for their views.

Justice William Brennan, a liberal and the court's only Catholic, was the first to speak up. "Vagueness" was not enough, he wrote. He urged Blackmun to get to the "core constitutional question." Douglas quickly agreed.

The *Doe* draft came on May 25, 1972. It was meatier and said directly that a woman's "fundamental personal decision" whether to have a child is protected by the Ninth and Fourteenth Amendments, though that right diminishes as the pregnancy advances.

Other justices saw flaws in the *Doe* draft, but they quickly agreed to join both the *Doe* and *Roe* decisions in hopes of getting them released before the term expired at the end of June. They gambled that they could get Blackmun to bulk it up once a majority had signed on.

But Blackmun also continued to be uneasy with the complexity of the case and felt like *Doe*, in particular, should be reargued in front of a full court. That was an option the more liberal justices wanted to avoid. They feared that including the new Nixon appointees might convince Blackmun to switch sides and shift the vote. At the moment, they counted five votes toward finding the Texas law unconstitutional, a clear majority out of seven.

Once raised, however, the idea of a reargument seemed to take root. After hearing some of his colleagues' suggestions, Blackmun indicated that he wanted to do more research and dig deeper into the medical issues around abortion. He was less certain which of the cases was more important. On May 31, he sent another memo to the full court.

"Although it would prove costly to me personally, in light of the energy and hours expended, I have now concluded, somewhat reluctantly, that reargument in <u>both</u> cases at an early date in the next term, would perhaps be advisable," he said.

Among other things, he wrote, "I believe, on an issue so sensitive and so emotional as this one, the country deserves the conclusion of a nine-man, not a seven-man court, whatever the ultimate decision may be."

His suggestion drew fast replies. Chief Justice Burger weighed in quickly, voting that the cases be reargued. "This is as sensitive and difficult an issue as any in this Court in my time," he wrote, "and I want to hear more and think more when I am not trying to sort out several dozen other difficult cases."

But the justices who were supporting Blackmun's decision made clear that they didn't see any reasons for more arguments, especially when there was a firm majority. Douglas was especially emphatic.

This time, however, the new justices weighed in. Lewis Powell, who had joined the court in January, had not previously participated in any *Roe* or *Doe* discussions. But he felt like he should participate in the discussion about holding another round of arguments. He was in favor of that, he said, because Blackmun himself thought the cases should be heard again. "His position, based on months of study, suggests enough doubt on an issue of large national importance to justify the few months delay," Powell wrote.

Rehnquist, the other new justice, agreed with Powell. And when all the votes were tallied, four justices wanted the decisions to be released before the end of June and five wanted the cases to be reheard in the fall. Of those five, four were Nixon appointees.

Justice Douglas blew his stack.

In an unusual move, he dashed out a personal dissent, had it printed up, and threatened to release it to the public. In one draft that circulated among the court, Douglas renewed his original complaint that the chief justice had inappropriately assigned the case. When "the minority" view does that, Douglas charged, "There is a destructive force at work in the Court."

The decisions had already taken too long to be drafted, he said. Now, he said, the move to rehear the cases was "merely another strategy by a minority somehow to suppress the majority view."

Then, he made a more damning accusation: The court was allowing politics to influence its decision. Typically, Douglas wrote, the minority honored the majority, even when they fiercely disagreed. But, he went on, "This is an election year. Both political parties have made abortion an issue."

That wasn't the court's business, he added. "We decide questions only on their constitutional merits," he wrote. "To prolong

Chief Justice Warren Burger meets with President Nixon, June 14, 1972, shortly after the court agreed to rehear *Roe v. Wade*.

these *Abortion Cases* into the next election would in the eyes of many be a political gesture unworthy of the Court."

He called for Blackmun's opinions to be released.

Had politics actually come into play? There was no evidence that Nixon had said anything to the chief justice. But it was well known inside the court that Chief Justice Burger had held a private meeting with Blackmun shortly before the reargument issue came up.

One insider account of the 1971–72 term had an interesting nugget: Douglas said that Blackmun had confided that the chief justice had tried to pressure him "by emphasizing President Nixon's public commitment to antiabortion forces in New York."

However, Blackmun later denied that to another justice.

Douglas left for vacation in Goose Prairie, Washington, with the issue still up in the air. But by the end of June, he had calmed down—or at least realized the damage his written statement would do. When the court announced that *Roe v. Wade* and *Doe v. Bolton* would be heard a second time in the fall of 1972, the order simply noted that Justice Douglas dissented from that decision.

Normally, nothing more would be said about the internal drama. But on July 4, the *Washington Post* ran an un-bylined, front-page story saying that Chief Justice Burger's actions might shift the court's position on the abortion cases. It then recounted, in detail, Douglas's complaints and the fact that a majority of the justices had been ready to strike down the laws as unconstitutional.

The *New York Times* carried a similar story the next day.

The stories roiled the court. Though Douglas was thought to be the source of the articles, he didn't even have a phone in Goose Prairie. (Likely, another justice was the source.) Douglas had learned about the story only when he called his wife, and he immediately sent a handwritten note to Burger, saying, "I am upset and appalled."

Burger responded with a four-page, single-spaced letter, defending each of his actions, "to keep the record straight."

Douglas, humbled, was willing to let it go. "That chapter in the Abortion Cases," he wrote back, "is for me gone and forgotten."

People on both sides of the issue were left guessing what the second arguments before the full court would mean—though it wasn't looking good for abortion rights advocates. Inside the court, even liberal Justice Brennan was willing to bet that Harry Blackmun would soon be switching sides.

ROE, AGAIN

August–October, 1972

While the Supreme Court was out of session in the summer of 1972, the waiting continued for Weddington and Coffee. It continued for Dr. Hallford of Texas and Dr. Hodgson, now in D.C., for Reverend Hare, and for the women of Jane in Chicago, who were now facing serious criminal charges.

Meanwhile, Justice Harry Blackmun returned to Minnesota to spend two weeks researching the history of abortion in the Mayo Clinic library. He was surprised to learn that it hadn't been a serious crime until the previous century, especially before quickening, and that many cultures accepted it.

He also looked into the history of the Hippocratic oath, a series of pledges outlining ethical standards for doctors that dated back to the time of Socrates and Plato. Among the original statements was a pledge to refuse to provide a woman with pessary—a preparation inserted in the vagina—to cause an abortion.

During his years as Mayo Clinic's lawyer, Blackmun saw framed versions of the oath in examining rooms, and he knew some medical schools still incorporated it into their graduation ceremonies. He was disturbed that none of the lawyers had mentioned it in the first round of arguments; it seemed like a relevant and important issue to him.

But his investigation dug up an unexpected history: Greek doctors of the era commonly helped women with abortions, especially in the early stages of pregnancy. Though the oath was attributed to Hippocrates, considered the father of medicine, modern scholars don't believe he wrote it or that his contemporaries followed it. Instead, they believe a small group with a minority point of view wrote it after his death. (The oath also promised to scrupulously avoid surgery for kidney stones. And that well-known phrase from Hippocrates, "First, do no harm"? It isn't in the oath at all.)

Blackmun was also in regular touch with his law clerk and working on an updated opinion on the two cases. There was no guarantee that he would be in the majority the second time around—or that he would be assigned to write the opinion again. But if he was, he would be more prepared.

Getting ready was much tougher for Sarah Weddington this time around. She

A small sign from Weddington's campaign for the state legislature.

was busy campaigning to become one of the very few women in the Texas legislature and also working to elect other Democratic candidates.

The court notified her in early September that the second hearing would be on October 11, and she had to scramble to fit in practice time. She especially wanted to be able to handle the barrage of questions the justices might throw at her.

Once again, she presented in front of other advocates and lawyers. And after she and Ron drove to Washington, D.C., from Austin in early October, she rehearsed again before some of the top lawyers on the issues.

Once again, she arrived early to the court for the 10 a.m. hearing. Ron and Linda Coffee joined her at the counsel's table; Roy Lucas, who had again tried unsuccessfully to argue the case, was in the crowd.

The first time, she had been interrupted with a question just two minutes into her presentation, and the exchanges kept her focused. This time, to her surprise, she was able to present for more than ten minutes before a justice asked a substantive question.

She gave some updates, noting that in New York, the maternal death rate and the infant mortality rate had declined since abortion became legal. In states where abortion was more available, the birth rate of women on public assistance had also fallen, she noted, a nod to some conservatives' criticism that poor women who received public assistance had too many children.

First and foremost, she said, women needed the court to answer "whether or not they will be forced by the state to continue an unwanted pregnancy."

This time, she didn't forget to cite constitutional reasons, saying their case relied on the Fifth, Ninth, and Fourteenth Amendments. She cited cases where rights not specifically spelled out in the Constitution were granted in court rulings, such as the 1967 *Loving v. Virginia* case, which struck down laws prohibiting interracial marriages.

There are, she said, "a great body of cases decided in the past by this Court in the areas of marriage, sex, contraception, procreation, childbearing, and education of children which says that there are certain things that are so much a part of the individual concern that they should be left to the determination of the individual."

When the judges finally interrupted her, they focused largely on the issue of fetal rights, pushing her on whether a fetus has constitutional rights and whether those rights changed as a pregnancy progressed.

Weddington dodged and parried, saying several times that a fetus was not a person under the Constitution or the law and offering only birth as the point where a fetus should be treated as a person. Instead, she urged the justices to find that the Texas law was unconstitutional and to conclude that a woman has "a fundamental constitutional right" to make decisions about her pregnancy.

Toward the end of her time, Justice Potter Stewart pushed harder on the point, asking: "If—*if*—it were established that an unborn fetus is a person within the protection of the Fourteenth Amendment, you would have almost an impossible case here, would you not?"

"I would have a very difficult case," she admitted, laughing nervously.

It was a misstep: A more seasoned lawyer likely would have found a way to avoid conceding that point.

Soon after, she concluded, saving a few minutes for a rebuttal at the end.

For the second round of arguments, Robert Flowers, Jay Floyd's boss and the head of the attorney general's enforcement division, represented the state of Texas. Flowers had thought from the beginning that the legal issues were clear-cut: To him, a fetus was human from conception and the questions around abortion belonged to the state legislature, not the courts.

Flowers was so sure of these arguments that he hadn't bothered to write out an outline or practice his presentation. While Weddington had coordinated with her *Doe* counterpart, Margie

Robert Flowers, 1978.

Pitts Hames, Flowers had never spoken with Dorothy Beasley, the articulate lawyer for Georgia. None of that had seemed necessary at the time. Later, he would say that he regretted not preparing more.

His office was also in some turmoil. The attorney general, Crawford Martin, had lost in the May primary election, and Flowers, Floyd, and many of their colleagues would soon be leaving their jobs. (Martin, who had significant health issues, was with Flowers and Floyd at the counsel's table, mainly because he was headed to Baltimore for medical treatment after the hearing. The fifty-six-year-old attorney general was sicker than most realized. On his last day of work in December, he died of a heart attack.)

Some years after the case, Flowers also admitted that he personally had "a feeling of great inner confusion" about abortion even as he argued for the state. Despite his legal positions, he could see reasons when it might make sense.

"I recognized it as a most difficult case, and I was hoping that the brilliant minds on the Supreme Court could resolve it," he said.

Those minds, no doubt, wanted some insight from Flowers and the state of Texas, but his presentation offered little. He started off declaring that a person is created at conception but then quickly got knotted up on whether it was a question for a legislature or a constitutional question for the court. In responses to questions, he seemed confused about when the Fourteenth Amendment was added (in 1868, after the Civil War) or what it said.

Justice White pointed out that if the fetus were a person, "the state would have great trouble permitting an abortion, wouldn't it?"

Flowers agreed.

What about "to save the life of a mother or her health or anything else?" White asked.

"Well," Flowers answered, "there would be a balancing of the two lives." The state chose the mother, he said.

Justice Thurgood Marshall couldn't resist poking a little fun at his contradictions: "Well, did the State of Texas say that if it is for the benefit of the health of the wife, [it is okay] to kill the husband?"

"I wouldn't think so, sir," Flowers answered.

The state's attorney soon returned to his main argument, that the fetus was a person under the Constitution. At one point, he turned to the dramatic language of the right-to-life movement, noting that the court had diligently protected the rights of minorities. "And gentlemen," he said, "we say that this is a minority, a silent minority, the true silent minority. Who is speaking for these children? Where is the counsel for these unborn children?"

He added, "Are we to place this power in the hands of a mother and a doctor?"

But he couldn't cite any medical studies saying that life began at conception and admitted that doctors don't agree when life begins. At one point, a couple of justices even tried to help him argue that a fetus might have other rights, even if it wasn't a person. But Flowers didn't catch on.

He sat down feeling like the court had been much tougher on him than on Weddington.

Weddington took full advantage of her remaining few minutes. Having bobbled an earlier question from Justice Blackmun about the Hippocratic oath, she pointed out that it was written when abortion was dangerous and possibly life-threatening for women.

While Flowers had essentially ignored whether a woman had any rights, she reiterated them. "We are not here to advocate abortion. We do not ask this Court to rule that abortion is good or desirable in any particular situation," she said.

"We are here to advocate that the decision as to whether or not a particular woman will continue to carry or will terminate a pregnancy is a decision that should be made by that individual, that she, in fact, has a constitutional right to make that decision for herself."

She wrapped up with the relevant line from Justice Brennan's opinion in the *Eisenstadt* case: "If the right of privacy is to mean anything, it is the right of the individual, whether married or single, to make determinations for themselves."

It was a solid argument for the twenty-seven-year-old lawyer.

Blackmun took sparse notes this time, a sign that perhaps he had already made up his mind. But he gave Weddington a B grade, an improvement over her first argument.

Flowers, however, got a D.

The court turned next to *Doe v. Bolton*, the companion case that challenged whether Georgia could restrict abortions to just a few reasons and whether women had to jump through multiple hoops to get one.

Margie Pitts Hames, in her arguments challenging the Georgia law, made the case that the law's exceptions for the benefit of women's health didn't help many women. More than twice as many Georgia women got abortions in New York in 1971 as in Georgia, she noted—and that didn't include women who went to the District of Columbia or California. Because of the many approvals required, a Georgia abortion cost $400 to $600, while an abortion in New York, including airfare, cost about $225. Poor women, unable to travel or wade through the state's maze of regulations, still resorted to cheap abortions from illegal, unlicensed providers, she said.

Dorothy Beasley, again the most energetic and clear-thinking speaker, didn't insist that a fetus was a person as Flowers had but recognized "a gray area" where some kind of life was present. A woman had rights, she said, but they were limited when another entity was involved.

Amid presentations from Margie Pitts Hames and Dorothy Beasley, at least a few of the justices wrestled with another issue: If a woman had a right to have an abortion, at what point during her pregnancy should the fetus's potential become a factor?

Neither Weddington nor Flowers had been any help on this, with Weddington ducking the question. Time limits on abortion weren't an issue in the Texas law, she said.

But Hames said she believed a time limit at some point in the pregnancy would be constitutional. And Beasley acknowledged that a state could legitimately have one set

Dorothy Toth Beasley, right, at an Atlanta event with Sarah Weddington, 1980.

of standards for the first third or first half of a pregnancy and a different standard beyond that.

It was a curious line of questioning. Neither law being challenged addressed any time limits or fetal development.

Justice Blackmun took a few more notes on *Doe*. Hames, he noted, "drones." He gave her a C-. Beasley won the highest grade of all, a B+.

Justice William Brennan listened to the questions that his colleague Blackmun had asked from the bench and concluded that Blackmun had, in fact, switched positions on the cases. Counting Blackmun and the two Nixon-appointed justices, Brennan tallied five votes to uphold the states' restrictive abortion laws and only four to overturn them.

Weddington left the court feeling like "most of them had already made their minds up," she told Ginny Whitehill in a letter soon after the arguments.

Still, she was cautiously optimistic. "I may be wrong, but I think we are going to win this case," she wrote her friend. "Not sure what grounds or how good the opinion will be, but really think we'll win."

OPINIONS

October 1972–January 1973

Two days after the second set of arguments, on October 13, 1972, the justices met to vote on the cases they had just heard. This time, they considered *Roe* and *Doe* together. With two new justices, no one knew exactly what to expect.

Chief Justice Warren Burger went first. He had been indecisive about *Roe* before, but this time he was specific: The Texas law was too restrictive in limiting abortions only to save a mother's life, he said. It needed to go. However, he was less certain about the Georgia law.

Justices William O. Douglas, William Brennan, and Thurgood Marshall all continued to support Harry Blackmun's previous proposed opinions overturning both laws. Potter Stewart still agreed with the previous decisions, too, but he felt strongly that the court needed to clearly state that a fetus wasn't a person under the Constitution, though it may still have rights.

Blackmun, intending to defend his months of work, had brought detailed notes with him to the meeting, tiny letters scratched out on a legal pad, with his own abbreviations, like *n* for not and *b* for be. He wanted to share outlines for the decisions he had been rewriting.

While few of his words are recorded in the notes of other justices, his scrawled talking points said he was pleased the case had been deferred because it had given him time to think and read more about the issues.

He didn't know whether the cases would be assigned to him again, but he had a lot of personal investment in them. "It is n[ot] a happy assignment—will b[e] excoriated," he wrote, adding, "I am revising and expanding t[he] proposed opinions to command a majority."

His colleague Brennan had been wrong. Blackmun hadn't changed sides at all. Nor did he see the cases differently than he had in the previous term. He still wanted to find the Texas law unconstitutionally vague and to make Georgia the lead case.

Blackmun also acknowledged the impact of the decisions, in both his notes and his comments to his fellow justices: If the Texas law falls, he wrote,

1. *A majority of state statutes go down the drain*
2. *It will be an unsettled period for a while*
3. *But most State legislatures will meet in '73.*

If the Supreme Court decision were released by early 1973, state lawmakers would have enough notice to come up with new laws that met the court's standards.

Next up was Lewis Powell, weighing in for the first time. His position was a surprise: He agreed with Blackmun. But he and

Harry Blackmun's notes, which read: "Mandate
1. A majority of state statutes go down the drain
2. It will be an unsettled period for a while
3. But most State legislatures will meet in '73
4. Any point in withholding the mandate? To 4/1"

some of the other judges urged Blackmun to find *Roe v. Wade* unconstitutional based on the Fourteenth Amendment, not because it was vague. He also thought *Roe* should be the lead case.

As expected, Justice White planned to dissent because he believed states had the right to make laws restricting abortion. Further, he said, he could not support abortion on demand. The other new justice, Rehnquist, agreed with him.

Blackmun was again asked to write the opinions. Though he had some new guidance from the other justices, he also had a strong majority: The vote was six or seven to two, with Burger undecided about *Doe.*

On Election Day, November 7, 1972, Sarah Weddington easily won a seat in the Texas House of Representatives, one of just five women elected that year to the statehouse.

Republican President Richard Nixon won reelection in a landslide over Democrat George McGovern, who had been painted as a radical liberal for supporting amnesty for those who evaded the military draft. (McGovern was also alleged to support abortion rights, though he actually believed the issue was up to individual states.) Nixon won the Catholic vote that had gone to Democrats in the three previous presidential elections, though abortion had not become a big issue in the campaign.

However, an unusual summer burglary of the Democratic National Committee headquarters in the Watergate office building was making headlines. Republican campaign money was linked to the break-in. Before long, reporters would be following trails that led toward Nixon himself.

Politics and the unpopular Vietnam War dominated the news. Meanwhile, groups on both sides of the abortion debate seemed to be building momentum. After the National Right to Life Committee's third annual convention in the summer of 1972, some Minnesota Right to Life leaders began lobbying for a national organization independent of the Catholic Church. By late in the year, organizers from several states were meeting to create a framework for a separate entity.

Right-to-life activists also fought a proposal in Michigan that would have allowed abortions up to the twentieth week of pregnancy. Catholic churches raised $200,000 (or about $1.2 million today) to help fight the referendum and mailed out a million pamphlets featuring fetal development. Meanwhile, a Protestant-led group called Voice of the Unborn flooded the state with images of eighteen-week- and nineteen-week-old fetuses, even though such abortions were rare and usually related to fetal deformities.

The group also mailed 250,000 flyers to African Americans that tied abortion to racial discrimination. Just before the election, Dr. Edgar Keemer's office was raided, and he was charged, again, with providing illegal abortions.

All the mailings and photographs had an impact. In November, the proposal was overwhelmingly defeated.

At the same time, more courts were striking down state abortion laws than upholding them. Feminists were also making gains in their demands for full and equal rights: In March 1972, the U.S. Senate approved the Equal Rights Amendment, a constitutional amendment that would outlaw discrimination based on sex. More than twenty states of the thirty-eight needed quickly ratified it.

Despite the Michigan vote, overall public opinion nationwide seemed to be moving rapidly in favor of abortion rights. A Gallup poll conducted in the summer of 1972 found that 64 percent of the public now believed that a decision about an abortion "should be made solely by a woman and her physician"—up from less than 15 percent of the public in 1968. Even a majority of Catholics agreed. Most of those polled also supported providing birth control information and counseling to teens.

Notably, Justice Blackmun had tucked a copy of the *Washington Post*'s Gallup story into his files.

In late November, nearly six weeks after the second arguments were heard, Blackmun circulated a much different draft of his *Roe* opinion to his fellow justices than his May version. It was long—close to fifty pages—and it included a thorough history of abortion and the Hippocratic oath, as well as a review of how professional organizations, like the American Medical Association, had changed their views on the procedure in recent years.

Finally, at the bottom of page thirty-seven, Blackmun got to the point: The court had long recognized that a right of privacy exists under the Constitution. Whether that right is found in the Fourteenth Amendment's concept of liberty or the other rights covered by the Ninth Amendment, he wrote, it "is broad enough to encompass a woman's decision whether or not to terminate her pregnancy." (Later, he stated that the Texas law violated the due process clause of the Fourteenth Amendment, which says the state can't deny a person life, liberty, or property without due process of law.)

But, he went on, that right to privacy isn't unlimited. It has to be weighed against the state's interest in the woman's health and in the growing potential life of the fetus.

He attached a memo with the opinion, presenting the "1972 fall edition" with a personal note: "This has proved for me to be both difficult and elusive."

He pointed out what would become one of the most controversial parts of the decision: specifying what kind of state interference could be allowed during each of the three trimesters of a woman's forty-week pregnancy. "You will observe," he wrote, "that I have concluded that the end of the first trimester is critical."

Indeed, at almost the end of his draft opinion, he wrote that a decision about abortion during the first trimester of pregnancy should be left to a woman's physician. Beyond that, the state could limit abortions to "stated reasonable therapeutic categories."

He didn't have to be so specific. The court could have simply struck down the Texas and Georgia laws as unconstitutional and left it to state legislatures to figure out laws that protected a woman's right to privacy. Some clerks thought he was acting as a legislature in including so much detail and referred to the draft as "Harry's abortion." Many critics later agreed.

But others saw it as necessary. Without guidance, states might adopt many different laws. The court could be tied up for years defining and redefining constitutional rights while leaving women still unable to have a safe procedure.

Where the abortion-rights-by-trimester approach came from isn't clear. Blackmun later said he had been influenced by abortion history—that for a long period of time, ending a pregnancy before quickening wasn't illegal. He may also have been reflecting the suggestions of the law clerk who worked on the opinion or decisions reached in lower courts.

In his cover letter to the other justices, Blackmun didn't explain why or how he settled on the first trimester, saying only, "This is arbitrary, but perhaps any other selected point, such as quickening or viability, is equally arbitrary."

He apologized "for the rambling character of the memorandum and for its undue length," and ended on a cautionary note. "It has been an interesting assignment," he wrote. "As I stated in conference, the decision, however made, will probably result in the Court's being severely criticized."

Separately, Blackmun sent a personal note to Justice Brennan, asking him to review references to the Catholic Church. "I believe they are accurate factually, but I do not want them to be offensive or capable of being regarded as unduly critical by any reader," he said.

One of the first judges to respond in detail was one of the new Nixon appointees, Lewis Powell, who was thought to be a conservative. Unknown to his fellow judges, Powell had come back to the court in the fall with his mind made up. He invited his law clerk, Larry Hammond, to a fancy lunch; to Hammond's shock, Powell announced that he thought a woman had a right to control her own body early in pregnancy. Powell believed that such a right benefited both women and their children.

"You could have knocked me over," Hammond recalled years later.

Powell may have had some insight from family connections. His father-in-law had been a prominent obstetrician, and his wife's two brothers were also doctors.

Powell was also deeply affected by a painful personal experience. When he was still practicing law in Richmond, a young man who worked at his law firm called him one night crying and in terrible distress, asking to meet. The young man explained that his girlfriend had gotten pregnant and asked for his help in inducing an abortion. Something went wrong, and she bled to death.

Powell met with the local prosecutor, who didn't press charges. But the experience seared in the lawyer an understanding that desperate women would seek abortions regardless of the law, and that keeping the procedure illegal only added to the danger.

In a private note that was hand-delivered to Blackmun, Powell complimented the "impressive scholarship and analysis" of the opinion. Then, he urged Blackmun to draw the line at "viability"— when the fetus can survive outside the womb—rather than at the end of the first trimester. He quoted a recent Connecticut federal court opinion, noting that at the point of fetal viability, the state's interest is easy to understand.

Blackmun wrote back, saying that at first blush, he preferred to leave the cutoff at the first trimester, with the understanding that a state could make it later if it wished.

A week later, Powell tried again, passing a note to Blackmun while they were on the bench, saying that he still thought viability "is a more logical & supportable time," but that he would support Blackmun's opinion without the change.

Soon after, Blackmun sent a memo to all the justices, saying that one judge had suggested that fetal viability would be better than the first trimester as the point where the state could regulate abortion. He could see arguments for both, he wrote, and would be willing to change his written opinion.

"May I have your reactions?" he asked.

Responses came quickly. Like Powell, Justices Marshall and Brennan supported a different time frame, and each offered suggestions for when and why the state might intervene. Justice Stewart was worried that the option might be too "legislative" in dictating when the state could act and urged Blackmun to give states more latitude. Douglas was okay with state regulation after the first trimester.

White and Rehnquist planned to write their own opinions.

Only Chief Justice Burger was vague and noncommittal, saying, "I have more 'ploughing' to do on your memo."

In mid-December, Blackmun responded that he would revise the opinions based on the suggestions and circulate another draft soon. There was some urgency: He wanted the cases to come down no later than mid-January "to tie in with the convening of most state legislatures."

A week later, he sent around new drafts with more details. Given that early abortions were safer than childbirth, abortions would be up to a doctor, in consultation with the patient, during the first trimester of pregnancy. During that time, the state could not interfere.

In the second trimester, however, when the procedures are more complicated, the state could impose regulations that "reasonably relate to the preservation and protection of maternal health." That could include requirements for doctors or facilities where the procedures are done.

At the point that the fetus is viable, the state can impose regulations to protect fetal life, "except when it is necessary to preserve the life or health of the mother," Blackmun wrote.

At a time when women still were fighting to be heard and recognized, the decision wasn't a feminist one. Blackmun declined to leave the choice primarily to women. Instead, he wrote in a summation, the abortion decision is "inherently, and primarily, a medical decision and basic responsibility for it must rest with the physician."

The other justices didn't see fit to ask for edits to include the woman's decision in the equation.

But they did go along. Before Christmas, Justices Douglas, Brennan, Stewart, and Marshall joined the decision, and Powell came on board early in the new year.

Justices White and Rehnquist, as expected, took the opposite position. In a stinging dissent, Byron White called the decision "an exercise of raw judicial power" and wrote that the court was saying that the Constitution "values the convenience, whim, or caprice of the putative mother more than the life or potential life of the fetus," until the fetus was viable.

He didn't think the Constitution granted such rights to women; he believed the issue should be left to the states. "In a sensitive area such as this, involving as it does issues over which reasonable men may easily and heatedly differ, I cannot accept the Court's exercise of its clear power of choice by interposing a constitutional barrier to state efforts to protect human life and by investing mothers and doctors with the constitutionally protected right to exterminate it," he wrote.

Justice Lewis Powell kept a scorecard of how each justice would vote.

Rehnquist joined White's dissent and wrote his own, questioning whether privacy was an issue in the case.

Even with the two dissenters, Blackmun now had a firm majority of six. But Chief Justice Burger was still dragging his feet, and none of the justices knew why.

By the second week of 1973, the decision, the dissents, and a few additional comments from justices were ready to go. In addition to the abortions allowed under *Roe*, the court was cutting away the red tape in the *Doe* case, throwing out the residency requirement or the need for a woman to get the approval of additional doctors and a committee.

The *Roe* opinion was Blackmun's work, to be sure, reflecting months of deliberation and thought. But it also reflected multiple views—Powell's, Marshall's, and Brennan's thoughts on when and how the state could step in; Douglas's writing in *Griswold*; and Stewart's specific request that the opinion state that the "unborn" is not a person under the Fourteenth Amendment.

Blackmun had molded a strong majority or, in legal lingo, "commanded a court." Now, he just had to wait for the chief justice to set a date for the decision to be announced.

THE DECISION

What was taking Chief Justice Burger so long? No one seemed to know exactly.

At one point, one justice suggested they release a decision with only eight votes.

During the court's regular conference on Friday, January 12, 1973, Blackmun made a point of asking that the opinions be announced the following Wednesday, January 17. Burger said he thought he could reach a decision by then, and steps were taken to set Wednesday as the date.

The Tuesday before, Potter Stewart passed Blackmun a handwritten note: "Are <u>Doe</u>, <u>Roe</u>, etc. going to be announced tomorrow?"

"Who knows?" Blackmun wrote back, saying he doubted they would. He was hoping for the following Monday, January 22. "They <u>must</u> come down," he added.

Later that day, Burger sent around a formal memo, saying that he would vote with the majority. He was working on short concurrences, agreeing with the decisions but with his own twist. He expected to deliver them the next day. "I see no reason why we cannot schedule these cases for Monday," he said.

Blackmun "was noticeably upset" at the delay, one justice said later. But there was nothing he could do about it.

Other justices had a theory. The chief justice was swearing in President Nixon for his second term on Saturday, January 20. Maybe he didn't want to face the president—the man who named him to his job—right after announcing a dramatic abortion decision that contradicted the president's previously stated views.

Chief Justice Warren Burger swears in President Richard M. Nixon for his second term, January 20, 1973.

Finally, during inauguration weekend, Burger shared a three-paragraph concurrence. He didn't think the court was exceeding the scope of its duties, he wrote. He didn't think the decision would be as dire as the dissenters White and Rehnquist predicted.

Then, perhaps speaking primarily to an audience of one president of the United States, he added, "Plainly, the Court today rejects any claim that the Constitution requires abortion on demand."

While he waited for the chief justice, Blackmun drafted an eight-page statement to read from the bench, acknowledging the sensitive and emotional nature of the decision.

On Monday, January 22, just after 10 a.m., the court began to reveal its decisions for the week.

Blackmun shared the highlights of the opinion, including the unusual breakdown of each trimester of pregnancy. With that, he added, "We thus strike a balance between the interests of a pregnant woman and the interests of the state in health and potential life." And he repeated the chief justice's conclusion: "I fear what the headlines may be, but it should be stressed that the Court does not today hold that the Constitution compels abortion on demand."

He had invited his wife, Dottie, to be at the court that day, without telling her why. (Blackmun later claimed that his wife and three daughters hadn't lobbied him at all; however, a late 1970s book about the court said she told one of his law clerks that she was working on him to lift the restrictions.)

Afterward, she told him she was proud of the decision.

Lewis Powell, perhaps anticipating the response that was to

come, sent Dottie a handwritten note. "Harry has written an historic opinion, which I was proud to join. His statement from the Bench this morning also was excellent," he said, adding, "I am glad you were here."

Despite Blackmun's worry, the initial headlines were direct. The *Dallas Times Herald*, an afternoon paper, noted in a relatively brief story that the Texas abortion law was overruled, but that states could still impose regulations.

Just about the time that paper hit doorsteps, there was another breaking story: Lyndon B. Johnson, the only living former president, died that day of a heart attack at his Texas ranch. That huge news grabbed the top of every major newspaper. (It even took up the entire front page of the next day's *Dallas Morning News*, pushing the story about the Dallas lawsuit to page five.)

The next day, Nixon announced a long-awaited peace agreement and cease-fire for the Vietnam War, another enormous news story. For all the months of angst and negotiation that had gone into the *Roe* opinion, the other news events made the decision seem almost unimportant.

Even if the stories weren't as prominent as they might have been, newspapers of the day understood the significance. Both the *Washington Post* and the *New York Times* headlines noted that abortions would be fully legal in the first three months of pregnancy. The *Times* called the decision "a historic resolution of a fiercely controversial issue" that would require rewriting almost every state law.

Both papers noted that three of the four justices appointed by Nixon voted with the majority. In fact, Republican presidents had appointed five of the seven justices who voted to legalize abortion.

Time magazine, which had been reporting ahead of the decision, actually published a story the day the opinion came out, predicting that the court's ruling would create a firestorm.

"No decision in the court's history, not even those outlawing public school segregation and capital punishment, has evoked the intensity of emotion that will surely follow this ruling," it said. "The pronouncement, ending 13 months of wrangling among the Justices, is certain to be met with passionate resistance by abortion opponents and to stir new controversy across the nation."

Nixon and the White House were silent, offering no public comment or press release on the decision. But according to fuzzy tapes released decades later, Nixon took notice. Chatting briefly with an aide the day after the decision, he seems to conclude that the decision will give women too much freedom. "A girl goes and gets knocked up," he appears to say, "the popular word is, she doesn't have to worry about the Pill anymore. She goes down to the doctor [and] has an abortion for five dollars or whatever."

A little later, he adds, "I'm having a hard time [believing] that abortions are necessary, I know that—unless you have a black and a white," he said, apparently referring to interracial couples, "or a rape. I just say that matter-of-factly. You know what I mean? There are times."

Sarah Weddington was in Austin at the Capitol starting her workday as a new state representative when reporters began calling

(AT2)AUSTIN,Tex.,Jan 22--PLEASED WITH COURT DECISION--
State Rep.Sarah Weddington of Austin submitted a bill
Friday to repeal the Texas abortion law. Now she
can drop it. Ms. Weddington, a lawyer, filed the
class action suit that resulted today in the U.S.
Supreme Court decision holding the abortion statute
unconstitutional. Rep.Weddingtion said she was
pleased with the decision.(AP WIREPHOTO)twp21130twp73

A photo of Sarah Weddington that the Associated Press sent out January 22, 1973, the day the court announced the landmark *Roe* decision.

both her law office and her state office. She remembers chaos as the phones rang, friends called to congratulate her, and people dropped by or sent flowers in celebration.

Around noon, she got a telegram from the Supreme Court with the rulings. The opinions would be "airmailed," the fastest mail available at the time.

Linda Coffee heard the news on the radio on the way to work. She and Weddington rejoiced on the phone. Then, both reached out to friends in Washington, D.C., who might tell them what the decision said, since the court's decision wouldn't show up for a few days.

For the lawyers and for abortion rights activists in general, the decision was far more than most of them dared to hope for, unconditionally making abortion available when it hadn't been before.

Weddington was grateful for the seven-to-two vote and the agreement that women had a fundamental right to abortion. The trimester approach, however, surprised her. No one had discussed trimesters in their oral arguments or in the briefs filed with the court, though doctors certainly performed different procedures depending on how far along a woman was. She said the details were "a very practical kind of response" to the many lawsuits that might be headed to the court.

Ginny Whitehill was jubilant, calling the decision "more important for women than getting the vote." The reason? "This truly gives women control over their own bodies for the first time in human history," she said.

Linda Coffee was more analytical. She was disappointed that the opinion didn't more specifically give rights to women instead of doctors. But, "as a practical matter," she said, "it doesn't make any difference."

The thirty-year-old lawyer was philosophical a few days later in an interview with the *Baptist Press*, the newspaper of the Southern Baptist Convention. In 1971, Southern Baptists passed a resolution calling for members to work for legislation that would permit abortion in cases of rape, incest, severe fetal deformity, or if there was a likelihood of damage to the mother's emotional, mental, and physical health.

Coffee told reporter Robert O'Brien that while she believed in the legal right of women to have an abortion, each individual still had to make her own moral decisions. "From my personal perspective as a Christian, it would tear me up to have to make a decision on abortion except in the early stages," she said. Even then, she added, "I would have to have a compelling reason."

From a legal standpoint, she said, she believed the state should leave abortion questions to the woman and her doctor. But for herself, she added, "I would have little personal sympathy for the use of abortion as a contraceptive or to avoid personal responsibility."

O'Brien also reached out to Norma McCorvey, who agreed to shed her Jane Roe identity for the interview.

Three years before, "I was a woman alone with no place to go and no job," McCorvey said. "I felt there was no one in the world who could help me."

Now twenty-five, she called the Supreme Court decision a "wonderful thing." The decision had brought back painful memories for her, and she was glad to know "that other women will not have to go through what I did," she said.

"I want to think about the future now, not the past."

The Supreme Court ruling put an end to the prosecution of Dr. Jane Hodgson, Reverend Robert Hare, Dr. Edgar Keemer, and the women of Jane. One by one, the cases were dismissed or simply disappeared. Dr. Hodgson continued to work as a legal abortion provider, as did Dr. Keemer. The woman of Jane considered continuing their work but decided to move on to the next stages of their lives, leaving the procedures to true professionals.

NARAL, which had been the National Association for the Repeal of Abortion Laws, became the National Abortion Rights Action League.

The decision outraged the Catholic Church and other abortion opponents. Cardinal John Krol of Philadelphia, who was president of the National Conference of Catholic Bishops, said the decision was "an unspeakable tragedy for the nation" and "a monstrous injustice."

The archbishop of Washington, Cardinal Patrick O'Boyle, asked every pastor in the archdiocese—more than one hundred of them—to preach that "abortion is morally evil" at all masses on the first Sunday after the ruling. Like others in the church, he compared the ruling to the pre–Civil War *Dred Scott* decision— perhaps the worst Supreme Court decision ever—that concluded that African Americans could not be citizens and slavery could continue.

By February, members of the Catholic Church were warned

that they could be excommunicated if they had an abortion or performed one. The court's decision also rallied the Right to Life umbrella group, which finally incorporated as a nonprofit in the spring and formally separated from the Catholic Church, allowing it to raise money and build a more effective organization.

The state of Texas tried to appeal the decision, but the court wasn't interested. In rejecting the appeal, the court also sent a number of pending abortion cases back to the lower courts to be reconsidered in light of the *Roe* and *Doe* rulings.

While Justice Blackmun knew the decision would be controversial, no one at the court was quite prepared for the tsunami that followed. More than seventy thousand letters poured in, mostly to him and Justice Brennan, many in opposition. Some came from clergy, some from parishioners, and many from entire classes of schoolchildren, who seemed to be fulfilling class assignments. The justices were called murderers and compared with Hitler, and faced regular death threats. Some also called for the Catholic Church to excommunicate Brennan.

Brennan shrugged off the responses as part of the job, but Blackmun read nearly everything that came in. On a trip to give a speech shortly after the decision, he was met for the first time with picketers opposing the opinion. For many years after, protestors showed up whenever he spoke. Though dismayed by the ugly responses, he remained firmly in support of his decision.

Polls taken after the ruling found that a majority of Americans approved of the decision, indicating that perhaps the opposition was a small but vocal minority and the controversy would cool. After all, almost 80 percent of Americans had opposed a 1962

Supreme Court decision that found prayer in schools unconstitutional, and more than 70 percent had disapproved of a 1967 decision striking down laws that banned interracial marriage.

Despite the Supreme Court's ruling, some states initially declined to allow abortions, and many hospitals chose not to offer the procedure. Few or no abortions were performed in Louisiana, Mississippi, Utah, North Dakota, or West Virginia in 1973.

Though legal, abortions were still more easily available to women with money and to those who lived in urban areas. Only 15 percent of public hospitals—which serve the poor—offered abortions by early 1974. More than half the procedures were done in clinics, typically located in large cities and usually requiring payment at the time of the service.

In New Jersey, state officials wrangled over regulations until well into 1974; there and in other states, providers simply opened clinics and operated without a license.

In Dallas, Dr. Curtis Boyd, who had been performing abortions for the clergy referral service, opened the first abortion clinic in February 1973. Others opened a second clinic a few months later. Some Planned Parenthood affiliates around the country gradually began to offer abortions along with birth control services.

By 1974, roughly 900,000 legal abortions were performed in the U.S., up about 50 percent from 1972, when New York, California, and the District of Columbia were offering the bulk of the legal abortion services.

Unable to access legal procedures, some women still sought illegal abortions: About twenty-five women died from illegal abortions in 1973, compared with twenty-two who died from legal ones. And experts estimated that even by the mid-1970s, hundreds of thousands of women who needed abortions could not get them because of cost or the distance they had to travel.

Still, except for the Catholic Church, the backlash to the court's decision was tempered. Even the conservative Southern Baptist Convention was willing to compromise. Well into the 1970s, Southern Baptists supported their 1971 position that abortion should be allowed in cases of rape, incest, severe fetal deformity, or the likelihood of emotional, mental, or physical damage to the mother.

Still, some in Congress favored a constitutional amendment to grant human rights to fetuses, but the effort never gained much support. Despite Nixon's modest efforts during the 1972 campaign, abortion wasn't a major political issue during the 1970s. Republican president Gerald Ford's wife, Betty, was a vocal supporter of abortion rights. And when Ford nominated John Paul Stevens to the Supreme Court to replace Justice Douglas, he wasn't asked one question about abortion or *Roe*.

With improvements in contraception and access to safe and legal birth control and abortions, many women finally had control over their reproduction and their bodies. Also aided by new equal-rights laws, they made great gains in the 1970s, attending law schools and medical schools in growing numbers, moving into the workforce, and demanding better pay and more opportunities. After such a long fight for reproductive control, supporters of abortion rights began to feel like the issue was settled.

They were mistaken.

PREGNANT PAUSE:
Forced Sterilization

In June 1973, just a few months after the *Roe v. Wade* decision, a nurse took fourteen-year-old Minnie Relf and her twelve-year-old sister, Mary Alice, from their Montgomery, Alabama, home, supposedly for birth control shots.

Instead, the two girls were admitted to a hospital. The next morning, a doctor tied their tubes, leaving them unable to ever have children.

Even as women fought for the right to control their own child-bearing, the U.S. government was helping others make decisions for broad swaths of poor or marginalized women and girls, who were sterilized without their consent.

The American College of Obstetricians and Gynecologists in 1969 had dropped its rule of 120, which limited voluntary sterilization. Instead, in 1970, it approved guidelines making tubal ligations a decision between a patient and a doctor. However, many middle- and upper-class women who wanted to have their tubes tied to prevent future pregnancies had to sue to force hospitals to let their doctors perform the procedures.

By the mid-1970s, voluntary sterilization passed the Pill as the most popular birth control method. But involuntary sterilizations also continued.

The Relf girls, whose family lived on public assistance, had previously been referred to a federally funded birth control clinic because "boys were hanging around." They were given experimental birth control shots, and when those were discontinued, the clinic recommended surgery.

Their mother, who could not read, signed a consent form with an X but did not understand that her daughters, one of whom had severe learning issues, would be sterilized. Their disabled father wasn't home.

When the surgery came to light, a federal investigation found that the clinic had sterilized eleven girls, nearly all of them African

In the center, from left, lawyer Morris Dees, twelve-year-old Mary Alice Relf, and her fourteen-year-old sister Minnie Lee Relf, after the young girls were sterilized without proper consent in 1973.

American, like the Relfs. Nationwide, at least eighty minors were sterilized at federally funded clinics.

New guidelines were put in to stem abuses, but those often were ignored. Studies estimated that the Indian Health Service sterilized 25 percent—or more—of Native American women of childbearing age during the 1970s. That included two fifteen-year-olds who went in for appendectomies.

Often, women were sterilized during or just after childbirth, sometimes because the doctor thought they were too poor or already had enough children. Sometimes, they were told their children would be taken away or they would lose public assistance if they didn't consent.

In Aiken, South Carolina, one of the few obstetricians refused to deliver babies for women on public assistance, who were often black, unless they either paid him in full in cash or agreed to be sterilized. A whistleblower accused a Los Angeles County hospital of coercing many Mexican American women into steriliza-tions and hysterectomies during labor.

In the later 1970s, amid lawsuits, stricter rules were put in place, requiring consent be given well in advance. But the cases were a reminder that even after *Roe*, there was a divide between rich and poor, white and nonwhite, and that women's bodies weren't always theirs to control.

PART IV

AFTER *ROE*

. . . Reproductive rights rest on the recognition of the basic right of all couples and individuals to decide freely and responsibly the number, spacing, and timing of their children and to have the information and means to do so, and the right to attain the highest standard of sexual and reproductive health. It also includes their right to make decisions concerning reproduction free of discrimination, coercion, and violence. . . .

—Beijing Declaration and Platform for Action,
Fourth World Conference on Women, Beijing, China,
September 1995

POLITICS

1975–1980

In the summer of 1975, Joseph Charles Stockett attended a party in Eugene, Oregon, had a few beers, and smoked some hashish. People there remembered that he went on a rant about abortion and contraception. He left the house when the party ended but came back later with gasoline.

Soon after, he splattered the gasoline inside a Planned Parenthood clinic across the street and set it on fire, damaging the second-floor examining rooms. His reason: He believed Planned Parenthood was responsible for his ex-wife's abortion.

The clinic provided birth control and offered pregnancy tests, but it referred those wanting an abortion elsewhere. Even so, it was the first recorded act of violence over abortion, one of what would become thousands of instances of vandalism, arson, trespassing, and threats against clinics and doctors.

By the end of the 1970s, a dozen more clinics had been burned or bombed. Aggressive abortion opponents pushed their way into other clinics, sometimes chaining themselves to furniture or sitting down inside to block the clinic's operations.

These first attacks on clinics paralleled a rise in organized opposition to abortion and a growing conservatism in the country. Abortion rights supporters—who now called themselves "prochoice"—grew complacent as abortion became widely available across the United States. The number of abortions performed grew to 1 million in 1975 and 1.5 million in 1979.

Meanwhile, Congress energized antiabortion activists when it passed the Hyde Amendment, a 1976 rider tacked on to the money allocated for the next budget of the U.S. Department of Health and Human Services. Sponsored by Henry Hyde, a Catholic and a Republican representative from the Chicago area, it barred the use of federal funds to pay for abortions, except to preserve a woman's life. That meant poor women who qualified for Medicaid health coverage would have to pay for an abortion out of their own pockets.

A federal judge blocked the Hyde Amendment from going into effect right away, saying it was unconstitutional. But in June 1977, in a separate case involving a Connecticut law called *Maher v. Roe*, the U.S. Supreme Court ruled that states don't have to use state money to pay for an abortion, even if the state pays for the costs of childbirth.

In the majority opinion, Justice Lewis Powell wrote that a woman's right to abortion still exists without Medicaid, even though her financial situation may make it impossible for her to pay for one.

Later, in a five-to-four vote on *Harris v. McRae*, the Supreme

Court upheld the Hyde Amendment itself, saying that the federal government and the states don't have to pay for abortions. In response, some states decided to use state Medicaid money to pay for abortions for poor women, but most did not. Once again, women with money or connections had easy access to abortions, while poor women—often women of color— did not.

Meanwhile, the right-to-life movement began to gather steam. Under the leadership of Mildred Jefferson, the first African American woman to graduate from Harvard Medical School, the National Right to Life Committee claimed three thousand chapters and eleven million supporters in 1977.

Southern Baptists had seen some need for abortions in the early 1970s. But that began to change as Southern Baptists and other evangelicals became increasingly uncomfortable with the remarkable social revolution of the previous two decades, especially gains by women, affirmative action for minorities, sex education in schools, abortion rights, gay rights, and a more relaxed attitude toward sex, made possible by the Pill's effectiveness. Another sore spot: Internal Revenue Service rulings that Christian schools had to accept nonwhite children if they wanted to keep their nonprofit status.

For the first time since Nixon's short-lived effort to recruit Catholics, political strategists saw an opportunity to bring evangelicals, conservative Catholics, Mormons, and Orthodox Jews into the Republican tent. At the time, about as many Republicans supported abortion rights as did Democrats.

In the late 1970s, with the support of the Republican Party, a television evangelist named Jerry Falwell energized these groups

Ronald Reagan and Jerry Falwell, 1984.

with a call for "old-time morality," which he defined as "pro-family policies" and love of country. On television and during "I Love America" rallies, he preached against the Equal Rights Amendment, abortion, and gay rights. He called his growing organization the Moral Majority.

That conservative surge, coupled with a deep dissatisfaction with the troubled economy under President Jimmy Carter, helped sweep former California governor Ronald Reagan into office in the 1980 elections.

THE SUPREME COURT, AGAIN

1980–1992

By the time he became president, the Ronald Reagan who had helped liberalize the California abortion laws as governor was now openly opposed to abortion, calling it the taking of an unborn life. During a radio address on the tenth anniversary of *Roe v. Wade* in 1983, he announced that it was time to end "abortion on demand."

He appointed abortion opponents to key federal jobs, including surgeon general, and took other steps to discourage abortion around the world. But he never asked Congress to limit abortion, focusing his legislative efforts on the economy, the military, and cutting taxes. Instead, like Nixon, he tried to appoint justices to the U.S. Supreme Court who would make the court more conservative and who might scale back or overturn *Roe v. Wade*.

His first opportunity came just a few months into his presidency, when Justice Potter Stewart announced his retirement.

Reagan had campaigned on a promise to nominate the first woman to the Supreme Court. To the dismay of his top aides, who were hoping for an ultraconservative justice, Reagan was determined to stick with his pledge.

But there wasn't a deep bench of experienced women judges, especially conservative ones. Most law schools offered only a few spots for women until the early 1970s. In 1980, there were fewer than seventy-five women federal judges in the United States and just sixty on state appeals courts.

Reagan's team came up with a short list that included Sandra Day O'Connor, a fifty-one-year-old Arizona state appeals court judge and former majority leader in the state senate. She had been a standout at Stanford University Law School, as was her classmate William Rehnquist.

After law school, Rehnquist became a clerk for a Supreme Court justice. However, Sandra Day was unable to land even an interview with a big law firm—though one firm suggested she might become a legal secretary if she could type well enough. She married John O'Connor, and they settled in Phoenix, where she opened her own law office before entering politics. Rehnquist and his wife, Nan, also settled in Phoenix, where he practiced law for many years before moving to Washington, D.C. Both couples were active in Republican politics.

The conservative Rehnquist let Reagan's team know that he supported O'Connor's candidacy—in fact, he might have recommended her.

In meetings with Reagan officials, O'Connor said she found abortion "personally repugnant," but she didn't say how she would rule as a judge. However, she said she believed judges should not make law. The court could overrule previous decisions, she added, but that should happen only rarely.

On July 7, Reagan announced that he was nominating O'Connor as the first woman to the U.S. Supreme Court.

The National Right to Life Committee and Moral Majority immediately began to push back, claiming that she had supported abortion as a state legislator. But there was little evidence of that, with one exception. During her first months in the state legislature, she had voted in a committee to repeal the state's law that made abortion a criminal act. The proposal never made it to a formal vote.

Despite the opposition, her obvious intelligence, charm, and poise won over the most conservative senators. In September, the U.S. Senate confirmed her nomination unanimously.

Sandra Day O'Connor is sworn in as the first woman on the U.S. Supreme Court, 1981.

Her first abortion test came during the 1982–83 term, a decade after *Roe*. The city of Akron, Ohio—along with some other cities and states—had passed a number of restrictions intended to make abortions more difficult to get. Among other things, second-trimester abortions had to be performed in a hospital, women had to wait twenty-four hours after signing consent forms before they could have the procedure, and minors had to get a parent's consent. In addition, a doctor was forced to tell them that "the unborn child is human life from the moment of conception," that abortion was major surgery, and that they faced potential complications intended to make abortion sound dangerous, even though the true risks of complication were low.

In a six-to-three decision, issued in June 1983, the court ruled that those restrictions failed to contribute to a woman's health or make an abortion safer. The waiting period increased the cost, the required lecture interfered with the doctor-patient relationship, and the required parental consent did not allow a young woman to prove she was mature enough to make her own decision.

O'Connor disagreed with the decision and wrote the dissent, which the two *Roe v. Wade* dissenters, Rehnquist and White, joined. She particularly took issue with the trimester approach, calling it "unworkable" because medical technology changes. Viability would get earlier, she predicted, while abortion procedures would get easier and safer, ultimately colliding with each other.

(Today, infants born at twenty-five weeks have a fair chance of survival with intensive medical care, though most will have some disabilities. A small percentage of infants born at twenty-two weeks can survive, but nearly all will have disabilities. Fetuses born earlier than that do not have the skin, lungs, or bodily systems to survive.)

O'Connor wrote that the state has an interest in protecting the unborn throughout the whole pregnancy—as long as it doesn't "unduly burden" a woman's freedom to terminate her pregnancy. She concluded that none of the Akron restrictions created an undue burden on women.

Though the dissent didn't carry any legal weight, it laid the groundwork for her future positions—and confirmed Harry Blackmun's assumption that she would oppose abortion rights.

As the court was grappling with efforts from mostly southern and midwestern states to restrict abortions, violence against abortion providers surged. In 1984, more than two dozen abortion clinics or related offices were bombed or set on fire. One man was convicted of four arsons in Washington State, while two men and two women were convicted of bombing four clinics in Florida.

Three suburban Maryland men in their thirties, described as "fervent Christians," were arrested just before Reagan's second inauguration in January 1985 and tied to ten attacks. The bombings and arsons were aimed at clinics as far north as Delaware and as far south as Norfolk, Virginia, as well as Planned Parenthood, National Abortion Federation, and American Civil Liberties Union offices in the Washington, D.C., area.

More bombs were found at the home of Thomas Eugene Spinks, a roofing contractor who activated the bombs. At his trial, Spinks told the court, "I did what I felt was necessary before God." He was sentenced to fifteen years in prison.

Weeks after the arrests, a bullet came through the window of

Justice Harry Blackmun's Arlington, Virginia, apartment. Police eventually concluded it had randomly been fired from a distance and wasn't related to his work. But since Blackmun had long been the target of death threats and picketers, security was stepped up for him.

In addition to his safety, Blackmun had other reasons to worry about abortion rights. The remaining colleagues who had voted with him on *Roe* were well into their seventies and wouldn't be on the court much longer. In September 1986, Chief Justice Warren Burger retired. The Nixon conservative William Rehnquist was named the new chief justice, and he was replaced with another staunch conservative, Antonin Scalia.

The next year, Justice Lewis Powell retired. After Reagan's first two nominees flamed out, Anthony Kennedy, a California conservative, joined the court in 1988. Many people began to count enough votes to damage or overturn *Roe*.

In early 1989, just before Republican George H. W. Bush was sworn in as president, the Supreme Court agreed to hear a case out of Missouri called *Webster v. Reproductive Health Services*. Missouri legislators had dubbed their abortion law the "kitchen sink bill" because there were so many restrictions, including forbidding abortions at public hospitals or by public employees, except to save a woman's life, and requiring special testing of the fetus after twenty weeks to be sure it wasn't viable.

Bush had once been a Planned Parenthood supporter, but as his party shifted to oppose abortion rights, so did he. His administration's Justice Department asked the Supreme Court to overturn *Roe*.

The court was deeply divided. Chief Justice Rehnquist, believing the majority wanted to allow all the new restrictions and more, assigned the opinion to himself. In his early drafts, he took aim at *Roe*'s trimester approach, calling it "unsound" and "unworkable." Then, he sought to "modify and narrow *Roe*" with a new test for abortion regulations: Would an abortion law reasonably further "the state's interest in protecting potential human life" throughout the pregnancy?

It was an obvious about-face, switching the court's standard from a woman's right to make a personal decision with her doctor to the state's right to protect only its perceived interests in her fetus. In short, it would gut the protections that *Roe* granted. Several justices protested, including a newer justice, John Paul Stevens.

The woman's interest "is given no weight at all" in this "newly minted standard," he said in a memo to Rehnquist. In addition, almost any requirement would meet the standard. "A tax on abortions, a requirement that the pregnant woman must be able to stand on her head for fifteen minutes before she can have an abortion, or a criminal prohibition would each satisfy your test," he wrote.

Stevens said he was opposed to overturning *Roe*. But he said that if Rehnquist wanted to do it, "I would rather see the Court give the case a decent burial instead of tossing it out the window of a fast-moving caboose."

Harry Blackmun wrote a fiery dissent, noting that "*Roe* no longer survives."

Sandra Day O'Connor had been quiet during the debate. But after Rehnquist scheduled the decision for June 29, 1989, the last day of the term, she circulated a draft of her own. The restrictions were constitutional, she agreed, but she refused to change the standards set in *Roe*. This wasn't the case or the time, she said.

Her surprising position required Rehnquist to push back the decision for four more days, to July 3, as everyone else edited what they had written. In a divided and emotional five-to-four vote, the justices agreed the Missouri rules were constitutional, meaning states could restrict abortions even in the first three months of a woman's pregnancy. But only three justices joined Rehnquist's move to create a new standard. Since that wasn't a majority, *Roe* continued to stand.

In practice, not much changed in Missouri. Clinics remained open and busy. A small number of women who had gone to a particular Kansas City, Missouri, hospital for later-term abortions because of fetal defects instead had to go to Kansas for their procedures. But the court's ruling was essentially an invitation to conservative state legislatures to pass new laws to test *Roe* again.

In his *Webster* dissent, Blackmun worried about the liberty and equality of millions of women. "For today, at least," he wrote, "the law of abortion stands undisturbed. For today, the women of this Nation still retain the liberty to control their destinies. But the signs are evident and very ominous, and a chill wind blows."

While Reagan and Bush opposed abortion rights, the Republican Party was slower to catch up. In the 1960s and 1970s, attitudes toward abortion tended to be determined more by one's religion than by one's political affiliation. Republican politicians shifted first, but it wasn't until the late 1980s or even early 1990s when

Republicans were more reliably opposed to abortion rights than Democrats.

During George H. W. Bush's single term as president, the court continued to change. In 1990, David Souter, a New Hampshire conservative, replaced the reliably liberal William Brennan. In the fall of 1991, the deeply conservative Clarence Thomas succeeded the civil rights icon Thurgood Marshall. Harry Blackmun was now the only justice left who had voted for *Roe*, though Rehnquist and White, the two dissenters in the case, were still there as well. With five Republican nominations in a decade, the court appeared to have become far more conservative.

When the Supreme Court agreed in early 1992 to hear arguments in a case known as *Planned Parenthood of Southeastern Pennsylvania v. Casey*, many predicted that the nineteen-year-old *Roe* decision would be shredded. The Planned Parenthood lawyers even took that expectation into consideration. Public opinion polls showed most Americans supported abortion rights, and 1992 was a presidential election year. If *Roe* was overruled, they thought, the election might hinge on the abortion question.

The case challenged Pennsylvania's Abortion Control Act, which included several restrictions the court had shot down in 1983: Women had to wait twenty-four hours before the abortion could be performed and listen to lectures about the risks of abortion and alternatives to it; if married, women had to notify their husbands; and if they were minors, they needed the permission of at least one parent, with some exceptions.

The Justice Department again asked the court to overrule *Roe*.

After the oral arguments in April, the justices met to discuss the case. This time, Rehnquist counted five votes to allow the

The justices on the 1991–92 Supreme Court seated, from left, are John Paul Stevens, Byron R. White, Chief Justice William H. Rehnquist, Harry A. Blackmun, and Sandra Day O'Connor. Standing, from left, David Souter, Antonin Scalia, Anthony Kennedy, and Clarence Thomas.

Pennsylvania restrictions, and he again assigned the opinion to himself. A month later, he shared a draft that aggressively dismantled the promises of *Roe*. The Constitution did not have an "all-encompassing right of privacy," he wrote, backing off *Roe*'s basic premise. And, he said, the court erred when it said a woman had a fundamental right to end a pregnancy.

If four other justices joined the opinion, a woman's right to an abortion would no longer exist.

Blackmun braced himself and worked on a dissent.

Two days later, Anthony Kennedy sent him a handwritten note. "Dear Harry," it read, "I need to see you as soon as you have a few free moments. I want to tell you about some developments in *Planned Parenthood v. Casey*, and at least part of what I say should come as welcome news." It was signed, "Yours, Tony."

When they met the next day, Kennedy explained that he had been meeting privately with Sandra Day O'Connor and David Souter. They were working on a rare joint opinion from the three of them, instead of from one justice, to underscore its importance. They would dismantle *Roe*'s trimester framework, which had protected all abortions during the first twelve weeks of pregnancy and restricted regulations in the second trimester to protecting a woman's health.

In its place would be O'Connor's "undue burden" standard. That meant any number of regulations could be imposed that had nothing to do with a woman's health or well-being, as long as judges didn't find them too burdensome.

Under that standard, they would uphold most of the Pennsylvania restrictions as constitutional because they didn't think they imposed an undue burden on a woman's right to an abortion. The requirement that a woman had to notify her husband, however, would be struck down.

But most significantly, they would reaffirm that a woman has a constitutional right to an abortion—formally making abortion a woman's right rather than a medical decision. The essence of the *Roe v. Wade* decision would remain.

Blackmun was relieved. The remaining four conservative

justices were left to write dissents arguing that *Roe* was wrongly decided and should be overturned.

In their joint opinion, O'Connor, Kennedy, and Souter affirmed "the right of the woman to choose to have an abortion before viability," considered between twenty-four and twenty-eight weeks after a woman's last menstrual period. Before the fetus is viable, they wrote, the state cannot prohibit abortion or impose a "substantial obstacle." After the fetus is viable, the state could restrict abortions as long as there are exceptions for a pregnancy that threatens a woman's life or health.

In addition, they wrote, the state "has legitimate interests" in protecting a woman's health and her fetus throughout the pregnancy.

Even though some of them found abortion personally offensive, they said, "Our obligation is to define the liberty of all, not to mandate our own moral code."

They based their decision on the legal principle of *stare decisis*, which calls for upholding what has become established law, and on constitutional grounds, including the right to make the very personal choice of whether to have a child.

Blackmun called the joint opinion "an act of courage and constitutional principle." He and Stevens joined the trio in upholding a woman's essential right to an abortion. Both, however, found the waiting period and required lectures unconstitutional. And Blackmun fretted in his opinion that just one different vote in the future could eliminate a woman's right to an abortion altogether.

When the decision was announced, neither side was happy. Pro-life factions were disappointed that abortion was still legal, and pro-choice supporters were concerned about what new restrictions might be imposed.

But David Garrow, a law professor who has written extensively about abortion, argued that the joint decision was historic because it "resolved the basic constitutional question of abortion *for all time*."

That may have been wishful thinking.

PUSHBACK

1992–2000

Every year around the January 22 anniversary of *Roe*, thousands of people opposed to abortion rights gather in Washington, D.C., for a March for Life. Both Reagan and Bush addressed the crowds via telephone hookups.

On January 22, 1993, tens of thousands of participants, including many teens from parochial schools and church youth groups, participated in the March for Life. But the president wouldn't be speaking to them. Instead, Bill Clinton, a Democrat elected in 1992, spent his second day in office reversing several of Reagan's and Bush's abortion policies.

Among other things, Clinton abolished Reagan's so-called gag rule, which banned professionals at federally funded family planning clinics from recommending abortion as a medical option for pregnant women. (The Supreme Court had upheld the rule in 1991, but it was never implemented.) He reversed a prohibition on abortions in military hospitals overseas, allowing them as long as the patients paid the bill.

And he called for reviewing a ban on a French pill that induced abortions early in pregnancy. (Abortion medications, pills that can induce a miscarriage up to ten weeks from a woman's last menstrual period, finally become available in 2000, near the end of Clinton's term in office.)

Abortion rights activists cheered the changes. But the lack of substantive results under Reagan and Bush, followed by Clinton's election, seemed to fan the anger of radical antiabortion groups, like Operation Rescue.

Randall Terry and other protestors had started Operation Rescue in 1986, when Terry was still in his twenties. Their motto: "If you believe abortion is murder, act like it's murder." By the late 1980s, Operation Rescue had rallied antiabortion protesters to block clinic entrances and try to interrupt clinic operations in New York City and Atlanta. Protests spread to Charlotte, North Carolina; Chicago; and Missoula, Montana. More than forty thousand protesters were arrested, many of them several times. Many faced fines or jail time. Terry himself spent nearly four months in prison rather than pay a $500 fine.

In the summer of 1991, the group descended on Wichita, Kansas, home to one of the few late-term abortion clinics in the United States. For weeks, protestors blocked the way into three different clinics and disrupted life in the small, central Kansas city. More than two thousand people were arrested.

Around the country, vandalism, hate mail, harassing phone calls, clinic blockades, arsons, and threats climbed in what a *New York Times* editorial called "a crescendo of violence." Protesters also sometimes picketed in front of doctors' houses, at their churches, and even at their children's events.

Then, some went further: In March 1993, David Gunn, a doctor at clinics in Florida and Alabama, had just arrived at a clinic in Pensacola, Florida. He was walking from his car to the back door when a protestor shot him three times in the back, killing him.

The gunman, Michael Griffin, surrendered and was sentenced to life in prison. People on both sides condemned the murder. But some radical antiabortion activists considered the shooting justified. "While Gunn's death is unfortunate, it's also true that quite a number of babies' lives will be saved," said a spokesman for Rescue America, the group that was protesting that day.

Five months later, Rachelle "Shelley" Shannon shot Dr. George Tiller as he drove out of the driveway of his Wichita, Kansas, clinic. He was wounded in both arms, but not seriously, and returned to work the next day. She was sentenced to eleven years in prison for attempted murder, plus additional time for acid attacks and arsons at other clinics.

The escalating violence prompted Congress to pass the Freedom of Access to Clinic Entrances—or FACE—Act, making it a federal crime to block access to clinics, trespass, or damage a reproductive health facility. Penalties include prison time and hefty fines.

The law reduced the blockades and attacks against clinics. But six more people were murdered in abortion clinic violence in the 1990s, including a doctor and his escort in Pensacola; two clinic workers in Brookline, Massachusetts; a police officer in Birmingham, Alabama; and a doctor in Amherst, New York. Several others were injured in attacks.

* * *

With their blockades limited, the most radical protestors had fewer ways to get on the nightly news. But some found other ways to stay in the limelight.

In the spring of 1995, Reverend Flip Benham, now national director of Operation Rescue, rented space next door to a Dallas abortion clinic. Not coincidentally, the clinic employed someone who was rather famous: Norma McCorvey, who was the "Roe" in *Roe v. Wade*.

More than two decades after the decision, McCorvey had settled down some. She had moved in with Connie Gonzalez before *Roe* was decided, and the couple had been together twenty-three years. Though she had little actual involvement in the famous lawsuit, she was interviewed around *Roe*'s anniversary for many years, always supporting the decision and the hope that other women wouldn't be denied an abortion like she was.

In the late 1980s, she had been paid for a 1989 made-for-TV movie of her story, in which actress Holly Hunter won an Emmy for portraying "Roe" (who was given a pseudonym of Ellen Russell). She had also worked at abortion clinics and given plenty of speeches. In 1994, she published a memoir, *I Am Roe*.

But her differing stories also generated a stir. Starting in 1973, she had told interviewers that she had needed an abortion because she was raped. Then, in 1987, she admitted that she had made up the rape story; in fact, she had gotten pregnant while in a relationship with a man she liked.

Right to Life leaders saw the disclosure as discrediting the lawsuit—even though the alleged rape was never part of the lawsuit.

When Benham moved next door, McCorvey was initially hostile. She told a reporter that she called the police twice the first day to complain about comments Operation Rescue supporters were shouting at her. But before long, the two became friendly. Then, they started having lunch together.

About four months after he arrived next door, Benham baptized McCorvey in a suburban Dallas swimming pool, with a newspaper photographer in attendance. Two days later, McCorvey quit her abortion clinic job and said she would work for Operation Rescue.

"Jesus Christ has reached through the abortion-mill wall and touched the heart of Norma McCorvey," Benham said.

Whether she was actually now against abortion wasn't clear. In an interview soon after, she said she supported abortion during the first trimester.

Still, anti-abortion groups seized on her change of heart, and her conversion was national news. She began to make a living speaking against abortion.

Pro-choice supporters weren't completely sur-

Reverend Flip Benham of Operation Rescue baptizes Norma McCorvey in a suburban Dallas swimming pool, August 1995.

prised. She had often been in need of money and attention, and both had waned as the years since the lawsuit had passed. They pointed out that every woman should have a choice about abortion, including McCorvey.

Benham helped her get a new book deal, and she published *Won by Love* in 1997, saying she was appalled by abortion and homosexuality. In 1998, she converted to Catholicism with the help of Father Frank Pavone of Priests for Life. For years after, her new role provided her income through paid appearances, the Roe No More Ministry she created, and help from her antiabortion friends.

She still lived and traveled with Gonzalez, though she began introducing her as her aunt or cousin.

McCorvey's experience paralleled that of Sandra Bensing, the "Doe" in *Doe v. Bolton*. She said she had a change of heart in the late 1980s, when she was married to her fourth husband and using the name Sandra Cano. She began speaking out against abortion. She decided to be baptized in 2000.

After they switched sides, both women claimed their lawyers had misled them and taken advantage of them during a time of personal crisis—though signed legal documents, verified by others, said otherwise. Bensing Cano's criticism was especially stinging because her lawyers worked for free to help her get visitation rights with the children who had been taken from her.

At one point, McCorvey filed a lawsuit asking that *Roe v. Wade* be overturned because of new information. The suit was dismissed.

In time, McCorvey's support from pro-life groups fell off, too, though Pavone's church still helped her some. "She just fishes for money," Benham said later.

Sarah Weddington initially said she hoped the new attention would be "helpful to her." Later, however, she would say she wished they had chosen a different plaintiff.

PREGNANT PAUSE:
Pregnancy and Abortion

If a woman decides an abortion is the right decision for herself and her family, the procedure she has will depend on how long it has been since her last menstrual period. It will, like her monthly period, involve blood and cramping.

Since abortion pills were approved in 2000, women have had a choice between a medical and a surgical procedure up until about the tenth week of pregnancy. In a medical abortion, a doctor gives a woman a dose of medicine called mifepristone. The next day, she takes a second drug, misoprostol. Bleeding is expected to start within a few hours, and the bleeding and cramping is likely to be worse than a regular menstrual period.

Some states allow doctors to prescribe the drugs via telemedicine, and medication abortions now account for about four out of ten early-term procedures. Some women prefer being able to schedule the procedure around work or childcare and to do it in the privacy of their homes—but home isn't always private for every woman.

For those who prefer a quicker process and for pregnancies up to sixteen weeks, the typical surgical procedure is a vacuum aspiration abortion. A woman puts her feet in stirrups, knees bent, as she does for a pelvic exam. A tool called a speculum is inserted to hold the vaginal walls open. The doctor injects a shot of painkiller into the cervix, the opening to the uterus, and begins to dilate it.

When the cervix is open wide enough, a straw, or cannula, is inserted into the uterus and the walls are gently suctioned clean.

The process takes about five minutes. When it's over, the uterus cramps for a few minutes as it begins to return to its original size.

The woman is sent to recovery, and the doctor or a lab technician examines the suctioned material to be sure nothing was left behind in the uterus.

Abortions from sixteen weeks until around the end of the second trimester—and later if the fetus will not survive or the woman's health is at risk—require more technical skill and are more complex. The most common procedure is known as dilation and evacuation. The cervix must be dilated wider to accommodate the larger fetus, which may take a day. Then, forceps and suction are used to empty the uterus, a process that takes up to fifteen minutes.

More rarely, a medication abortion may be done in the second trimester, much like inducing labor in a later-term pregnancy.

RESTRICTIONS

2000–2016

By the early 2000s, antiabortion activists were realizing that neither Congress nor the courts were going to outlaw abortion. So if they couldn't ban them, they could at least make them harder to get.

Pregnant teens became a particular target.

Pro-life lobbyists found that requiring parental notification or consent was one of the easiest restrictions to win in state legislatures, since encouraging minors to talk to their parents was politically appealing—and teens have little ability to fight back.

The Virginia General Assembly voted in 2003 to require pregnant young women under the age of eighteen to get written permission from a parent before they could have an abortion.

A Republican legislator called it "the most profound bill we will have considered in a number of years," gloating that the new law would prevent thousands of abortions a year.

It would do that, noted a Democratic legislator, by forcing teen girls to have babies against their will.

By 2005, more states, like Oklahoma, were adding parental notification laws. Others, like Texas, changed their notification laws to require a parent's permission. The trend continued until most states required some parental involvement—even though younger teen moms are far less likely than other teens to complete high school or go to college and are more likely to be poor and need public assistance. In every case, the rules disproportionately affected poor, black, and Latina women, who were all more likely to get pregnant as teens.

While many young women are willing to talk to their parents, plenty of others live with parents who may be abusive, mentally ill, or unwilling to hear their daughters' decisions. Others may have been impregnated by a male relative or relative's boyfriend, complicating family relationships. Some young immigrants or children of parents who are in prison may have no parent to turn to. In addition, the U.S. Supreme Court had previously ruled that parents cannot have an absolute say over a daughter's right to an abortion.

As a result, virtually every parental notification or consent law allows a young woman to go before a judge if she doesn't feel like she can tell her parents. To get a so-called judicial bypass, she must demonstrate that she is mature and well informed enough to make the decision and that not telling a parent is in her best interest. It's a scary experience, even under the best of circumstances.

Arranging a court time can take from a few days to three weeks, even though every day counts when a woman needs an abortion. To get to court means missing school or work and sometimes lying to a parent. One young woman managed to get to court—and then the judge rescheduled her case.

Judges can ask a range of questions, requiring teens to share intensely personal information with a stranger. They likely will have to explain difficult or abusive family situations. They may be asked if they used birth control and if they didn't to explain why. They may be asked to explain the abortion procedure in detail and its potential risks, as well as whether they have considered having a baby and giving it up for adoption.

In Texas, a *guardian ad litem* is appointed for the young woman to look out for her interests. Judges in Alabama and Florida have appointed lawyers for the teens' fetuses—and the lawyers sometimes made up names for them.

Even those who prepare and make a strong case may be denied a judicial bypass. The magazine *Mother Jones* looked at forty cases and found judges sometimes denied teens' requests for "arbitrary, absurd, or personal reasons." Three judges refused to give teens permission because they became pregnant accidentally— as though that doesn't happen to women of every age. Another judge said a young woman should have discussed her decision with her priest.

In Texas, a young woman who played soccer, cared for younger siblings, and held an internship was told she didn't understand the emotional cost of an abortion. She tried to make her case: "You guys keep telling me that I'm not mature enough to make this decision and I don't know what I'm getting myself into, yet . . . if I'm not mature enough to make a decision like this, how am I mature enough to even have a baby?"

Her request was denied.

A denial can be appealed, but sometimes a young woman may be better off going to another state without the requirements.

After talking with twenty young women in Texas who sought a judicial bypass, researchers concluded that the process "functions as a form of punishment" for young women and allows judges and others "to humiliate adolescents for their personal decisions."

Teens weren't the only ones targeted. One particularly long abortion fight was over a medical procedure used in later second and third trimesters.

Women need later-term abortions for a number of reasons, just as they did when the Jane group in Chicago was performing illegal abortions in the early 1970s. Teenagers may be slow to realize they are pregnant, and poor or uninsured women often struggle to get funds together or to find a provider, especially if they live far from a major city. Sometimes, women are in conflict with their male partner or fear violence, which delays them from getting help.

In addition, many fetal or genetic deformities aren't evident until near the twentieth week of pregnancy. Occasionally, women face serious health issues that require a late-term procedure.

About 90 percent of abortions are performed in the first 12 weeks, when the procedure is safe and simple. Later-term abortions remain more difficult and complex, requiring more experienced and skilled doctors.

In some later-term abortions, doctors used a dilation-and-extraction method in which the fetus was removed intact, though the skull was reduced to allow it to pass through the cervix; the method was sometimes considered a safer option than the more traditional method because it reduced the risk of infection or uterine perforation.

But after hearing of a doctor's blunt description of the method in the 1990s, antiabortion activists worked for years to have it banned, portraying the medical procedure in gruesome terms. They dubbed it "partial-birth abortion."

Congress twice passed laws forbidding the procedure in the 1990s, and President Bill Clinton vetoed them both. In 2000, the U.S. Supreme Court ruled, in a five-to-four decision in *Stenberg v. Carhart*, that the state of Nebraska's version violated *Casey* and *Roe* in criminalizing the procedure.

After Republican George W. Bush became president, Congress again passed legislation outlawing the procedure, without an exception to preserve the health of the woman. This time, Bush signed it. And this time, the U.S. Supreme Court ruled in 2007, in *Gonzales v. Carhart*, that a narrower law banning the procedure wasn't an undue burden. The difference? Sandra Day O'Connor had retired and Samuel Alito Jr. had replaced her.

Though the most aggressive attacks on abortion clinics abated some in the 2000s, the anger toward them did not disappear. In states where abortion was controversial, picketers continued to gather, sometimes yelling at and harassing both clinic staff and patients. Doctors and staffers were often on high alert, taking different routes to work and always keeping an eye out.

They were reminded why in 2009. George Tiller, the doctor who had been injured in a 1993 attack, was handing out church bulletins as an usher at his Wichita, Kansas, church on May 31. A man

with a handgun approached and fatally shot Tiller. He pointed his
gun at others who tried to stop him and then fled.

Tiller—a sixty-seven-year-old father of four and grandfather
of ten—died in his church foyer.

Dr. George Tiller, center, of Wichita, Kansas, in 2009.

Tiller's death rattled the abortion clinic community. He was
one of a small number of doctors in the country who performed
third-trimester abortions, and he had continued to try to provide health care to women even as he was investigated repeatedly
based on claims by antiabortion activists. In the aftermath, other
doctors pledged to continue his work.

Scott Roeder, a fifty-one-year-old abortion opponent, told a jury that he had planned to kill the doctor for years and had even gone into the church with a gun in the past. He was convicted of murder and sentenced to life in prison.

The murder also put the women's health care community back on high alert—even as they were under attack in new ways. In the years between 2010 and 2016, states hostile to abortion adopted more than three hundred new regulations to chip away at abortion rights, almost one-third of all the regulations that had been adopted since 1973.

Abortion opponents came up with a raft of new ways to restrict abortions, including a new strategy: encouraging state legislation aimed at creating stricter regulations for abortion clinics than for other medical facilities. Some new rules, for instance, called for wider hallways, required clinics to be near hospitals or meet the standards of surgical centers, or demand that doctors have admitting privileges at hospitals—none of which were needed during the first three decades that abortion was legal.

The regulations even had a name: TRAP laws, for "targeted regulation of abortion providers." In 2016, however, the Supreme Court struck down regulations in Texas that had led a number of abortion clinics to close.

Despite continued attacks on abortion, women in the twenty-first century had more contraceptive and abortion options than any women in history. The Pill is more effective with lower doses of hormones. Intrauterine devices, or IUDs, with or without hormones, safely prevent sperm from getting to their destination, and they are effective for years.

In 2006, drugstores were permitted to sell an emergency contraceptive called Plan B (and sometimes "the morning-after pill") over the counter. The pills help prevent a pregnancy by affecting ovulation, or when an egg is released.

In addition, the Affordable Care Act, sometimes called Obamacare, has helped many uninsured Americans get health insurance. It also required insurance coverage for birth control, making it available to more women than ever.

With more effective options, fewer women are getting pregnant. The birth rate, or births per one thousand women between fifteen and forty-four years old, has dropped dramatically, to the lowest level in more than thirty years. The birth rate has declined most sharply for teens.

Meanwhile, the abortion rate has fallen to below the 1973 level, when *Roe v. Wade* was decided. In 2014, the actual number of abortions performed in the United States fell below one million for the first time since 1975.

Some of the drop is certainly tied to better contraception. Some may mean that more pregnancies are intended rather than unwanted. And some may reflect the difficulty poor women and teens have in accessing abortions, especially in states with strict regulations. For many women, coming up with the average cost of about $500 for a first-trimester abortion is a challenge—before paying travel expenses if the only clinic is far away. A woman who makes $10 an hour must have more than a week's wages to cover the procedure.

Regardless, many women wrestle with the decision every day. The majority of women who have abortions in the United States are already raising children. Most are not married and most are poor. Black women have abortions at nearly three times the rate of white women, and Latina women at twice the rate.

In addition, trans and non-gender-conforming people also need reproductive health care.

For many, abortion is not really about choice, but about making services women need accessible. That's why more and more people are calling for reproductive justice, a term coined by a group of African American women in 1994 that has won a broader audience. In its simplest form, reproductive justice is the right to control your own body, to have a child or to not have a child, and to raise children in safe and sustainable communities. It's a broad issue that includes the impact of poverty and discrimination, as well as access to effective schools, affordable housing, and good jobs. Access to contraception and abortion are only a part of it.

PREGNANT PAUSE:
Birth Control Today

American women have a greater range of birth control choices today than ever before—from hormonal patches and pills to condoms and sponges to methods that can be inserted and left for years.

Because a woman may be fertile from her preteens into her fifties, different kinds of contraceptives may work best for her at different times in her life. During all those years, of course, the most effective birth control is abstinence, or not having sex.

For teens who are sexually experienced, the most commonly used birth control is the male condom, which also prevents sexually transmitted infections. The next most common is the

Pill. Both methods are effective if used properly—but not if the condom is forgotten or the Pill isn't taken every day.

About one in five teens claim to use old-fashioned *coitus interruptus*, or the withdrawal method, which fails more often than the Pill or condoms.

More reliable methods are available. Hormone implants, which are injected under the skin, and intrauterine devices, some with hormones and some without, can last for years after they are inserted. They cost more initially but are covered by insurance.

Hormone shots, patches, and vaginal rings work similarly to the Pill. A new shot is required every three months, rings must be changed monthly, and patches need to be changed each week. Using a condom with another form of birth control can increase reliability.

In addition, the Plan B emergency contraception sold at drugstores is available if a condom breaks, a woman forgets to take her Pill, or no birth control was used. It can be taken up to three days following intercourse.

Among women of all ages who use contraceptives in the United States, the most popular method is sterilization, either a vasectomy for men or a tubal ligation for women, when they are done having children. One in four women uses the Pill. Condoms are the next most commonly used, followed by IUDs, which have grown more popular because of their effectiveness and the availability of insurance for prescription contraceptives.

EPILOGUE

Almost daily, I drive past an abortion clinic in my hometown of Dallas, Texas, one of a handful in the area. I know it's there because nearly every day but Sunday, in sizzling summer heat and soaking winter rain, protestors gather on the corner of the driveway, sometimes holding signs or posters, sometimes kneeling in prayer.

The clinic, it turns out, is run by Dr. Curtis Boyd, the same doctor who started doing abortions in East Texas in the late 1960s to help the Clergy Consultation Service. In fact, he runs two clinics—one in Dallas and another in Albuquerque, New Mexico.

He might as well be working on two different planets: Texas has some of the nation's most restrictive abortion laws, while New Mexico lets women decide without interference when and if they want an abortion, without any specific time limits.

In the more than forty-five years he has operated a Dallas clinic,

Boyd has faced death threats and bomb threats, his home has been picketed, and nails have been strewn about in the staff parking area. On Christmas Eve 1988, the clinic was set on fire; two years later, Operation Rescue members burst in, knocked down a doctor and counselor, and chained themselves to medical equipment.

Dr. Curtis Boyd still owns clinics in Dallas and Albuquerque.

New Mexico is one of seven states and the District of Columbia that have no restrictions on when an abortion can be performed, and one of sixteen states where state Medicaid funds pay for abortions for poor women. But protestors picket there as well.

Now in his eighties, Boyd mostly teaches doctors how to perform abortions rather than doing them himself. But he remains deeply committed to allowing any woman who wants an abortion to have one. "I choose to do abortions, despite the unpleasantries and the risks," he once wrote in an essay, "because I believe that abortion is a good and moral choice. And I know of no one better qualified to make the choice than the pregnant woman." Women don't make those important decisions lightly, he added.

In many places, however, American women can no longer exercise that right easily. Three out of four states require a minor to either notify a parent or get a parent's or a judge's permission. The Hyde Amendment has been renewed every year since the early 1980s, meaning federal funds cannot be used to pay for a poor woman's abortion except in cases of rape, incest, or if a woman's life is in danger. The amendment also prevents women serving in the military overseas from getting an abortion at a military hospital, even if she pays, unless it is for one of those three exceptions. It also extends to the Indian Health Service, which won't provide abortions on reservations.

Most states also refuse to use their Medicaid funds to pay for abortions for poor women, except for the usual exceptions. Some states, including Indiana, Kansas, Michigan, and Texas, even restrict private health insurance plans from covering abortion care. The nation's federal employees do not have insurance coverage for abortions, either.

About half the states forbid abortions after the twentieth or twenty-fourth week of pregnancy—before the fetus is viable—unless the woman's life or health is in danger. And about half the states require a woman to be counseled at least a day before she has an abortion, forcing her to wait for care.

From Boyd's point of view, so many hurdles exist in so many states that the right to abortion already is at risk. In Texas, for instance, a woman must see a doctor and have a sonogram, and then come back at least twenty-four hours later to have her abortion. That means low-income women, who are less likely to have paid sick leave and who may have to travel to a clinic in another city, will miss at least one day of pay and maybe more.

The state's laws require doctors to make the heartbeat audible and describe what they see on the sonogram, though the woman does not have to listen. They also must provide "state-mandated information," including the false statement that having an abortion increases a woman's risk of having breast cancer. Boyd shares this, but then explains that he doesn't believe it.

"We don't have to like it," he said of the requirements. "We just have to do it."

As a result, a woman's options today may depend on her bank account, her race, her age, and where she lives, just as it has for much of the past 150 years.

Aggression against abortion providers began to pick up in 2015. In November that year, a man opened fire on a Planned Parenthood clinic in Colorado Springs, Colorado, killing three people and injuring nine others; later, he said he was "a warrior for the babies."

The number of trespassing incidents at clinics increased tenfold between 2015 and 2018. The number of picketers also soared.

Republican Donald Trump, who once supported abortion rights, was elected president in 2016 with a promise to help overturn *Roe*. Like his Republican predecessors Reagan and both Bushes, Trump hasn't asked Congress for specific legislation on abortion. But he has nominated conservative federal judges at all levels. His greatest impact on abortion rights, however, will come from his Supreme Court appointments.

In 2017, after the death of Antonin Scalia, Trump nominated Neil Gorsuch. Then, in 2018, Anthony Kennedy retired. Kennedy had been a believer in individual rights and was for years the swing vote on the Supreme Court on abortion rights and gay rights. Trump nominated Brett Kavanaugh to replace him, and the Senate approved him after contentious hearings.

Both Gorsuch and Kavanaugh attended the same prestigious Catholic boys high school in Washington, D.C., and Ivy League universities, and both were clerks for Kennedy as young men. Both were considered deeply conservative.

Many court watchers believed that for the first time since the Reagan administration, there were truly five votes to overturn the abortion rights granted in *Roe* and *Planned Parenthood v. Casey*.

In response, legislatures in several very conservative states raced to pass unusually restrictive laws in hopes of being the one that convinces the Supreme Court to overturn its long-standing abortion ruling. In 2019, several states passed laws banning abortion when the early fluttering of a fetal heartbeat can be heard, which can be as soon as six weeks. That's sometimes before a woman knows she is pregnant. Alabama went further, essentially outlawing abortion in the state except to prevent a serious health risk to the woman. There was no exemption for rape or incest. Doctors who perform abortions could face up to ninety-nine years in prison.

So far, courts have blocked all these efforts, but the Supreme Court could decide to hear one or more of the cases.

No one knows what might happen with the more conservative court. A majority could rule that, under the principle of *stare decisis*, abortion rights are settled law, allowing *Roe* and *Casey* to stand. Some think the court might approve so many restrictions that abortion rights would exist in name only.

The justices on the Supreme Court in 2019 seated, from left, are Stephen G. Breyer, Clarence Thomas, Chief Justice John G. Roberts, Ruth Bader Ginsburg, and Samuel A. Alito Jr. Standing, from left, Neil M. Gorsuch, Sonia Sotomayor, Elena Kagan, and Brett M. Kavanaugh.

Others think *Roe* and *Casey* would be overturned.

What would that look like? The court could declare that life begins at conception—but experts said that seems unlikely. Instead, a majority of the court could rule, as William Rehnquist tried to do in 1989 and 1992, that *Roe* and *Casey* were incorrectly decided. That is, more than forty-five years after *Roe*, the court could say that women actually do *not* have a constitutional right to terminate a pregnancy before viability. Should the court rule that way, abortion would not become illegal in the United States but would be up to individual states. Some states have laws on the books allowing abortion. Other states—at least a handful, and perhaps even a majority—might outlaw abortion or drastically limit it.

Such an outcome would have a much greater impact on poor women and women of color than on wealthier women who could afford to travel for an abortion.

In restrictive states, there might be exceptions to protect the life or health of a woman, and also perhaps in cases of rape, incest, or fetal deformity—which would mean someone else would decide whether a woman could have an abortion. It would mark a return to the early 1970s, when hospital committees made decisions for most women, while abortion was essentially legal in New York, California, and Washington, D.C.

Justice Potter Stewart was sarcastic when he said, during oral arguments in *Roe v. Wade* in 1971, that maybe a woman makes her choice not when she gets pregnant but "when she decides to live in Texas." If the Supreme Court overturns *Roe*, a woman's options will indeed depend on where she lives.

Even outlawed, abortion will not go away. In the history of the world, it never has. No birth control is 100 percent effective, and women will always get pregnant accidentally. Couples will break up or divorce, or a man will turn abusive or disappear when a woman is expecting. Women will face unexpected health problems or financial issues. Any number of things could happen.

When they do, some women in restrictive states will manage to get to places where abortion is legal. Others will seek out medication to bring on a miscarriage, try to induce an abortion themselves, or find illegal providers, who are certain to pop up to meet an obvious demand. Already, the combination abortion pills, mifepristone and misoprostol, are available without a prescription in Mexico and can be purchased online. Already, researchers say, women are turning to the internet for ways to induce an abortion themselves.

As the late New York legislator Constance Cook said in 1970, "The issue is not whether we do or don't have abortions. The issue is where."

Imagine that you're pregnant, or your girlfriend is pregnant. What does that mean to you? What does that mean to your life from now on?

What do you want to do? What should you—or another woman—be able to do?

What are you going to do?

As of 2019, abortion is still legal in the United States, protected by the Supreme Court's *Roe* and *Casey* decisions.

Over and over, Americans say they support abortion rights. A 2018 Gallup poll found that almost two out of three Americans believe *Roe v. Wade* should stand. A *Wall Street Journal*/NBC poll found even more, 71 percent, were opposed to overturning *Roe*.

The recent political climate has energized many people, especially young people who have the power to speak up and be heard.

Dr. Boyd urges you to ask, "What kind of society do I want?"

Once you know, he adds, you're "going to have to work towards that end."

Given the history, there will be plenty of opportunities ahead. No matter what the U.S. Supreme Court does, the reality remains: The fights over whether, when, and how a woman may decide to have a child are far from over.

GLOSSARY OF LEGAL AND MEDICAL TERMS

Abortifacient—A drug or chemical that causes an abortion. The pills that cause a miscarriage, mifepristone and misoprostol, are abortifacients. Some pro-life organizations contend that intrauterine devices, morning-after pills, and even the Pill are abortifacients because they prevent a fertilized egg from implanting in a woman's uterus. But scientists say all of them are intended to prevent fertilization, not to prevent implantation.

Affidavit—A written statement, given under oath, containing facts that can be admitted as evidence in legal proceedings. An affidavit can take the place of live testimony in court.

Amicus curiae—The term is Latin for "friend of the court." People or groups that are not part of a lawsuit but have a strong interest in a case may file *amicus curiae* briefs that present their legal viewpoints, hoping to influence the outcome.

Class action lawsuit—A lawsuit filed by one or a few people on behalf of a whole class of people who are affected. In *Roe v. Wade*, Jane Roe represented the class of women wanting an abortion who are pregnant or might become pregnant in the future.

Conception—Like so much in the abortion discussion, this term is the subject of differing viewpoints. About once a month, an egg leaves a woman's ovary and travels down a fallopian tube. If the woman has had intercourse recently, a sperm may fertilize the egg during that five-day trip, and the single cell begins to multiply. Pro-life advocates say that conception happens at fertilization. The American College of Obstetricians and Gynecologists says that *conception* is not a scientific or medical term. Instead, pregnancy begins when the cell cluster reaches the uterus and implants in the uterine wall. After that point, enough hormones are released to confirm a pregnancy. An unknown number of fertilized eggs fail to implant in the uterus and exit a woman's body.

Courts, state and federal—State courts handle cases covered under state laws, including most criminal cases. Federal courts handle cases where there are constitutional issues, issues under federal laws or treaties, or differences between residents of different states. Typically, cases heard in state district court may be appealed to a state appeals court and then to the state's supreme court, and in limited cases, to the U.S. Supreme Court. Federal cases may be appealed to a federal circuit court of appeals and then to the U.S. Supreme Court.

Diaphragm—A form of birth control especially popular in the twentieth century, a diaphragm is a dome-shaped flexible cup that is inserted into the vagina and covers the cervix. Typically, it is used with a spermicide jelly or cream, and it blocks sperm from reaching the egg.

Dilation and curettage—Also called a D&C, dilation and curettage is a procedure for removing tissue from inside the uterus. A woman's cervix is dilated and a surgical tool called a curette is used to gently scrape the uterine walls. Until the 1970s, many early abortions were performed with a D&C procedure.

Dilation and evacuation—Dilation and evacuation is the most common second-trimester abortion. A woman's cervix is dilated and the contents of her uterus are removed with forceps and suction.

Embryo—A developing pregnancy from cell division up to eight weeks of gestation, or about ten weeks after a woman's last menstrual period.

Eugenics—A popular scientific belief in the early decades of the 1900s that most traits are inherited and the population could be improved through better breeding. *Positive eugenics* encouraged the voluntary union of "superior citizens." *Negative eugenics* was more invasive, attempting to prevent people deemed "unfit" or genetically deficient, such as criminals, alcoholics, and epileptics from having children, sometimes through laws that allowed forced sterilization. The concept was denounced after Nazi Germany adopted some of the ideas to justify extermination of Jews and others in the 1930s and 1940s.

Fertilization—Fertilization occurs when a sperm and an egg combine in a woman's fallopian tube.

Fetus—The growing pregnancy from nine weeks of gestation until birth.

Fourteenth Amendment—The Fourteenth Amendment to the U.S. Constitution was ratified after the Civil War to help establish equal rights for the formerly enslaved. The portion that is often cited in court cases reads, "No state shall make or enforce any law which shall abridge the privileges or immunities of citizens of the United States; nor shall any state deprive any person of life, liberty, or property, without due process of law; nor deny to any person within its jurisdiction the equal protection of the laws." The U.S. Supreme Court has ruled that the *due process clause*, among other things, grants individuals a right to privacy in areas of marriage, birth control, and abortion. The *equal protection clause* requires that states have a good legal reason for treating an individual differently than others in similar circumstances.

Indictment—A formal accusation or charge against someone accused of committing a crime.

Injunction—A court order requiring a person or entity to stop doing something that violates another party's rights or to do something to prevent harm to another party.

Ninth Amendment—The Ninth Amendment to the U.S. Constitution acknowledges that people have rights that are not specifically spelled out in the Bill of Rights. It reads, "The enumeration in the Constitution, of certain rights, shall not be construed to deny or disparage others retained by the people."

Pessary—A device inserted into the vagina to provide support. Years ago, pessaries sometimes functioned as birth control, covering the cervix and preventing sperm from reaching an egg. Today, pessaries are used to support pelvic organs.

Pregnancy—Medically speaking, a pregnancy begins when a fertilized egg is implanted in the uterus. Though the embryo begins to grow before that, it may not implant. The length of a normal pregnancy is forty weeks, starting with the first day of a woman's last menstrual period. Babies born at thirty-seven weeks or later are considered full term.

Rhythm method—A form of birth control that calls for abstaining from sex on the days when a woman is believed to be fertile. It requires carefully tracking a woman's menstrual cycles, which can vary for many reasons.

Sterilization—A permanent option, sterilization involves surgery that prevents someone from having children in the future. The most common procedure for women is a tubal ligation, in which the fallopian tubes are cut or blocked—sometimes called having your "tubes tied." A woman without a uterus or ovaries is also unable to have children. For men, the most common procedure is a vasectomy, which blocks sperm from leaving the body.

Vacuum aspiration abortion—The most common abortion procedure for pregnancies up to about sixteen weeks, the vacuum aspiration method gently suctions out the contents of the uterus through a cannula or narrow tube.

Viability—The point at which a fetus can survive outside the womb. Survivability will depend on the individual fetus and the medical care available. In rare cases, extremely premature babies born at twenty-two weeks after a woman's last menstrual period can survive, but most of them will have permanent disabilities. Most hospitals offer intensive medical care for infants born at twenty-four weeks, with odds of survival of roughly 50 percent, though surviving children may have disabilities.

TIMELINE

March 3, 1873: The Comstock Act is signed by President Grant.

April 1, 1878: Abortion provider Madame Restell is found dead on the day of her trial.

October 16, 1916: Margaret Sanger opens America's first birth control clinic in Brooklyn, New York. The state shuts it down ten days later.

February 5, 1917: Sanger is sentenced to thirty days in jail for dispensing birth control information.

1936: Federal judges rule that birth control devices can be used for patients' health, ending the impact of the federal Comstock Act.

May 21, 1959: The American Law Institute recommends that states allow abortion in cases of rape, incest, likely severe birth defects, or serious threat to the mental or physical health of the mother.

May 9, 1960: FDA approves sale of Enovid, the first birth control pill.

November 1, 1961: Estelle Griswold and Dr. Lee Buxton open a Planned Parenthood clinic in New Haven, Connecticut, offering contraceptives. The state shuts it down days later.

May 24, 1962: The American Law Institute includes the 1959 abortion recommendations as part of a proposed major overhaul of state criminal codes.

Summer 1962: Sherri Chessen takes thalidomide pills early in pregnancy, unaware that they can cause severe birth defects. Unable to obtain a legal abortion in Arizona, she travels to Sweden to end her pregnancy.

1964: Two-year nationwide rubella outbreak begins, raising awareness of birth defects caused by exposure to rubella early in pregnancy.

April 1965: *Life* magazine publishes images of embryos in development, which antiabortion groups later use to further their mission.

June 7, 1965: The Supreme Court overturns Griswold's and Buxton's convictions, concluding that a constitutional right to privacy extends to married couples who want to use birth control.

June 30, 1966: National Organization for Women (NOW) is founded.

Spring 1967: Colorado, North Carolina, and California become the first states to relax abortion laws, allowing procedures in cases of rape and incest and to protect a woman's health.

April 1967: National Conference of Catholic Bishops votes to spend $50,000 on a nationwide education campaign aimed at halting abortion reform.

May 22, 1967: The Clergy Consultation Service on Abortion, a group of New York ministers and rabbis, goes public with plans to connect women seeking abortions with safe providers.

1968: National Right to Life Committee is created by the U.S. Catholic Conference's Family Life Bureau.

July 25, 1968: Pope Paul VI issues the encyclical *Humanae Vitae*, which declares that the rhythm method and abstinence are the only acceptable forms of contraception for Catholics and that abortion and sterilization are to be "absolutely excluded."

March 3, 1970: *Roe v. Wade* is filed in Dallas.

March 11, 1970: Hawaii becomes the first state to legalize abortion. Soon after, legislatures in Alaska and New York also vote to legalize abortion.

April 29, 1970: Jane Hodgson performs an abortion in a Minnesota hospital on a woman who had rubella early in her pregnancy.

May 22, 1970: Three federal judges in Dallas hear *Roe v. Wade*.

June 17, 1970: Three federal judges decide that Texas abortion laws are unconstitutionally vague, but refuse to block the state from enforcing them. Dallas County District Attorney Henry Wade says he will continue to prosecute abortion cases.

July 1, 1970: Abortion becomes legal in New York State.

August 1970: Lawyers for Jane Roe ask the U.S. Supreme Court to hear their appeal of *Roe v. Wade*.

November 19, 1970: Jane Hodgson is convicted in Minnesota of performing an illegal abortion.

April 21, 1971: The Supreme Court rules in *United States v. Vuitch* that the D. C. abortion law is constitutional, but offers a broad definition in allowing abortions for the health of a woman.

May 3, 1971: The Supreme Court announces that it will hear both *Roe v. Wade* from Texas and *Doe v. Bolton* from Georgia.

Fall 1971: Supreme Court justices Hugo Black and John Harlan II resign from the court because of illness.

December 13, 1971: A seven-member Supreme Court hears oral arguments in *Roe v. Wade* and *Doe v. Bolton*.

January 7, 1972: Nixon appointees Lewis F. Powell Jr. and William H. Rehnquist join the court.

March 22, 1972: In *Eisenstadt v. Baird*, the Supreme Court rules that unmarried people also have a right to use birth control.

May 3, 1972: Chicago homicide detectives arrest seven Jane women for performing abortions.

June 1972: The Supreme Court announces that *Roe v. Wade* and *Doe v. Bolton* will be held for reargument.

October 11, 1972: The Supreme Court again hears oral arguments in *Roe v. Wade* and *Doe v. Bolton*.

November 7, 1972: Nixon is reelected, and Sarah Weddington wins a seat in the Texas House of Representatives.

January 20, 1973: Nixon is sworn in for his second term.

January 22, 1973: In a 7–2 vote, the Supreme Court rules in *Roe v. Wade* that women have a constitutional right to terminate a pregnancy before a fetus is viable.

1976: Congress passes the Hyde Amendment, preventing the use of federal funds to pay for abortions except to save a woman's life. The Supreme Court later upholds the amendment.

July 3, 1989: The Supreme Court, in *Webster v. Reproductive Health Services*, allows Missouri's abortion restrictions, saying they don't put an undue burden on a woman's constitutional right. Four justices say they are ready to overturn *Roe v. Wade*.

June 29, 1992: The Supreme Court, in *Planned Parenthood of Southeastern Pennsylvania v. Casey*, reaffirms a woman's constitutional right to an abortion before a fetus is viable but eliminates Roe's trimester framework. The ruling allows restrictions throughout pregnancy as long as they don't impose an "undue burden."

April 7, 2017: Trump nominee Neil Gorsuch joins the Supreme Court after the death of Antonin Scalia.

October 6, 2018: Trump nominee Brett Kavanaugh joins the Supreme Court after the retirement of Anthony Kennedy, the swing vote on abortion issues.

SIGNIFICANT SUPREME COURT CASES
ON ABORTION AND REPRODUCTIVE RIGHTS

The U.S. Supreme Court has ruled in many cases that affect reproductive rights and abortion. Here are cases mentioned in this book, as well as other significant cases.

Buck v. Bell (1927): In an 8–1 decision, the court ruled that a Virginia law allowing forced sterilization of inmates of institutions was constitutional.

Tileston v. Ullman (1943) and ***Poe v. Ullman*** (1961): In *Tileston*, the court concluded that a physician could not challenge Connecticut's law banning the use of birth control. In *Poe*, the court said that patients who had not been arrested or prosecuted for using birth control could not challenge the law.

Griswold v. Connecticut (1965): In a 7–2 groundbreaking decision, the court ruled that the Constitution includes a right to privacy that extends to married couples who want to use birth control.

United States v. Vuitch (1971): In a 5–4 decision, the court upheld as constitutional a District of Columbia law allowing abortion to preserve the life or health of the woman, but also offered a broad definition of health that allowed more abortions than before.

Eisenstadt v. Baird (1972): In a 6–1 decision, the court ruled that if married people have a right to use birth control, so do unmarried people. Knowing that abortion cases were pending, Justice Brennan wrote in the opinion, "If the right of privacy means anything, it is the right of the individual, married or single, to be free from unwarranted governmental intrusion into matters so fundamentally affecting a person as the decision whether to bear or beget a child."

Roe v. Wade (1973): In a landmark 7–2 decision, the court ruled that the right to privacy included a woman's right to an abortion in consultation with her doctor. The decision created a trimester framework: In the first trimester of pregnancy, an abortion was up to a woman and her doctor. During the second trimester, the state could pass regulations preserving a woman's health. Once a fetus was viable, the state could regulate or prohibit abortion, as long as there were exceptions to protect the life or health of the woman.

Doe v. Bolton (1973): In a companion case to *Roe*, the court in a 7–2 decision struck down a Georgia law that added additional hurdles to getting an abortion, including requirements that two additional doctors recommend the abortion, along with the woman's physician, and that a hospital committee approve the procedure.

Planned Parenthood of Central Missouri v. Danforth (1976): The court, in a 6–3 decision, ruled that laws requiring a minor to get parental consent for an abortion and a wife to get her spouse's consent were unconstitutional. The court said parents cannot have an absolute veto over a minor female's abortion. Further, if a husband and wife disagree, the woman may decide, since she bears the child and is more immediately affected.

Maher v. Roe (1977): In a 6–3 decision, the court ruled that Connecticut did not have to use state Medicaid dollars for abortions even if the state provided Medicaid funding for childbirth.

Bellotti v. Baird (1979): The court ruled, by an 8–1 vote, that states can require minors to notify a parent or get a parent's consent for an abortion only if the minor has an alternative option, such as getting a judge's permission. The court has consistently upheld the requirement that minors must have an alternative to notifying a parent or getting parental consent.

Harris v. McRae (1980): The court, in a 5–4 decision, upheld the Hyde Amendment, which banned the use of Medicaid money for abortions unless the woman's life was in danger. (Today, Medicaid funds also cover abortions in cases of rape or incest.)

Akron v. Akron Center for Reproductive Health (1983): In a 6–3 decision, the court struck down provisions that made a woman wait twenty-four hours before having an abortion and required a doctor to give her specific information intended to make an abortion sound dangerous.

Webster v. Reproductive Health Services (1989): A deeply divided and more conservative court, in a 5–4 decision, ruled that Missouri could forbid abortions at public hospitals or by public employees and impose other regulations. Four justices said they were willing to overturn *Roe v. Wade*.

Rust v. Sullivan (1991): In a 5–4 decision, the court held that the Department of Health and Human Services could impose a so-called gag rule on federally funded family planning providers, prohibiting them from counseling about abortion or providing abortion referrals. The rule also required abortion services to be physically separate from family planning services. President Clinton overturned the rule, but the Trump administration revived it in 2019.

Planned Parenthood of Southeastern Pa. v. Casey (1992): In an unusual decision written by three justices, the court, in a 5–4 decision, upheld a woman's constitutional right to an abortion but allowed regulation in the first trimester. The court upheld restrictions, such as a mandatory, twenty-four-hour waiting period and requirements for pre-abortion counseling, as long as they don't create an "undue burden" on a woman's ability to get an abortion.

Stenberg v. Carhart (2000): In 5–4 decision, the court struck down a Nebraska law that prohibited the use of the dilation-and-extraction method, (dubbed "partial-birth abortion" by pro-life advocates), saying it put an undue burden on a woman's right to abortion.

Gonzales v. Carhart (2007): Reversing itself in another 5–4 decision, the court upheld Congress's ban of dilation-and-extraction abortions, saying the law wasn't unconstitutionally vague and didn't impose an undue burden on a woman's right to an abortion.

Whole Woman's Health v. Hellerstedt (2016): The court, in a 5–3 decision, struck down Texas's strict regulations on abortion providers and abortion facilities. The court said the regulations, which caused about half the state's facilities to close, did not add medical benefits and created an undue burden on a woman's right to an abortion.

ACKNOWLEDGMENTS

I was thirteen years old and living in Dallas when *Roe v. Wade* was decided. It was a fascinating time to be a young teen. The year before, new equal rights laws for women had passed in Congress, allowing young women like me to dream that we might graduate into a world where women could be whoever they wanted to be.

All around me, attitudes and expectations about women were changing. I vividly remember the day my mother got a credit card in her own name because Sarah Weddington had convinced the Texas legislature that banks shouldn't require a husband to sign his wife's application.

There was so much hope.

So when Simon Boughton, then with Roaring Brook Press, called to ask about my interest in a book on reproductive rights and *Roe*, the memories came flooding back. Sure, it was a big complicated subject. Sure, it *is* divisive. But it sure is fascinating, compelling, and important, too.

As with all my projects, I owe thanks to many people. My agent, Susan Cohen, listened to my worries and ideas, and immediately told me I had to do this.

I am profoundly indebted to my patient and enthusiastic editor, Emily Feinberg, as well as the whole wonderful Roaring Brook team: Jen Besser, Avia Perez, Dawn Ryan, Nicole Wayland, Monique Sterling, Jen Keenan, Celeste Cass, Hayley Jozwiak, Jill Freshney, Katie Halata, Melissa Croce, Cierra Bland, Lucy Del Priore, Johanna Allen, and Kelsey Marrujo.

Research is often a team sport. In the Manuscripts Reading Room of the Library of Congress, where I spent days reading the papers of Supreme Court justices, a kind person directed me to insightful annual recaps written by Justice Brennan's clerks. At Wesleyan University, Suzy Taraba, director of Special Collections and Archives, opened the reading room early so I could look at Roy Lucas's papers.

Margaret Justus researched NARAL papers at the Schlesinger Library at Harvard and downloaded invaluable Family Planning oral histories. Jen

McCartney read letters at the Archdiocese of Los Angeles Archival Center and Scott McCartney scanned materials from Claude Evan's family papers at Duke University's Rubenstein Library. Kari Gould helped me go through boxes and boxes of Virginia Whitehill's and Vivian Castleberry's unprocessed papers at Southern Methodist University. As the deadline hovered, Megan Marshall helped with the timeline, photos, and last-minute research.

For special assists, I owe thanks to Pamalla Anderson and Samantha Dodd at SMU's DeGolyer Library; Barbara Rust at the National Archives; Eric Wong and Paul Watler of Jackson Walker; Nina Flournoy; Gail Griswold; Becky Paterik; Naomi Aberly; and especially Margaret Whitehill. I also truly appreciate all the people who gave their time for interviews.

Authors Ellen Chesler, David Garrow, Linda Greenhouse, Jonathan Eig, Joshua Prager (who is working on an adult book on *Roe v. Wade* and Norma McCorvey), and Daniel K. Williams graciously took the time to chat and answer questions, and Greenhouse, Eig, and Prager read all or part of the manuscript and offered feedback. Dr. Jan Goss, Polly Holyoke, Abby McCartney, Jen McCartney, Laney Nielson, Sarah Patzer, David Stern, Melanie Sumrow, Jamila Taylor, and Ann Zimmerman also read the manuscript or parts of it and made helpful suggestions.

There are never enough thanks for my family—for my grown daughters for listening and reading, and for my husband, Scott. He and I haven't gone anywhere in the last two years where we didn't detour to a library for research. I am grateful for our partnership every day.

BIBLIOGRAPHY

This project started as a look at abortion through a history of the famous lawsuit *Roe v. Wade*. But in trying to understand *Roe*, I needed to understand how the lawsuit came about—and then how the laws behind the lawsuit came about.

Before too long, I was enmeshed in a much bigger story about women's rights, reproductive rights, racial discrimination, medicine, and religion.

To research it, I broke it down in parts, just as I have broken down the sources into sections here. In addition to books, I sought out oral histories, news articles from the time, autobiographies and biographies, court documents, and personal papers, especially the papers of the justices on the Supreme Court at the time, and of Roy Lucas, who worked on the lawsuit with Sarah Weddington and Linda Coffee.

I also became a big fan of the website Oyez.org. From that site, you can look up Supreme Court justices, cases, and decisions and actually listen to tapes of Supreme Court oral arguments. (You can also be like Justice Blackmun and grade them.)

Virginia Whitehill, a Dallas feminist icon who worked with Weddington to change the Texas law, had a great appreciation of history and preserved meeting minutes, correspondence, brochures, and other key documents. She gave much of that material to the DeGolyer Library at Southern Methodist University, which granted me access before the papers were processed. In addition, her daughter Margaret generously shared some of Ginny's personal files.

Whitehill was in failing health and not up to an interview, but I was able to interview many others to fill in the gaps between what has been written and what I wanted to know. Nearly a half century after the fact, many of them were in their seventies, eighties, and nineties.

One piece of this project proved particularly challenging. To get the state's side of the story, I wrote the Texas State Library and Archives to request copies of the state's *Roe* case files.

Oddly, the state archives could not find the files and referred me to the state attorney general's office. Author David J. Garrow kindly loaned me his microfilm copies of the files, and I spent days at the library scrolling through more than four thousand pages. Eventually, I asked for a digital version through a Texas Open Records request filed with the state attorney general's office.

The state released most of the papers, but withheld several hundred pages as "attorney-client privilege" and "work product," including Jay Floyd's handwritten notes that are on page 207. With the help of lawyers Eric Wong and Paul Watler, who volunteered their time through the Freedom of Information Foundation of Texas, I appealed to the attorney general's office to get all the files. It ruled against me.

Suing the state, the lawyers informed me, would cost way more than I could afford. So I paid to have the microfilm digitized and have shared those files with the Dallas Public Library and some law school libraries.

The many sources listed here are the major resources I consulted. You will find many more in the Notes. If you have any questions about sources, feel free to contact me through my website, karenblumenthal.com.

Key resources on *Roe v. Wade* and beyond *Roe*

Blackmun, Sally. Introduction, in Gloria Feldt, *The War on Choice*. New York: Bantam Books, 2004. Kindle edition.

Boyd, Curtis. "The Morality of Abortion: The Making of a Feminist Physician." *St. Louis University Public Law Review*, 1993.

Cheek, Jeannette Bailey. Interview with Sarah Weddington, March 12, 1976. Family Planning Oral History Project Interviews, 1973–1977. Schlesinger Library, Harvard University.

Duke, Patricia. Oral Memoirs of Linda Coffee, April 17, 1973. Baylor University Institute for Oral History, Baylor University.

Duke, Patricia. Oral Memoirs of Sarah Weddington, March 30, 1973. Baylor University Program for Oral History, Baylor University.

Evans, J. Claude. J. Claude Evans Family Papers, 1930–2002. David M. Rubenstein Rare Book and Manuscript Library, Duke University.

Faux, Marian. *Roe v. Wade: The Untold Story of the Landmark Supreme Court Decision That Made Abortion Legal.* New York: Macmillan, 1988.

Forsythe, Clark D. *Abuse of Discretion: The Inside Story of Roe v. Wade.* New York: Encounter Books, 2013.

Fowlkes, Diane and Charlene Ball. Interview with Sarah Weddington, April 15, 1998. Georgia Women's Movement Oral History Project, Special Collections, Georgia State University Library.

Garrow, David J. "Abortion Before and After *Roe v. Wade*: An Historical Perspective." *Albany Law Review*, 1998–99.

Garrow, David J. "How *Roe v. Wade* Was Written." *Washington and Lee Law Review*, Vol. 71, 2014.

Garrow, David J. *Liberty and Sexuality: The Right to Privacy and the Making of Roe v. Wade.* Berkeley, CA: University of California Press, 1998.

Gorney, Cynthia. *Articles of Faith: A Frontline History of the Abortion Wars.* New York: Touchstone, 2000.

Greenhouse, Linda, and Reva B. Siegel. "Before (and After) *Roe v. Wade*: New Questions about Backlash." *Yale Law Journal*, June 2011.

Greenhouse, Linda, and Reva B. Siegel. *Before Roe v. Wade: Voices That Shaped the Abortion Debate before the Supreme Court's Ruling.* New York: Kaplan Publishing, 2010.

Griswold, Gail. Interview with Virginia Whitehill, multiple dates, 2003. Personal papers, Whitehill family.

Harlan, Christi. "Roe vs. Wade Didn't Look Like History Maker." *Dayton Daily News*, Jan. 19, 1998.

Karrer, Robert. "The National Right to Life Committee." *Catholic Historical Review*, July 2011.

Lucas, Roy. Roy Lucas Abortion Litigation Papers, 1967–1973. Special Collections and Archives, Olin Library, Wesleyan University.

Luker, Kristin. *Abortion and the Politics of Motherhood.* Berkeley, CA: University of California Press, 1984.

Marcello, Ronald E. Interview with Judge Sarah T. Hughes, Aug. 23, 1979. Oral History Collection, #489, University of North Texas.

McCorvey, Norma, with Andy Meisler. *I Am Roe: My Life, Roe v. Wade, and Freedom of Choice.* New York: HarperCollins Publishers, 1994.

McCorvey, Norma, with Gary Thomas. *Won by Love*. Nashville, TN: Thomas Nelson Publishers, 1997.

McGee, Alexandra. "The Politics of Protection: The Forgotten History of Georgia Feminists and *Doe v. Bolton*." Thesis, Georgia State University, 2015.

Milbauer, Barbara, in collaboration with Bert N. Obrentz. *The Law Giveth: Legal Aspects of the Abortion Controversy*. New York: Atheneum, 1983.

Parker, Dr. Willie. *Life's Work: A Moral Argument for Choice*. New York: Atria Books, 2017.

Paulk, Janet. Interview with Judith Rooks. Georgia Women's Movement Oral History Project, Special Collections, Georgia State University Library.

Prager, Joshua. "The Accidental Activist." *Vanity Fair*, Jan. 18, 2013.

Prager, Joshua. "*Roe v. Wade*'s Secret Heroine." *Vanity Fair*, Jan. 19, 2017.

Robenault, James. *January 1973: Watergate, Roe v. Wade, Vietnam, and the Month That Changed America Forever*. Chicago: Chicago Review Press, 2015.

Rubin, Eva R., editor. *The Abortion Controversy: A Documentary History*. Westport, CT: Greenwood Press, 1994.

Shapiro, Fred C. "'Right to Life' Has a Message for New York State Legislators." *New York Times*, Aug. 20, 1972.

Solinger, Rickie, editor. *Abortion Wars: A Half-Century of Struggle*, 1950–2000. Berkeley, CA: University of California Press, 1998.

State of Texas case files, *Roe v. Wade*. Texas Attorney General's office. Supplied digitally and redacted in 2017 by the Texas Attorney General's office and on microfilm and unredacted in the 1990s by the Texas State Archives.

Tribe, Laurence H. *Abortion: The Clash of Absolutes*. New York: W.W. Norton & Company, 1990.

Vilardo, Lawrence J. and Howard W. Gutman. "With Justice from One: Interview with Hon. Irving L. Goldberg," *Litigation*, Spring 1991.

Weddington, Sarah. *A Question of Choice*. New York: Penguin Books, 1993.

Whitehill, Virginia. Virginia Whitehill Papers, 1880–2018, and Virginia Whitehill Women's and Children's Rights Collection, 1958–2018. DeGolyer Library, Southern Methodist University.

Wilkie, Dr. and Mrs. J.C. *Handbook on Abortion*. Cincinnati, Ohio: Hayes Publishing Co., Inc., 1979.

Williams, Daniel K. "The GOP's Abortion Strategy: Why Pro-Choice Republicans Became Pro-Life in the 1970s." *Journal of Policy History*, volume 23, no. 4, 2011.

Key resources on the history of reproduction and abortion

Baker, Jean H. *Margaret Sanger: A Life of Passion*. New York: Hill and Wang, 2011.

Brodie, Janet Farrell. *Contraception and Abortion in 19th Century America*. Ithaca, NY: Cornell University Press, 1994.

Browder, Clifford. *The Wickedest Woman in New York: Madame Restell, the Abortionist*. Hamden, CT: Archon Books, 1988.

Calderone, Mary Steichen, editor. Abortion in the United States: A Conference Sponsored by the Planned Parenthood Foundation of America, Inc. New York: A Hoeber-Harper Book, 1958.

Carlson, A. Cheree. *The Crimes of Womanhood: Defining Femininity in a Court of Law*. Urbana, IL: University of Illinois Press, 2009.

Chesler, Ellen. *Woman of Valor: Margaret Sanger and the Birth Control Movement in America*. New York: Simon & Schuster, 1992.

Comstock, Anthony. *Frauds Exposed; or How the People Are Deceived and Robbed and Youth Corrupted*. New York: J. Howard Brown, 1880.

Dolnick, Edward. *The Seeds of Life: From Aristotle to da Vinci, from Sharks' Teeth to Frogs' Pants, the Long and Strange Quest to Discover Where Babies Come From*. New York: Basic Books, 2017.

Dreifus, Claudia, editor. *Seizing Our Bodies: The Politics of Women's Health*. New York: Vintage Books, 1977.

Dunaway, Wilma A. *The African-American Family in Slavery and Emancipation*. Cambridge, UK: Cambridge University Press, 2003.

Gordon, Linda. *Women's Body, Women's Right: A Social History of Birth Control in America*. New York: Grossman Publishers, 1976.

Keemer, Ed M.D. *Confessions of a Pro-Life Abortionist*. Detroit: Vinco Press, 1986.

Kluchin, Rebecca M. *Fit to Be Tied: Sterilization and Reproductive Rights in America, 1950–1980*. New Brunswick, N.J.: Rutgers University Press, 2009.

Largent, Mark A. *Breeding Contempt: The History of Coerced Sterilization in the United States*. New Brunswick, NJ: Rutgers University Press, 2008.

Mohr, James C. *Abortion in America: The Origins and Evolution of National Policy, 1800–1900*. New York: Oxford University Press, 1978.

Mohr, James C. "The Historical Character of Abortion in the United States Through World War II," in *Perspective on Abortion*, edited by Paul Sachdev. Metuchen, NJ: The Scarecrow Press, 1985.

Reagan, Leslie J. *When Abortion Was a Crime: Women, Medicine, and Law in the United States, 1867–1973*. Berkeley, CA: University of California Press, 1997.

Riddle, John M. *Eve's Herbs: A History of Contraception and Abortion in the West*. Cambridge, MA: Harvard University Press, 1997.

Roberts, Dorothy. *Killing the Black Body: Race, Reproduction, and the Meaning of Liberty*. New York: Pantheon Books, 1997.

Roberts, Dorothy. "Margaret Sanger and the Racial Origins of the Birth Control Movement." In *Racially Writing the Republic: Racists, Race Rebels, and Transformations of American Identity*, Bruce Baum and Duchess Harris, eds. Durham, NC: Duke University Press, 2009.

Schwartz, Marie Jenkins. *Birthing a Slave: Motherhood and Medicine in the Antebellum South*. Cambridge, MA: Harvard University Press, 2016.

Solinger, Rickie. *Pregnancy and Power: A Short History of Reproductive Politics*. New York: New York University Press, 2005.

Storer, Horatio Robinson M.D. *Why Not? A Book for Every Woman*. Boston: Lee and Shepard, 1866.

Tone, Andrea. *Devices and Desires: A History of Contraceptives in America*. New York: Hill and Wang, 2001.

White, Deborah Gray. *Ar'n't I a Woman: Female Slaves in the Plantation South*. New York: W.W. Norton & Co., 1985.

Key resources on reproductive rights in the 1960s

Bailey, Martha J. "'Mama's Got the Pill': How Anthony Comstock and *Griswold v. Connecticut* Shaped U.S. Childbearing." Cambridge, MA: National Bureau of Economic Research Working Paper 14675.

Carmen, Arlene and Howard Moody. *Abortion Counseling and Social Change: From Illegal Act to Medical Practice.* Valley Forge, PA: Judson Press, 1973.

Caron, Simone M. "Birth Control and the Black Community in the 1960s," *Journal of Social History,* Spring 1998.

Cheek, Jeannette Bailey. Interview with Estelle Griswold, March 7, 1976. Family Planning Oral History Project Interviews, 1973–1977. Schlesinger Library, Harvard University.

Cheek, Jeannette Bailey. Interview with Patricia Maginnis, Nov. 16–18, 1975. Family Planning Oral History Project Interviews, 1973–1977. Schlesinger Library, Harvard University.

Chesler, Ellen. Interview with Arlene Carmen, Jan. 7, 1976. Family Planning Oral History Project Interviews, 1973–1977. Schlesinger Library, Harvard University.

Chesler, Ellen. Interview with Constance Cook, Jan. 13, 1976. Family Planning Oral History Project Interviews, 1973–1977. Schlesinger Library, Harvard University.

Chesler, Ellen. Interview with Lonny Myers, M.D., Sept. 24, 1976. Family Planning Oral History Project Interviews, 1973–1977. Schlesinger Library, Harvard University.

Chisholm, Shirley. *Unbought and Unbossed.* Boston: Houghton Mifflin Company, 1970.

CWLU Herstory Project, articles about the Chicago abortion service Jane, cwluherstory.org/jane-abortion-service.

Dirks, Doris Andrea and Patricia A. Relf. *To Offer Compassion: A History of the Clergy Consultation Service on Abortion.* Madison, WI: University of Wisconsin Press, 2017.

Eig, Jonathan. *The Birth of the Pill: How Four Crusaders Reinvented Sex and Launched a Revolution.* New York: W. W. Norton & Company, 2014.

Fessler, Ann. *The Girls Who Went Away: The Hidden History of Women Who Surrendered Children for Adoption in the Decades before Roe v. Wade.* New York: The Penguin Press, 2006.

Guttmacher, Alan F. M.D. *Babies by Choice or by Chance.* New York: Avon Book Division, 1961.

Jane: Documents from Chicago's Clandestine Abortion Service, 1968–1973. Baltimore, M.D.: Firestarter Press, 2004.

Joffe, Carole. *Doctors of Conscience: The Struggle to Provide Abortion Before and After Roe v. Wade.* Boston: Beacon Press, 1995.

Johnson, Linnea. "Something Real: Jane and Me. Memories and Exhortations of a Feminist Ex-Abortionist." CWLU Herstory Project, cwluherstory.org.

Kaplan, Laura. *The Story of Jane: The Legendary Underground Feminist Abortion Service.* Chicago: The University of Chicago Press, 1995.

Lader, Lawrence. *Abortion.* Boston: Beacon Press, 1966.

Lader, Lawrence. *Abortion II: Making the Revolution.* Boston: Beacon Press, 1973.

Moody, Howard. *A Voice in the Village: A Journey of a Pastor and a People.* Xlibris, 2009.

Morgan, Robin, editor. *Sisterhood Is Powerful: An Anthology of Writings from the Women's Liberation Movement.* New York: Vintage Books, 1970.

Reagan, Leslie J. *Dangerous Pregnancies: Mothers, Disabilities, and Abortion in Modern America.* Berkeley, CA: University of California Press, 2010. Kindle edition.

Schulder, Diane and Florynce Kennedy. *Abortion Rap.* New York: McGraw Hill Book Company, 1971.

Solinger, Rickie. *Wake Up Little Susie: Single Pregnancy and Race before Roe v. Wade.* New York: Routledge, 1992.

Williams, Daniel K. *Defenders of the Unborn: The Pro-Life Movement before Roe v. Wade.* New York: Oxford University Press, 2016.

Wolff, Joshua D. "Ministers of a Higher Law: The Story of the Clergy Consultation Service on Abortion." Senior paper, Amherst College, 1998.

Key sources regarding the U.S. Supreme Court

Blackmun, Harry A. Harry A. Blackmun Papers, 1913–2001. Manuscript Division, Library of Congress.

Brennan, William J. William J. Brennan Papers, 1945–1998. Manuscript Division, Library of Congress.

Clor, Harry M. "Constitutional Interpretation: An Interview with Justice Lewis Powell." *Kenyon College Alumni Bulletin*, Summer 1979.

Douglas, William O. William O. Douglas Papers, 1801–1980. Manuscript Division, Library of Congress.

Graetz, Michael J. and Linda Greenhouse. *The Burger Court and the Rise of the Judicial Right.* New York: Simon & Schuster, 2016.

Greenhouse, Linda. *Becoming Justice Blackmun: Harry Blackmun's Supreme Court Journey.* New York: Times Books, 2005.

Jeffries, John C., Jr. *Justice Lewis F. Powell, Jr.: A Biography.* New York: Charles Scribner's Sons, 1994.

Koh, Harold Hongju. The Justice Harry A. Blackmun Oral History Project. Recorded under the auspices of the Supreme Court Historical Society and the Federal Judicial Center. memory.loc.gov/diglib/blackmun -public/series.html?ID=D10.

Marshall, Thurgood. Thurgood Marshall Papers, 1949–1991. Manuscript Division, Library of Congress.

Powell, Lewis F. Jr. *Roe v. Wade.* Supreme Court Case Files Collection. Box 5. Lewis F. Powell Jr. Archives, Washington & Lee University School of Law, Virginia. law2.wlu.edu/powellarchives/page.asp?pageid=1341.

Rehnquist, William H. William H. Rehnquist Papers. Hoover Institution Archives.

Stone, Geoffrey. *Sex and the Constitution: Sex, Religion, and Law from America's Origins to the Twenty-First Century.* New York: Liveright Publishing Corporation, 2017.

Thomas, Evan. *First: Sandra Day O'Connor.* New York: Random House, 2019.

White, Byron R. Byron R. White Papers, 1961–1992. Manuscript Division, Library of Congress.

Woodward, Bob and Scott Armstrong. *The Brethren: Inside the Supreme Court.* New York: Simon & Schuster, 1979.

Author Interviews

Dr. Curtis Boyd, March 13, 2018

Frank J. Bradley Jr., D.O., Aug. 7, 2018

Vivian Castleberry, May 16, 2017

Sherri Chessen, March 17, 2018

Linda Coffee, Aug. 10, 2017; Aug. 16, 2019

Rev. Robert Cooper and Shirley Cooper, Feb. 13, 2018

Jeanne Galatzer-Levy, Dec. 19, 2017

"Helen," who gave a baby up for adoption, June 14, 2018

Dr. Irwin Kerber, Nov. 1, 2017

Sanford Levinson, April 2, 2019

Martin McKernan, Nov. 29, 2017

Loretta Ross, Feb. 9, 2019

Dr. Barry Schwarz, Oct. 20, 2017

Martha Scott, Jan. 8, 2018

Geoffrey Stone, Feb. 20, 2019

Imam Omar Suleiman, Sept. 5, 2019

Jamila Taylor, Feb. 13, 2019

John Tolle, Feb. 15, 2019

Ron Weddington, Sept. 6, 2017

Sarah Weddington, Sept. 5, 2017

Newspapers and Magazines

Austin American Statesman, *Baptist Press*, Catholic newspapers, *Dallas Morning News*, *Dallas Times Herald*, *Fort Worth Star-Telegram*, *New York Times*, *Time* magazine, *Washington Post*, and numerous articles accessed through a subscription to Newspapers.com. Many of these are accessible through library databases and to subscribers. The *Baptist Press* archive is online at the Southern Baptist Historical Library and Archives, sbhla.org/bp_archive /index.asp, and the Catholic press is online at Catholic News Archives, thecatholicnewsarchive.org/.

Videos

Dore, Mary, director/producer. *She's Beautiful When She's Angry*. Music Box Films, 2016.

Fadiman, Dorothy, director. *From Danger to Dignity: The Fight for Safe Abortion*. New York: Concentric Media, 1995. youtube.com/watch?v=Vg4B-UmgfG8.

Fadiman, Dorothy, director. *When Abortion Was Illegal: Untold Stories*. New York: Concentric Media, 1992. youtube.com/watch?v=O_IgnSEpKe8.

Jane: An Abortion Service. Documentary by Kate Kirtz and Nell Lundy. New York: Women Make Movies, 1996. DVD.

Websites

Guttmacher Institute, guttmacher.org.

LiveAction News, liveaction.org/news/.

National Abortion Federation, prochoice.org.

National Right to Life Committee, nrlc.org.

Oyez, oyez.org, which also links to Justia.com for court decisions.

Planned Parenthood, plannedparenthood.org.

NOTES

Prologue: Jane

Martha Scott and Jeanne Galatzer-Levy didn't: Author interviews with Jeanne Galatzer-Levy, Dec. 19, 2017, and Martha Scott, Jan. 8, 2018; Martha J. Bailey, "'Momma's Got the Pill,'" National Bureau of Economic Research, Working Paper 14675, p. 3; Martin Tolchin, "Doctors Divided on Issue," *New York Times*, Feb. 27, 1967; Laura Kaplan, *The Story of Jane*, pp. 27, 36, 38–42, 53–55, 92, 175; Linnea Johnson, "Something Real: Jane and Me," CWLU Herstory Project, cwluherstory.org/jane-abortion-service; *Jane: An Abortion Service*, documentary by Kate Kirtz and Nell Lundy; "Abortion Clinic Raided," *Alton (IL) Evening Telegraph*, May 4, 1972.

Part I: **Restrictions:**

Anthony Comstock, *Frauds Exposed*, p. 416.

Madame Restell

More than a century before: Clifford Browder, *The Wickedest Woman in New York*, pp. 3, 6–7, 155; Karen Abbott, "Madame Restell: The Abortionist of Fifth Avenue," smithsonian.com, Nov. 27, 2012; A. Cheree Carlson, *The Crimes of Womanhood*, pp. 111–112, 128; Robert Sneddon, "That Was New York: The Notorious Madame Restell," *New Yorker*, Nov. 15, 1941; "Female Monthly Pill," Advertisement, *Boston Post*, Nov. 30, 1840; "Mme. Restell," *New York Times*, Dec. 28, 1866; "The Wages of Sin: Madame Restell at the Bar of Justice," *Brooklyn Daily Eagle*, Feb. 24, 1878; "Mme. Restell Arrested," *New York Times*, Feb. 12, 1878; "Madame Restell," advertisement, *New York Daily Herald*, Aug. 13, 1843.

The services Madame Restell and others: John M. Riddle, *Eve's Herbs*, pp. 26–28, 35–36, 68, 233–35; Linda Gordon, *Women's Body, Women's Right*, pp. 35–39, note on 52–53; James C. Mohr, *Abortion in America*, pp. 3–5, 20–27, 39–43, 47, 53–60; Leslie J. Reagan, *When Abortion Was a Crime*, pp. 8–10.

Madame Restell was at the forefront: "The Evil of the Age," *New York Times*, Aug. 23, 1871; Abbott, "Madame Restell"; Sneddon, "That Was New York"; *National Police Gazette*, "Wonderful Trial of Caroline (sic) Lohman, Alias Restell," pp. 3–9, 38; Carlson, *Crimes*, pp. 123–128.

Advertising and the wide availability: Mohr, pp. 46–47, 50, 83–85, 98–114; "Rise of Industrial America, 1876–1900," Library of Congress, loc.gov/teachers /classroommaterials/presentationsandactivities/presentations/timeline/riseind/; Kate Manning, "What Abortion Was Like in the 19ᵗʰ Century," elle.com, Oct. 22, 2014; Gordon, pp. 4–5, 11, 48; "The Evil of the Age," *New York Times*; Roberts, *Killing the Black Body*, pp. 46–47; Deborah Gray White, *Ar'n't I a Woman*, pp. 78–90; Wilma A. Dunaway, *The African-American Family in Slavery and Emancipation*, pp. 114–127; Marie Jenkins Schwartz, *Birthing a Slave*, pp. 106–126.

By the 1850s: Mohr, *Abortion*, pp. 33–37, 147–170, 186–196, 200; Reagan, *When Abortion*, pp. 10–13; American Medical Association, "AMA History," ama-assn.org /about/ama-history/ama-history; Horatio Robinson Storer Papers, Biographical Sketches, Massachusetts Historical Society, masshist.org/collection-guides /view/fa0001; Horatio Robinson Storer, M.D., *Why Not? A Book for Every Woman*, pp. 15, 75–76, 85; "Report on Criminal Abortion," *Transactions of the American Medical Association*, vol. 12, 1859, pp. 75–78, D.A. O'Donnell and W.L. Atlee, "Report of the Committee on Criminal Abortion," May 3, 1871, *Transactions of the American Medical Association*, vol. 12, 1871, pp. 249–250; Gordon, pp. 95–115; Tracy A. Thomas, "Misappropriating Women's History in the Law and Politics in Abortion," *Seattle University Law Review 1 (2012)*, University of Akron School of Law, Legal Studies Research Paper Series, no. 12-03, pp. 3–4, 26; Riddle, *Eve's Herbs*, pp. 222–224.

Sidelined by an infection: Browder, *Wickedest Woman*, pp. 139–183; Abbott, "Madame Restell"; "The Wages of Sin," *Brooklyn Daily Eagle*, Feb. 24, 1878; "Madame Restell," *New York Daily Herald*, Feb. 24, 1878; "The Case of Mme. Restell," *New York Times*, Feb. 24, 1878; "End of an Infamous Life," *New-York Tribune*, April 2, 1878; Sneddon, "That Was New York"; Ernest Sutherland Bates, "Comstock Stalks," *Scribner's Magazine*, April 1930; Jennifer Davis, "James Joyce, Ulysses, and the Meaning of Obscenity," Library of Congress law blog, blogs.loc.gov/law/2016/02/james -joyce-ulysses-and-the-meaning-of-obscenity/.

Pregnant Pause: Where Babies Come From

Edward Dolnick, *The Seeds of Life*, pp. 16–17, 31, 70–75, 104, 114, 126, 132, 216–227, 256, 261–262; Laura Poppick, "The Long, Winding Tale of Sperm Science," Smithsonian, June 7, 2017, smithsonianmag.com/science-nature /scientists-finally-unravel-mysteries-sperm-180963578/; Robert Krulwich, "Two Glorious Science Experiments: One about Sex, the Other About Lunch," NPR, June 25, 2014.

Pregnant Pause: A Short History of Birth Control: Ancient Times to the 1870s

Gordon, p. 41; Mohr, pp. 7–10, 65; Riddle, pp. 31–32, 46–62, 124; Kate Manning, "Leeches, Lye and Spanish Fly," *New York Times*, Jan. 21, 2013.

Margaret Sanger

The legacies of Horatio Storer: Ellen Chesler, *Woman of Valor*, pp. 22, 44–45, 62–63, 97–104, 126; Jean H. Baker, *Margaret Sanger*, pp. 22–23, 49–52, 83, 99, 105–108; Cathy Moran Hajo, "Birth of a Movement: The Case of Sadie Sachs," Margaret Sanger Papers Project, sangerpapers.wordpress.com/tag/sadie-sacks/; Edwin M. Schur, "The Abortion Racket," *The Nation*, March 5, 1955; David J. Garrow, *Liberty and Sexuality*, p. 272; Margaret Sanger, "Birth Control or Abortion," *Birth Control Review*, Dec. 1918; Reagan, *When Abortion Was a Crime*, pp. 43, 113–116, 121–125; James C. Mohr, "The Historical Character of Abortion in the United States Through World War II," in *Perspective on Abortion*, p. 11; Jonathan Eig, *The Birth of the Pill*, pp. 41–54; Margaret Sanger, "Not Guilty!" Public Writings and Speeches of Margaret Sanger, nyu.edu/projects/sanger/webedition/app/documents/show .php?sangerDoc=309032.xml; James Waldo Fawcett, editor, "Jailed for Birth Control: The Trial of William Sanger, September 10th, 1915," accessed at babel .hathitrust.org/cgi/pt?id=hvd.32044050973734;view=1up;seq=13; "Clinic Opened Here for Birth Control; Challenges Police," *Brooklyn Daily Eagle*, Oct. 22, 1916; Jill Grimaldi, "Sanger's First Clinic," Margaret Sanger Papers Project, sangerpapers .wordpress.com/2010/10/26/sangers-first-clinic/; "Mrs. Sanger Fights as Police Seize Her in Raid on 'Clinic,'" *Brooklyn Daily Eagle*, Oct. 26, 1916; Andrea Tone, *Devices and Desires*, pp. 106–107; "Birth Control Organizations: American Birth Control League," "Birth Control Organizations: Birth Control Review," and "Tracing One Package—The Case That Legalized Birth Control," Margaret Sanger Papers Project, nyu.edu/projects/sanger/index.php; William Laurence, "Birth Control Is Accepted by American Medical Body," *New York Times*, June 9, 1937.

Without question, Sanger was a: Roberts, pp. 57–89; Amita Kelly, "Fact Check: Was Planned Parenthood Started to 'Control' the Black Populations," NPR, npr .org/sections/itsallpolitics/2015/08/14/432080520/fact-check-was-planned -parenthood-started-to-control-the-black-population; Eig, pp. 51–54; Baker, pp. 5, 249; Chesler, 2007 Afterword to *Woman of Valor,* accessed via Kindle; Emily Crockett, "Margaret Sanger's Grandson Hopes for a Future Where We Don't Need Planned Parenthood," *Vox.com*, Oct. 16, 2016; Dorothy Roberts, "Margaret Sanger and the Racial Origins of the Birth Control Movement," in *Racially Writing the Republic*, pp. 202–211; Rebecca M. Kluchin, *Fit to Be Tied*, pp. 15–16; Mark A. Largent, *Breeding Contempt*, pp. 79–80; *Buck v. Bell*, Justia, supreme.justia.com/cases/federal/us/274/200/case .html; Don Wharton, "Birth Control: The Case for the State," *The Atlantic*, Oct. 1939.

Pregnant Pause: When the Rabbit Died

Cari Romm, "Before There Were Home Pregnancy Tests," theatlantic.com, June 17, 2015, theatlantic.com/health/archive/2015/06/history-home-pregnancy-test /396077/; "A Timeline of Pregnancy Testing," National Institutes of Health, history .nih.gov/exhibits/thinblueline/timeline.html; Pagan Kennedy, "Who Made That Home Pregnancy Test?" *New York Times,* July 27, 2012.

A Crime

As they were training: Alan F. Guttmacher, M.D., "Abortion: Odyssey of an Attitude," *Family Planning Perspectives,* Oct. 1972; Betty DeRamus, "Abortion Pioneer Reflects on Years of Abuse, Shame," *Detroit Free Press,* May 7, 1973; Guttmacher, *Babies by Choice or by Chance,* pp. 10–11, 138–142; Jill Lepore, "This Is Forty: The Anniversary of *Roe v. Wade,*" *New Yorker,* Jan. 17, 2013; David Dempsey, "Dr. Guttmacher Is the Evangelist of Birth Control," *New York Times,* Feb. 9, 1969; Frederick S. Jaffe, "Alan Guttmacher, 1898–1974," *Family Planning Perspectives,* Winter 1974; "Suggests Doctors Relax 'Hypocrisy,'" *New York Times,* Jan. 31, 1942; Reagan, *When Abortion Was a Crime,* pp. 178–179, 200–213; Rickie Solinger, "Pregnancy and Power Before *Roe v. Wade,* 1950–1970," in *Abortion Wars,* pp. 23–24; Lawrence Lader, *Abortion,* pp. 24–31; Lawrence Lader, *Abortion II,* pp. 21–23.

When Edgar Bass Keemer Jr. was: DeRamus, "Abortion Pioneer"; Reagan, pp. 180–192; "Abortion Suspects Arraigned," *Detroit Free Press,* Sept. 1, 1956; "2 Doctors, 2 Aides Convicted," *Detroit Free Press,* Jan 22, 1958; "Two Detroit Doctors Convicted," *Pittsburgh Courier,* Feb. 15, 1958; Ed Keemer, M.D., *Confessions of a Pro-Life Abortionist,* pp. 170–171, 208–209.

In 1952, Guttmacher left: Guttmacher, "The Law That Doctors Often Break," *Redbook,* Aug. 1959; "Made Obstetrics Chief At Mount Sinai Hospital," *New York Times,* June 27, 1952; Guttmacher, "Abortion: Odyssey;" Mary Steichen Calderone, editor, *Abortion in the United States,* pp. 5, 59–63, 113; Reagan, p. 148; Lader, *Abortion,* pp. 42–51; "Four Charged in Abortion Case," *Baltimore Sun,* Sept. 1, 1950; Abortion in the U.S.," *Time,* June 2, 1958; Anthony Lewis, "Legal Abortions Proposed in Code," *New York Times,* March 22, 1959; Anthony Lewis, "Model Penal Code Is Approved by the American Law Institute," *New York Times,* May 25, 1962; Jaffe, "Guttmacher"; Guttmacher, "Abortion: Odyssey."

Pregnant Pause: Another Double Standard

Kluchin, pp. 22–24, 90–107; Leslie Aldridge Weston, "Why Six Million Have Deliberately Chosen an Ultimate Form of Contraception," *New York Times,* Sept. 29, 1974; Roberts, *Killing the Black Body,* pp. 89-98; Author interviews; DeNeen L. Brown,

"Civil Rights Crusader Fannie Lou Hamer Defied Men—and Presidents—Who Tried to Silence Her," *Washington Post*, Oct. 6, 2017.

Pregnant Pause: A Short History of Birth Control: 1870s to 1950s

"History of Condoms," Dittrick Medical History Center, artsci.case.edu/dittrick /collections/aritfacts/contraception-collection/history-of-contraception-videos /; Hallie Lieberman, "A Short History of the Condom," JStor daily, daily.jstor.org /short-history-of-the-condom/; Tone, pp. 14, 126–138; 158–160; Margaret Sanger, "Family Limitation," sixth edition, 1917; "Rhythm Method," Highlights of the Percy Skuy History of Contraception Gallery, Case Western Reserve University, case.edu /affil/skuyhistcontraception/online-2012/Rhythm-method.html.

Sherri Chessen

Sherri Chessen was just looking: Sherri Chessen, "Sherri Chessen, Rich Little Poor Girl," Veteran Feminists of America, veteranfeministsofamerica.org/legacy /Sherri%20Chessen.htm; Gene McLain, "Court Decision Delay Couple's Big Concern," *Arizona Republic*, July, 26, 1962; Ross Davis, "Sherri's TV Work Praised," *Arizona Republic*, July 26, 1962; Jules Loh, "Arizona Parents Searched Souls on Fate of Unborn Child," *Tampa Tribune*, Aug. 5, 1962; Julian DeVries, "Pill May Cost Woman Her Baby," *Arizona Republic*, July 23, 1962; James E. Cook, "Mother TV Star Here: Court Suit Filing Reveals Identity," *Arizona Republic*, July 26, 1962; James E. Cook, "Decision in Abortion Case Due Tomorrow," *Arizona Republic*, July 29, 1962; James E. Cook, "Finkbines Lose Bid in Court," *Arizona Republic*, July 31, 1962; Author interview of Sherri Chessen, March 17, 2018; Lader, *Abortion*, p. 15; "Pair Flees Phoenix in Disguise," *Arizona Republic*, Aug. 4, 1962; "Finkbines Take Flight to Sweden," *Arizona Republic*, Aug. 5, 1962; "Doctors Say Finkbine Baby Would Have Been Crippled," *Yuma Daily Sun*, Aug. 19, 1962; Jay Mathews, "25 Years After the Abortion," *Washington Post*, April 27, 1987; "Finkbine Abortion Crime: Vatican," *Arizona Republic*, Aug. 20, 1962; "Sweden's Church Upholds Finkbines," *Arizona Republic*, Aug. 21, 1962; Luise Leismer, "Present and Future Are What Count for Sherri Finkbine and Her Family," *Arizona Daily Star*, Sept. 12, 1971; Myra McPherson, "Some States Loosen Abortion Laws," *Arizona Republic*, Dec. 28, 1968; "Mrs. Finkbine to Make Film in Phoenix After Return From Swedish Operation," *Arizona Daily Sun*, Sept. 3, 1962.

Pregnant Pause: Illegitimate

"Unwed Fathers," words and music by John Prine and Bobby Braddock, used by permission; Ann Fessler, *The Girls Who Went Away*, pp. 7–13, 72, 110, 191–193, 198, 213–214, 232, 315–316; "Number, rate, and percent of births to unmarried women and birth rate for married women, United States, 1940–1999," *National Vital Statistics*

Report, vol. 48, no. 16, Oct. 18, 2000, p. 17; Rickie Solinger, *Wake Up Little Susie*, pp. 6, 13, 49–53, 90, 103–104; "Forced to Give Up Their Babies," *People*, Sept. 18, 2006; Diane Schulder and Florynce Kennedy, *Abortion Rap*, pp. 22-23.

Estelle Griswold

Sherri Chessen was pushed into: Jeannette Bailey Cheek, interview with Estelle Griswold, March 17, 1976, Schlesinger-Rockefeller Oral History Project, pp. ii, 4–5, 16–19, 26–28, 31–38, 47–48; Garrow, *Liberty and Sexuality*, pp. 16, 103–105, 131–133, 139–142, 212, 217, 224, 229, 233, 239; 249, 260, 262, 268–269; *Poe v. Ullman*, Oyez, oyez.org; "New Haven Police Shut Birth Clinic," *New York Times*, Nov. 11, 1961; Jack V. Fox, "Birth Control Law Under Challenge," *Pasadena (Calif.) Independent*, Dec. 7, 1961; Eig, pp. 3–4, 98–101, 299–302, 313, 315–316; "Contraception: Freedom From Fear," *Time*, April 7, 1967; Bailey, pp. 3, 9–16; "Caseloads: Supreme Court of the United States," Federal Judicial Center; *Meyer v. Nebraska* and *Pierce v. Society of Sisters*, Oyez, oyez.org; *Griswold v. Connecticut*, Oral Arguments, March 29 and 30, 1965, oyez.org/cases/1964/496, and decision, supreme .justia.com/cases/federal/us/381/479/#tab-opinion-1945662; "The Law: Emanations from a Penumbra," *Time*, June 18, 1965.

Pregnant Pause: Deaths from Abortions

"Table 290F: Deaths for Approximately 64 Selected Causes," (1950–1959), "Table 290A: Deaths for Approximately 60 Selected Causes," (1960–1969), and "Table 290A: "Deaths for 69 Selected Causes," (1968–1978), Centers for Disease Control/National Center for Health Statistics; Carole Novielli, "How Many Women Really Died From Illegal Abortion Prior to *Roe v. Wade*," LiveAction, liveaction.org/news/women-died-illegal-abortion-roe/; Edwin M. Schur, "The Abortion Racket," *The Nation*, March 5, 1955; Eve Edstrom, "Abortion Deaths Estimates Too High Conference Told," *Washington Post*, Sept. 7, 1967; Tolchin, *New York Times*; Glenn Kessler, "Planned Parenthood's False Stat," *Washington Post*, May 29, 2019.

Part II: Reform

Ellen Chesler, interview with Constance Cook, Jan. 13, 1976, Schlesinger-Rockefeller Oral History Project, p. 47.

Clergy

For decades, many women: Lader, *Abortion II*, pp. 27-28; Wallace Turner, "Abortion Classes Offered on Coast," *New York Times*, Dec. 4, 1966; Jeannette Bailey Cheek, interview with Patricia Maginnis, Nov. 16–18, 1975, Schlesinger-Rockefeller

Oral History Project, pp. 106–107; Keith Monroe, "How California's Abortion Law Isn't Working," *New York Times*, Dec. 29, 1968; Kaplan, pp. 7–12; Cynthia Gorney, *Articles of Faith*, pp. 29–31; "Unitarians Urge Legal Abortions," *New York Times*, May 19, 1963; "Lutherans Back Some Abortions," *New York Times*, Oct. 25, 1966; Doris Andrea Dirks and Patricia A. Relf, *To Offer Compassion*, p. 10.

Larry Lader, a journalist, became one of: Lader, *Abortion II*, pp. viii–ix, 24–25, 44; Lawrence Lader, "The Scandal of Abortion Laws," *New York Times*, April 25, 1965; Lader, *Abortion*, p. 1; Dirks and Relf, pp. 6, 21, 23–29, 31, 41, 51–53; Ed Gold, "Rev. Moody Reflects on 50 Years of Activism," *The Villager*, Dec. 30, 2003; Arlene Carmen and Howard Moody, "Abortion Counseling and Social Change," pp. 19, 21–26, 30–31, 61–63, 66; "35 Call Clergymen For Aid on Abortion," *New York Times*, May 24, 1967; Ellen Chesler, interview with Arlene Carmen, Jan. 7, 1976, Schlesinger-Rockefeller Oral History Project, pp. 13–16, 20–21, 25–27, 33, 99.

Pregnant Pause: Robert Douglas Spencer

"Dr. Robert Spencer, 79, Dies," *New York Times*, Jan. 22, 1969; Susan Brownmiller, "Dr. Spencer, 1889–1969: Last Trip to Ashland," *Village Voice*, Jan. 30, 1969; "Abortion Experts, Saying Women Should Decide on Birth, Ask to End Curbs," *New York Times*, Nov. 24, 1968; "King of the Abortionists," *Newsweek*, Feb. 17, 1969.

Right to Life

Far from New York: Jane E. Brody, "Vaccine For Measles," *New York Times*, May 1, 1966; "Rubella in the U.S.," Centers for Disease Control and Prevention, cdc.gov /rubella/about/in-the-us.html; Lader, *Abortion II*, pp. 62–71; Leslie J. Reagan, *Dangerous Pregnancies*, Kindle edition, Kindle locations 3080–3311; "The Agony of Mothers About Their Unborn," *Life*, June 4, 1965; Daniel K. Williams, *Defenders of the Unborn*, pp. 62–72; Keith Monroe, "How California's Abortion Law Isn't Working," *New York Times*, Dec, 29, 1968.

Reforming the abortion law: Letters and statements dated Sept. 28, 1966, Dec. 8, 1966, Dec. 9, 1966, from the Abortion—1966 folder, and letters and statements dated Jan. 27, 1967, "Objective," (undated), "Suggestions for the Parochial Support of the 'Right to Life League,'" June 15, 1967, from the Abortion—1967 folder, all from the Archives of the Archdiocese of Los Angeles; Williams, *Defenders*, pp. 72–84; Michelle Ye Hee Lee, "Donald Trump's Claim He Evolved into Pro-Life Views Like Ronald Reagan," *Washington Post*, March 31, 2016; Monroe, "How California's Abortion Law Isn't Working"; "Judge Throws Out Abortion Penalty in Measles Case," *Los Angeles Times*, Aug. 3, 1968.

The swift progress: Williams, *Defenders*, pp. 62, 68, 75, 89–100; Edward B. Fiske, "Bishops to Press Abortion Battle," *New York Times*, April 14, 1967; Donald Janson, "A.M.A., in Reversal, Favors Liberalizing of Abortion Laws," *New York Times*, June 22, 1967; "Bishop James T. McHugh, Third Bishop of Rockville Centre," biography, The Diocese of Rockville Centre, Long Island, NY; James T. McHugh to Most Rev. George Leech, Nov. 6, 1967; James T. McHugh, "Special Abortion Report," June 10, 1968, and McHugh letters to bishops, July 25, 1968, and Jan. 10, 1969, all from the U.S. Conference of Catholic Bishops; Robert N. Karrer, "The National Right to Life Committee," *Catholic Historical Review*, July 2011, pp. 539–540; "Encyclical Letter Humanae Vitae of the Supreme Pontiff Paul VI," The Vatican, vatican.va/content /paul-vi/en/encyclicals/documents/hf_p-vi_enc_25071968_humanae-vitae.html; Robert C. Doty, "Pope Bars Birth Control by Any Artificial Means," *New York Times*, July 30, 1968.

Pregnant Pause: Images

"Drama of Life Before Birth," *Life*, April 30, 1965; "Behind the Lens: An Interview with Lennart Nilsson," pbs.org/wgbh/nova/odyssey/nilsson.html; "Making Visible Embryos: The Lonesome Space Traveller," University of Cambridge, online exhibition, sites.hps.cam.ac.uk/visibleembryos/s7_4.html; Emily Langer, "Lennart Nilsson, Photographer Who Revealed Unborn Life, Dies at 94," *Washington Post*, Feb. 2, 2017.

Repeal

The late 1960s were: Williams, *Defenders*, pp. 105–106; Cheek, Maginnis, p. 102; Ellen Chesler, interview with Lonny Myers, M.D., Schlesinger-Rockefeller Oral History Project, Sept. 24, 1976, pp. 36–37; Dirks and Relf, pp. 55–56; "Progress Report on Liberalized Abortion," *Time*, Nov. 15, 1968; Lader, *Abortion II*, pp. 49, 85–86; Robert D. McFadden, "Flaw in Abortion Reform Found in an 8-State Study," *New York Times*, April 13, 1970; David Dempsey, "Dr. Guttmacher Is the Evangelist of Birth Control," *New York Times*, Feb. 9, 1969.

The repeal movement also gained: Betty Friedan, "Up from the Kitchen Floor," *New York Times*, March 4, 1973; Lader, *Abortion II*, pp. 36–37, 91, 93–95; Martha Weinman Lear, "The Second Feminist Wave," *New York Times*, March 10, 1968; Linda Greenhouse and Reva B. Siegel, eds., *Before Roe v. Wade*, pp. 38–39; Frances M. Beal, "Double Jeapardy: To Be Black and Female," in *Sisterhood Is Powerful*, pp. 346–350; Thomas A. Johnson, "Boycott of Sports by Negroes Asked," *New York Times*, July 24, 1967; Simone M. Caron, "Birth Control and the Black Community in the 1960s," *Journal of Social History*, Spring 1998, pp. 546–547; Dick Gregory, "My Answer to Genocide," *Ebony*, Oct. 1971; Roberts, *Killing the Black Body*, pp. 98–103; Shirley Chisholm, *Unbought and Unbossed*, pp. 113–114.

In March 1970: Lader, *Abortion II*, pp. 58–59, 116–120, 122–124; "Brydges Easing Opposition to New Abortion Law," *New York Times*, Feb. 19, 1970; Francis X. Clines, "State Senate to Act on Abortion Reform," *New York Times*, March 11, 1970; Bill Kovach, "Abortion Reform Approved, 31–26, By State Senate," *New York Times*, March 19, 1970; Chesler, Cook interview, pp. 28–29, 38, 43, 47–50, 70; "New York Assembly Debate on Abortion, 1969–1970," YouTube, youtube.com/watch?v=YBVSmuWL0Mk; "A Remarkable Life: Constance Eberhardt Cook, Pioneer and Politician," YouTube, youtube.com/watch?v=H7uGUHtA2xo; Bill Kovach, "Abortion Reform Beaten In the Assembly by 3 Votes," *New York Times*, March 31, 1970; Francis X. Clines, "Lobbies Included Wives and Clergy," *New York Times*, April 11, 1970; Bill Kovach, "Abortion Reform Is Voted By the Assembly, 76 to 73; Richard Mathieu, "Assembly OKs Abortion Reform Bill," *New York Daily News*, April 10, 1970; New York Legalizes Abortion, 1970, YouTube, youtube.com/watch?v=gOckXY6OmwA; "Final Approval Expected," *New York Times*, April 10, 1970; Linda Greenhouse, "After July 1, An Abortion Should Be As Simple To Have As A Tonsillectomy, But—," *New York Times Magazine*, June 28, 1970.

Pregnant Pause: A Short History of Birth Control: 1960s to 1990s

Planned Parenthood, "The Birth Control Pill: A History," June 2015; "Dalkon Shield," Percy Skuy History of Contraception Gallery, Case Western Reserve University, case.edu/affil/skuyhistcontraception/online-2012/IUDs.html; Philip J. Hilts, "Birth Control Backlash," *New York Times*, Dec. 16, 1990.

Courts

In the fall of 1969: Joshua Prager, "*Roe v. Wade*'s Secret Heroine," *Vanity Fair*, Jan. 19, 2017; "California Court Decision May Curb Abortion Prosecutions," *New York Times*, Sept. 14, 1969; Garrow, pp. 391, 395–399; Sarah Weddington, *A Question of Choice*, pp. 11–14, 18–20, 23, 29, 38–45; (McMurry College became McMurry University in 1990); Jeannette Bailey Cheek, interview with Sarah Weddington, March 12, 1976, Schlesinger-Rockefeller Oral History Project, pp. 3; Diane Fowlkes and Charlene Ball, interview with Sarah Weddington, April 15, 1998, Georgia Women's Movement Oral History Project, Special Collections, Georgia State University, p. 2; Dusty Burke, "A Woman Had a Place, and It Was Not Practicing Law," Texas Monthly.com, texasmonthly.com/politics/a-woman-had-a-place-and-it-was-not-out-practicing-law/; Kay Crosby, "The Law Clerks Are Girls," *Dallas Morning News*, Sept. 2, 1968; Author interview with Ron Weddington, Sept. 6, 2017; Marian Faux, *Roe v. Wade*, pp. 30–31, 36–41; "Law in Capital Barring Abortion Is Overruled by a Federal Judge," *New York Times*, Nov. 11, 1969; Linda J. Greenhouse, "Constitutional Question: Is There a Right to Abortion?" *New York Times*, Jan. 25, 1970; Barbara Milbauer, *The Law Giveth*, pp. 29–30.

As Coffee was quietly: Doris Middleton, "Alas *Roe v Wade*. . . . we know thee well," Virginia Whitehill Clippings Collection, box 7, folder 13, DeGolyer Library, Southern Methodist University; Gail Griswold, interview with Virginia Whitehill, Sept. 4, 2003; Faux, pp. 103–110; Charles C. Mann, "The Book That Incited a Worldwide Fear of Overpopulation," *Smithsonian*, Jan. 2018; "Organizational Meeting of the Dallas Association for the Study of Abortion," Feb. 11, 1970, box 4, folder 3, and "Contributions as of 3/15/71," box 17, folder 17, both in Virginia Whitehill Women's and Children's Collection, DeGolyer Library, SMU; Vivian Castleberry, "Claude Evans, The Reluctant Liberal," *Dallas Times Herald*, Oct. 16, 1977; Martha Man, "Face in the Crowd: Rev. Evans," *Dallas Times Herald*, April 14, 1970; "300 a Month Seek Advice," *Dallas Morning News*, Feb. 6, 1972; Author interview with Robert (Bob) and Shirley Cooper, April 27, 2018; Martha Man, "Methodists Back Abortion," *Dallas Times Herald*, April 24, 1970; "Abortion Resolution Wins Presbyterians' Approval," *Dallas Times Herald*, June 19, 1970; Dirks and Relf, pp. 62, 78–88; Lader, *Abortion II*, pp. 74–78; "Rabbi's Case to Be Dropped," *Chicago Tribune*, Jan 25, 1970.

Pregnant Pause: Curtis Boyd

Author interview with Curtis Boyd, March 13, 2018; Curtis Boyd, "The Morality of Abortion: The Making of a Feminist Physician," *St. Louis University Public Law Review*, 1993; Cooper interview.

Jane Roe

The Dallas Clergy Consultation: Joshua Prager, "The Accidental Activist," *Vanity Fair*, Jan. 18, 2013; Norma McCorvey with Andy Meisler, *I Am Roe*, pp. 41–56, 68–71, 78–80, 104–107; Monika Maeckle, "The Double Life of Norma McCorvey," *Dallas Times Herald*, Oct. 18, 1981; multiple emails and conversations with author Joshua Prager, May 30, 2018; Alex Witchel, "At Home With Norma McCorvey," *New York Times*, July 28, 1994; Interview with Frank J. Bradley Jr., D.O., Aug. 7, 2018; Michelle Green and Lois Armstrong, "The Woman Behind *Roe v. Wade*," *People*, May 22, 1989; Weddington, p. 51.

Linda Coffee and Henry McCluskey: Garrow, pp. 398–407; Faux, pp. 3–4, 10–24, 39–41; Recreating what happened decades ago can be challenging. Weddington remembers being at the pizza parlor meeting. But in a 1971 letter to Ginny Whitehill, describing what she had done during a recent trip to Dallas, she wrote, "Meeting Jane Roe was fascinating, indicating that she first met Roe more than a year later." After much discussion, she told author David Garrow in 1992, "I can tell you what I remember; I can't tell you what was true or not." Many of McCorvey's stories have been disproven. In addition, her doctors don't recall her saying she was raped. The Kings declined requests for an interview. "'Jane Roe' Holds Tight to Cause," *Fort Worth Star-Telegram*, Jan. 22, 1983; Author interviews with Linda Coffee, Aug. 10, 2017 and Aug. 16, 2019; Patricia Duke,

"Oral Memoirs of Linda Coffee," April 17, 1973; Prager, "*Roe v. Wade*'s Secret Heroine"; Weddington, pp. 52–57; Norma McCorvey with Gary Thomas, *Won by Love*, p. 29; *Jane Roe v. Henry Wade*, CA# 3-3690 and *John Doe and Mary Doe v. Henry Wade*, CA#3-3691, both in the U.S. District Court, Northern District of Texas, March 3, 1970; Christi Harlan, "*Roe vs. Wade* Didn't Look Like History Maker," *Dayton (Ohio) Daily News*, Jan. 19. 1988.

Pregnant Pause: The Texas Abortion Law

Roy Lucas, et. al, "Brief for Appellants," *Jane Roe, John Doe, Mary Doe, and James Hubert Hallford, M.D., v. Henry Wade*, Supreme Court of the United States, no. 70-18, 1971 term, Aug. 18, 1971.

Jane Hodgson

For years, Dr. Jane Hodgson: Victor Cohn, "Frogs Tell You If Baby Is on the Way," *Star Tribune*, May 29, 1952; "Jane Hodgson's Odyssey," *U.S. News and World Report*, Dec. 4, 1989; Sherrie Mazingo, "Doctor Risks License on Belief in Humanity," *Minneapolis Star*, May 2, 1970; Seth S. King, "Minnesota Gynecologist, a Mother, Risks Her Career to Test State's Abortion Law," *New York Times*, Nov. 15, 1970; Carole Joffe, *Doctors of Conscience*, pp. 8–18; Bob Lundegaard, "State Abortion Law Is Challenged," *Star Tribune*, April 17, 1970; Garrow, pp. 414–416; Sharon Blinco, "Dr. Hodgson Claims 'Hypocrisy' in Abortion Law," *Star Tribune*, Nov. 18, 1970; Paul Presbrey, "Abortion Sentence Is Stayed," *Minneapolis Star*, Nov. 21, 1970.

As Dr. Hodgson was protesting: Faux, pp. 96–98; Garrow, pp. 437–439; Author interview with John Tolle, Feb. 15, 2019; "Defendant's Original Answer," *Roe v. Wade*, U.S. District Court, Northern District of Texas, March 28, 1970; Weddington, p. 60; McCorvey, *I Am Roe*, pp. 125–126; "Affidavit of Jane Roe," *Roe v. Wade*, May 21, 1970; Prager, "Accidental Activist."

Federal Court

On May 22, 1970, *Roe v. Wade*: "Transcript of Oral Argument," *Roe v. Wade*, May 22, 1970; Coffee and Weddington, "Brief of Plaintiffs, Jane Roe, John Doe, and Mary Doe," *Roe v. Wade*, April 23, 1970; Tolle interview; Garrow, pp. 437–444; Chris Daniel, "Women Were Kept Off Texas Juries Until 1954," *Houston Chronicle*, July 31, 2014, chron.com/neighborhood/kingwood/opinion/article/DANIEL -Women-were-kept-off-Texas-juries-until-9705922.php; "Louise B. Raggio," State Bar of Texas, texasbar.com/AM/PrinterTemplate.cfm?Section=Search&template= /CM/HTMLDisplay.cfm&ContentID=14971; Carolyn Barta, "WEAL Finds Credit Discrimination," *Dallas Morning News*, Jan. 17, 1973; John B. Tolle, "Defendant's Brief," *Roe v. Wade*, May 18, 1970.

The judges didn't need: Ronald E. Marcello, interview with Judge Sarah T. Hughes, Aug. 23, 1979, North Texas State University Oral History Collection, #489; Lawrence J. Vilardo and Howard W. Gutman, "With Justice From One: Interview with Hon. Irving L. Goldberg," *Litigation*, Spring 1991; *Roe v. Wade*, 314 F. Supp. 1217, June 17, 1970; Garrow, pp. 451–455; "Key Point: Which Comes First?" *Dallas Morning News*, June 19, 1970; John Lumpkin, "Texas Abortion Laws Ruling Will Be Appealed," *Fort Worth Star-Telegram*, June 19, 1970; Dave McNeely, "Wade to Continue Abortion Trials," *Dallas Morning News*, June 19, 1970; Earl Golz, "State, Challengers Appeal Ruling on Abortion Laws, *Dallas Morning News*, Aug. 18, 1970.

Jane

By the time *Roe*: Kaplan, pp. 3–5, 12, 15, 37–43, 82–83, 86, 115–116; Madeleine Schwartz, "Jane Does," *Harper's Magazine*, April 2017; Trevor Jensen, "Jody Howard, 1940–2010," *Chicago Tribune*, Feb. 15, 2010; "'Jane' Leader Helped Women Get Abortions in '60s, '70s," *Chicago Tribune*, Sept. 1, 2004; Kirtz and Lundy, *Jane: An Abortion Service* documentary; "The *Hyde Park Voices* series on Jane," cwluherstory.org.

Though tens of thousands: Susan Edmiston, "A Report on the Abortion Capital of the Country," *New York Times*, April 11, 1971; Jane E. Brody, "At 17, the Road to Abortion Is Lonely," *New York Times*, Oct. 18, 1970.

Not long after: Kaplan, *The Story of Jane*, pp. 109–111, 126–30, 148–158, 174–175, 203, 224–225, 280; *Jane* documentary; *Hyde Park Voices*; Edmiston, "A Report"; Galatzer-Levy and Scott interviews, "Lib Groups Linked to Abortion," *Chicago Tribune*, May 5, 1972.

Part III: *Roe v. Wade*

Justice Harry Blackmun, statement from the bench, Jan. 22, 1973, Harry A. Blackmun Papers, 1913–2001, box 151, folder 3.

Appeal

The U.S. Supreme Court: Linda Greenhouse, *Becoming Justice Blackmun*, p. 74; Weddington, pp. 72–73; Clement E. Vose, interview with Roy Lucas, Feb. 4, 1973, box 25, Roy Lucas Abortion Litigation Papers, Special Collections & Archives, Wesleyan University Library; Garrow, pp. 335–340, 351–353, 381–382, 386–388, 461–462; Coffee interviews.

While a growing number: Bob Woodward and Scott Armstrong, *The Brethren*, pp. 6–7, 14, 143–144, 198, 207–208; Greenhouse, *Becoming*, pp. 6–8, 15, 18–19, 63, 72, 77–80; Garrow, pp. 470, 474, 480–482, 488–491; Margaret Engel, "Doctor Faces

License Battle," *Washington Post*, Nov. 11, 1984; Gesell memorandum opinion, *United States v. Vuitch*, 305 F. Supp. 1032, Nov. 10, 1969; "No. 84—*United States v. Vuitch*," Blackmun Papers, box 123, folder 8; *United States v. Vuitch*, Oyez, oyez.org /cases/1970/84 and decision, supreme.justia.com/cases/federal/us/402/62/#tab -opinion-1949317.

The day after the Vuitch: Greenhouse, *Becoming*, pp. 78–79; Garrow, pp. 423, 427–428, 457–458, 491; *Doe v. Bolton*, 410 U.S. 179, Justia, supreme.justia.com /cases/federal/us/410/179/#tab-opinion-1950139; Gayle White, "*Roe v. Wade* Role Just a Page in a Rocky Life Story," *Atlanta Constitution*, Jan. 23, 2003; Achsah Nesmith, "Abortion Act Rules Killed," *Atlanta Constitution*, Aug. 1, 1970; Virginia Whitehill, letter to her parents, Dec. 26, 1970, Whitehill personal papers; Weddington, pp. 75–83.

Pregnant Pause: Sally's Story

Greenhouse, *Becoming*, pp. 74–75; Sally Blackmun, Esq., Introduction, in Gloria Feldt, *The War on Choice*. Kindle edition.

Briefs

The pointed message from: Weddington, pp. 83-100; interviews with Sarah Weddington and Ron Weddington; Faux, pp. 203–204, 221–224; Sarah Weddington to Whitehill, approximately June 1971, Whitehill personal papers; Garrow, pp. 497– 502; Appellant's brief, *Roe v. Wade*, in the Supreme Court, p. 123, footnote 96, Aug. 18, 1971; Vose, Lucas interview; Roy Lucas memorandum, Dec. 19, 1970, Lucas Papers, box 25, Misc. correspondence—Sept.–Dec. 1970; Griswold, Whitehill interview, Oct. 9, 2003; Ruth McLean Bowman Bowers obituary, Legacy.com, April 22, 2013.

Like Roe's lawyers: Faux, pp. 136–137, 229; Williams, *Defenders*, p. 153; "The Anti-Abortion Campaign," *Time*, March 29, 1971; "HHH Opposes Abortions on Demand," *Minneapolis Star Tribune*, June 16, 1971; Karrer, "National Right to Life," p. 545; Author interview with Martin McKernan, Nov. 29, 2017; Martin F. McKernan Jr., to Alfred Walker, Esq., July 2, 1970, State of Texas *Roe v. Wade* case files, Texas Attorney General's office; Joseph P. Witherspoon to The Hon. Crawford C. Martin, et. al, Aug. 27, 1971, Texas *Roe* files; Alfred L. Scanlan to Hon. Jay Floyd, July 13, 1971, Texas *Roe* files; Alfred Scanlan et. al, *Amicus Curiae* brief for the National Right to Life Committee, *Roe v. Wade*, in the U.S. Supreme Court, Oct. 8, 1971, p. 2; Jerry Frazel to Jay Floyd, Sept. 9, 1971; Dennis Horan to Jay Floyd, Sept. 16, 1971, Sept. 21, 1971, and Sept. 24, 1971, all Texas *Roe* files; Appellee Brief, *Roe v. Wade*, in the U.S. Supreme Court, Oct. 19, 1971; Bruce McCabe, "*Roe vs. Wade*," *Boston Globe*, May 15, 1989; Martin F. McKernan Jr. to Hon. Jay Floyd, Nov. 5, 1971, Texas *Roe* files.

A few weeks before: Woodward and Armstrong, pp. 188–189, 197–198; Blackmun Papers, box 151, folder 3; Garrow, pp. 514–517; Weddington, pp. 100–106; Faux, pp. 229–236; Weddington to Whitehill, Nov. 23, 1971, Whitehill personal papers; Prager, "*Roe v. Wade*'s Secret Heroine"; Horan to Floyd, Sept. 24, 1971, Texas *Roe* files; Cheek, Weddington interview, p. 35.

Oyez, Oyez, Oyez

There is hardly: "Building Features," "The Court and Its Traditions," and "The Court and Its Procedures," at supremecourt.gov; On morning coat history, email from the Supreme Court Public Information Office, July 3, 2019; Famously, current Supreme Court Justice Elena Kagan declined to wear morning dress when she was solicitor general; Ann Farmer, "Order in the Closet," *Perspectives*, fall 2010; Weddington, pp. 105,109–115; Griswold, Whitehill interview; Fowlkes and Ball, Weddington interview; Marsha King letter to Whitehill, Feb. 12, 1973, Whitehill personal papers; *Roe v. Wade* oral argument recording, Dec. 13, 1971, Oyez, oyez .org/cases/1971/70-18; "No. 70-18-ATX—*Roe v. Wade*," Blackmun Papers, box 152, folder 2.

Immediately after Floyd: *Doe v. Bolton* oral argument recording, Dec. 13, 1971, oyez.org/cases/1971/70-40; "No. 70-40-ATX—*Doe v. Bolton*," Blackmun Papers, box 153, folder 1; In Blackmun's assessment of Weddington, there is an errant comma and the description reads, "large blond, hair, rather pretty, plump"; Margaret Shannon, "Matters of Life and Death," *Atlanta Constitution*, April 23, 1973; "Texas Defends Anti-Abortion Law in Court," *Washington Post*, Dec. 14, 1971; "2 Suits Contest Bans on Abortion," *New York Times*, Dec. 4, 1971.

Pregnant Pause: The Supremes

"About the Court," and "The Court as an Institution," U.S. Supreme Court, supremecourt.gov; "About the Supreme Court," United States Courts, uscourts.gov /about-federal-courts/educational-resources/about-educational-outreach/activity -resources/about; Elizabeth Nix, "7 Things You Might Not Know About the U.S. Supreme Court," history.com; Justice biographies, Oyez, oyez.org/justices.

Deliberations

Three days after: Garrow, pp. 529–534; Woodward and Armstrong, pp. 201–209; Paul Hoeber, Gerald Goldman, Robert B. Miller, C. Taylor Ashworth, "Opinions of William J. Brennan Jr.," October Term, 1971, Supreme Court of the United States, Brennan Papers, part II, box 6, folder 14; William O. Douglas Papers, box 1590, folder 5; William J. Brennan Jr. Papers, box 1280, folder 6; Douglas Papers, box

1589, folder 2, and box 1590, folder 6; Weddington, p. 132; Harold Hongju Koh, Harry A. Blackmun Oral History Project transcript, p. 489; Thurgood Marshall Papers, box 99, folder 1; Greenhouse, *Becoming*, p. 89.

While Blackmun worked: Charlotte Moulton, "High Court Topples Mass. Birth Control Law," and J. Jerome Sullivan, "Old State Law Hotly Debated Since 1967," *Boston Globe*, March 22, 1972; "Court Voids an Anti-Contraception Law," *New York Times*, March 23, 1972; Garrow, pp. 320–321; Opinion, *Eisenstadt v. Baird*, Justia, supreme.justia.com/cases/federal/us/405/438/#tab-opinion-1949624.

While members of the court waited: Wauhillau La Hay, "Potomac Patter," *El Paso Herald Post*, March 31, 1972; Gordon Slovut, "Dr. Hodgson Busy, but Wants to Come Home," *Minneapolis Star*, Jan. 2, 1973; Dirks and Relf, pp. 82–83; Bill Hendricks, "Quacks Still Inflicting Big Abortion Toll," *Dallas Times Herald*, April 28, 1972; Maryln Schwartz, "Abortion: Even When It's Legal It Still Isn't Easy," *Dallas Morning News*, Feb. 6, 1972; Problem Pregnancy Information Service Inc. price sheet, Nov. 6, 1972, Whitehill Women's and Children's Rights Collection, box 43, folder 2.

After the December 1971 arguments: Weddington, pp. 122–129; "Austin Woman Files For Race," *Austin Statesman*, Feb. 7, 1972; "Seven Runoffs Coming in Travis," *Austin Statesman*, May 8, 1972; Garrow, pp. 482–483, 547; Fred. C. Shapiro, "'Right to Life' Has a Message for New York State Legislators," *New York Times*, Aug. 20, 1972; "Thousands Here Urge Repeal of Abortion Statute," *New York Times*, April 17, 1972; Robert D. McFadden, "Lobbying on Abortion Increases at Capitol," *New York Times*, May 8, 1972; James F. Clarity, "Governor Reported Irked By Nixon's Abortion Views," *New York Times*, May 9, 1972; Greenhouse, *Becoming*, pp. 83–84; Daniel K. Williams, "The GOP's Abortion Strategy: Why Pro-Choice Republicans Became Pro-Life in the 1970s," *Journal of Policy History*, volume 23, no. 4, 2011, pp. 517–522; Linda Greenhouse and Reva B. Siegel, "Before (and After) *Roe v. Wade*: New Questions About Backlash," *Yale Law Journal*, June 2011; William E. Farrell, "Governor Vetoes Abortion Repeal As Not Justified," *New York Times*, May 14, 1972.

Pregnant Pause: What Religions Say

Dave Musci, "Where Major Religious Groups Stand on Abortion," Pew Research Center, June 21, 2016; Encyclical Letter *Humanae Vitae*; "Lutherans Focus on Women's Role," *New York Times*, Oct. 16, 1974; "Abortion," Social Statement Summary, Evangelical Lutheran Church in America, elca.org/Faith/Faith-and -Society/Social-Statements/Abortion; Interview with Imam Omar Suleiman, president, Yaqeen Institute, Sept. 5, 2019; Suleiman, "Islam and the Abortion Debate," March 20, 2017; "Abortion/Reproductive Choice Issues," Presbyterian Mission, Presbyterian Church (USA), presbyterianmission.org/what-we-believe/social

-issues/abortion-issues/; "Abortion Reform," 49th General Assembly, Nov. 1967 and "Reproductive Rights," 1990, Union for Reform Judaism, urj.org; "Baptists Urged to Work for Pro-Abortion Laws," *Baptist Press*, June 2, 1971; "On Celebrating the Advancement of Pro-Life Legislation in State Legislatures—2019," Southern Baptist Convention, sbc.net; "Reform of Abortion Statues, 1963 Resolution," and "Reproductive Justice," Unitarian Universalist Association, uua .org; "General Synod Statements and Resolutions Regarding Freedom of Choice," United Church of Christ; "Homosexual Marriages Opposed by Methodists," *New York Times*, April 27, 1972; "Social Principles: The Nurturing Community," What We Believe, United Methodist Church, umc.org/what-we-believe/the-nurturing -community#abortion.

Five months after: Blackmun Papers, box 151, folder 4; Brennan Papers, part I, box 285, file 9; Douglas Papers, box 1590, file 5; Blackmun Papers, box 151, file 3; Mr. Justice Douglas, 6th Draft, Dissent, June 1972; Powell, Supreme Court Case Files Collection, law2.wlu.edu/powellarchives/page.asp?pageid=1341; Hoeber, et. al; Brennan Papers, part II, box 6, file 14; Marshall Papers, box 99, folder 2; Garrow, pp. 548–560; Woodward and Armstrong, pp. 220–228; "Move By Burger May Shift Court's Stand on Abortion," *Washington Post*, July 4, 1972; "Abortion Cases Creating Friction on High Court," *New York Times*, July 5, 1972; Douglas Papers, box 1589, folder 2.

Roe, Again

While the Supreme Court: Blackmun Oral History Project transcript, pp. 197–198, 201; Hippocratic Oath, National Library of Medicine, nlm.nih.gov/hmd/greek /greek_oath.html; Opinion, *Roe v. Wade*, 410 U.S. 113 (1973), Justia, supreme.justia .com/cases/federal/us/410/113/#tab-opinion-1950137.

Getting ready was much tougher: Weddington, pp. 134–142; Garrow, pp. 563–568; *Roe v. Wade* oral reargument, Oct. 11, 1972, Oyez, oyez.org/cases/1971/70 -18; Faux, p. 284.

For the second round: Faux, pp. 137–138, 280–287; "Crawford Martin Dies at Age 56," *Dallas Morning News*, Dec. 30, 1972; Associated Press, "Lawyer Confused About Abortion," *Longview News-Journal*, Jan. 30, 1983; *Roe v. Wade* oral reargument, Oct. 11, 1972; Blackmun Papers, box 151, file 8.

The court turned next: *Doe v. Bolton* oral reargument, Oct. 11, 1972, Oyez, oyez .org/cases/1971/70-40; Blackmun Papers, box 53, folder 1; William J. Maledon, Gerald M. Rosberg, and Geoffrey R. Stone, "Opinions of William J. Brennan, Jr., October Term, 1972," Brennan Papers, part II, box 6, folder 16; Weddington letter to Ginny Whitehill, Oct. 16, 1972, Whitehill personal papers.

Opinions

Two days after: Conference notes: Douglas Papers, box 1590, folder 5; Blackmun Papers, box 151, folder 9; Brennan Papers, box 1280, folder 6; and Powell Papers, retrieved online; Blackmun Papers, box 151, file 8; Garrow, pp. 573–576; Greenhouse, *Becoming*, pp. 91–95; Dottie Fish, "They're Concerned with 'People Issues,'" *Austin Statesman*, Nov. 19, 1972; David S. Broder, "Nixon Wins Landslide Victory," *Washington Post*, Nov. 8, 1972; Williams, "The GOP's Abortion Strategy"; Karrer, "National Right to Life," pp. 550–553; Betty DeRamus, *Detroit Free Press*, "Abortion Pioneer Reflects on Years of Abuse, Shame," May 7, 1973; Williams, *Defenders*, pp. 190–193; Jack Rosenthal, "Survey Finds Majority in Shift, Now Favors Liberalized Laws," *New York Times*, Aug. 25, 1972; George Gallup, "Abortion Seen Up to Woman, Doctor," *Washington Post*, Aug. 25, 1972.

In late November: Blackmun Papers, box 151, folder, 6; Powell Papers; Woodward and Armstrong, p. 280; Garrow, pp. 580–585; James Robenault, *January 1973*, pp. 165–175; Martin Van Der Werf, *Roe v. Wade*, "Still Debated," *Arizona Republic*, Jan 22, 1988; John C. Jeffries Jr., *Justice Lewis F. Powell Jr.*, p. 347; Blackmun Papers, box 151, folders 4 and 8; Douglas Papers, box 1590, folder 5; Powell Papers, Byron White Papers, box 237, folder 8.

In mid-December: Blackmun Papers, box 151, folder 4; Powell Papers; Brennan Papers, part I, box 286, folder 1; *Roe v. Wade*, 410 U.S. 113 (1973). Most of the *Roe v. Wade* opinion can be found at Justia, supreme.justia.com/cases/federal/us/410/113/#tab-opinion-1950137. However, the dissenting opinion of Justice White and the concurring opinions of Chief Justice Burger and Justice Douglas are with opinions in *Doe v. Bolton*, 410 U.S. 179 (1973), Justia, supreme.justia.com/cases/federal/us/410/113/#tab-opinion-1950137.

The Decision

What was taking Chief Justice Burger: Woodward and Armstrong, pp. 220, 284–286; Brennan Papers, part II, box 6, folder 16; Blackmun Papers, box 151, folder 3; Koh, Blackmun oral history, p. 199; John P. MacKenzie, "Supreme Court Allows Early-Stage Abortions," *Washington Post*, Jan 23, 1973; Warren Weaver Jr., "High Court Rules Abortion Legal the First 3 Months," *New York Times*, Jan. 23, 1973; "The Sexes: Abortion on Demand," *Time*, Jan. 29, 1973; Richard Nixon and Charles Colson, White House Tapes Conversation #407-18, between 6:22 and 7:23, Jan. 23, 1973; Richard Nixon Presidential Library; Nina Totenberg, "Tape Reveals Nixon's Views on Abortion," NPR, npr.org/templates/story/story.php?storyId=105832640.

Sarah Weddington was in Austin: Weddington, pp. 146–150, 161–162; Cheek, Weddington interview, p. 28; Barbara Richardson, "Abortion Ruling," *Dallas Times Herald*, Jan 23, 1973; Robert O'Brien, "Abortion Court Decision Interpreted by Attorney," *Baptist Press*, Jan. 29, 1973; "Baptists Urged to Work for Pro-Abortion

Laws," *Baptist Press*, June 2, 1971; Robert O'Brien, "Abortion Case Plaintiff Sheds 'Jane Roe' Identity," *Baptist Press*, Jan. 29, 1973.

The Supreme Court ruling: Gwenyth Jones, "State Supreme Court Overturns Abortion Law, Two Convictions," *Minneapolis Star*, Feb. 2, 1973; Dirks and Relf, p. 88; Kaplan, pp. 278–279; Michael Maidenberg and Dolores Katz, "State Doctors Set for Abortion Rise," *Detroit Free Press*, Jan. 23, 1973; MacKenzie, *Washington Post*, Jan 23, 1973; Marjorie Hyer, "Cardinal O'Boyle Asks Pastors to Preach Against Abortion Rule," *Washington Post*, Jan. 25, 1973; "Catholics Warned to Avoid Abortions," *New York Times*, Feb. 15, 1973; Press release, Texas Attorney General, Feb. 15,1973, Texas *Roe* files; Wayne King, "Supreme Court Bars a Review of Abortion Decision," *New York Times*, Feb. 27, 1973; Koh, Blackmun oral history, pp. 492–493; Greenhouse, *Becoming*, pp. 133–138; Brennan Papers, part II, box 6, folder 16; Stone, *Sex and the Constitution*, pp. 394–395; Jane Brody, "National Study Finds Many Unable to Get Abortion in '74 Despite Supreme Court's Easing of Curbs," *New York Times*, Oct. 7, 1975; "Rules on Abortion Clinics Filed," *New York Times*, Aug. 11, 1974; Linda Little, "2nd Abortion Clinic Opens in Dallas Area," *Dallas Morning News*, April 26, 1973; Jane E. Brody, "Legal Abortions Up 53% Since Court Ruled in '73," *New York Times*, Feb. 3, 1975; David Roach, "How Southern Baptists Became Pro-Life," *Baptist Press*, Jan. 16, 2015; Williams, "The GOP's Abortion Strategy."

Pregnant Pause: Forced Sterilization

Joel Dreyfuss, "The Relfs: Did They Understand?" *Washington Post*, July 8, 1973; "Mother of 3 to Fight Sterilization Ban," *New York Times*, Aug. 29, 1971; Weston, "Why Six Million," *New York Times*, Sept. 29, 1974; B. Drummond Ayres, Jr., "The Nation: Sterilizing the Poor," *New York Times*, July 8, 1973; Kluchin, pp. 103–105, 108–111, 116–120; Jane Lawrence, "The Indian Health Service and the Sterilization of Native American Women," *American Indian Quarterly*, Summer 2000; Nancy Hicks, "Sterilization of Black Mother of 3 Stirs Aiken, S.C.," *New York Times*, Aug. 1, 1973; Claudia Dreifus, "Sterilizing the Poor," in *Seizing Our Bodies*, pp. 105-120.

Part IV: After *Roe*

Beijing Declaration and Platform for Action, Fourth World Conference on Women, Sept. 4–15, 1995, p. 91.

Politics

In the summer of 1975: Don Mack, "Arson Blamed in Early Morning Fire," *Eugene Register-Guardian*, June 27, 1975; "*State v. Sockett*," Justia, law.justia.com/cases/oregon/supreme-court/1977/278-or-637-6.html; Violence Statistics, Arsons and Bombings, and NAF Violence and Disruption Statistics, National Abortion Foundation, prochoice.org/education-and-advocacy/violence/violence-statistics-and-history/; Lawrence Lader,

"Abortion Opponents' Tactics," *New York Times*, Jan. 11, 1978; Number of Abortions, Guttmacher Institute, data.guttmacher.org/states/trend?state=US&topics=66&dataset =data; Heidi Williamson and Jamila Taylor, "The Hyde Amendment Has Perpetuated Inequality in Abortion Access for 40 Years," Center for American Progress, Sept. 29, 2016; "Chronology on Abortion Issue," *New York Times*, July 1, 1980; William Robbins, "Abortion Foes Look to Ultimate Victory," *New York Times*, June 19, 1977; Greenhouse and Siegel, "Before (and After) *Roe*"; Williams, "The GOP's Abortion Strategy;" John Dart, "'New Face' Emerging in Protestant Fundamentalism," *Los Angeles Times*, Oct. 13, 1979.

The Supreme Court, Again

By the time he became president: Ronald Reagan, on *Roe v. Wade,* history.com, history.com/topics/us-presidents/ronald-reagan-on-roe-v-wade-video; Bill Peterson, "Abortion Foes Gain Key Federal Posts," *Washington Post*, March 6, 1981; Evan Thomas, *First: Sandra Day O'Connor*, pp. 36, 39, 43, 56–61, 84, 123–124, 127–128, 131,135–143, 234; Georgia Dullea, "Women as Judges: The Ranks Grow," *New York Times*, April 26, 1984; Steven R. Weisman, "White House Rebuts Charges that Nominee Has Voted for Abortions," *New York Times*, July 9, 1981; Lou Cannon, "Reagan Names Woman to Supreme Court," *Washington Post*, July 8, 1981; Steven R. Weisman, "Reagan Nominating a Woman, An Arizona Appeals Judge, To Serve On Supreme Court," *New York Times*, July 8, 1981; *Akron v. Akron Center for Reproductive Health*, Justia, supreme.justia.com /cases/federal/us/462/416/#tab-opinion-1955113; Pam Belluck, "Premature Babies May Survive at 22 Weeks, If Treated, Study Finds," *New York Times*, May 6, 2015; Greenhouse, *Becoming*, pp. 143–145, 182; Evan Thomas, "How Supreme Court Justice Sandra Day O'Connor Helped Preserve Abortion Rights," *New Yorker*, March 27, 2019; Violence Statistics, National Abortion Federation; Victoria Churchville and Martin Weil, "3 Arrested In Series of Bombings," *Washington Post*, Jan. 20, 1985; Ruth Marcus and Joe Pichirallo, "Intensive Investigation Led to Clinic Bombing Arrests," *Washington Post*, Jan. 21, 1985; Paul W. Valentine, "3rd Abortion Clinic Bomber Sentenced to 15 Years," *Washington Post*, July 27, 1985; Michael Specter, "Shot Fired Through Blackmun's Window," *Washington Post*, March 5, 1985.

In addition to his safety: Greenhouse, *Becoming*, pp. 190–194; Benjamin Weiser and Bob Woodward, "Roe's Eleventh Hour Reprieve," *Washington Post*, May 23, 1993; Thomas, *First*, pp. 261–264; Al Kamen, "5–4 Ruling Stops Short of Overturning *Roe*," *Washington Post*, July 4, 1989; Linda Greenhouse, "Supreme Court, 5–4 Narrowing *Roe v. Wade*, Upholds Sharp State Limits on Abortions," *New York Times*, July 4, 1989; Opinions, *Webster v. Reproductive Health Services*, Justia, supreme.justia.com /cases/federal/us/492/490/#tab-opinion-1958093; Cynthia Gorney, "Missouri, In Webster's Wake," *Washington Post*, July 3, 1990.

While Reagan and Bush: Greenhouse and Siegel, "Before (and After) *Roe*"; Greenhouse, *Becoming*, pp. 202–206; Thomas, *First*, pp. 278–281; Ruth Marcus, "Abortion

Rights Groups Expect to Lose," *Washington Post*, April 22, 1992; Linda Greenhouse, "Documents Reveal the Evolution of a Justice," *New York Times*, March 4, 2004; *Planned Parenthood of Southeastern Pa. v. Casey*, Justia, supreme.justia.com /cases/federal/us/505/833/#tab-opinion-1959105; Ruth Marcus, "5–4 Court Declines to Overrule *Roe*," *Washington Post*, June 30, 1992; David J. Garrow, "Abortion Before and After *Roe v. Wade*: An Historical Perspective," *Albany Law Review*, 1998–99.

Pushback

Every year around the January 22 anniversary: Robin Toner, "Settling In: Easing Abortion Policy," *New York Times*, Jan. 23, 1993; "Title X 'Gag Rule' is Formally Repealed," *Guttmacher Policy Review*, Aug. 1, 2000; The Supreme Court case is *Rust v. Sullivan* (1991); Charles E. Shepard, "Operation Rescue's Mission to Save Itself," *Washington Post*, Nov. 24, 1991; "Operation Rescue: True History," Operation Rescue, operationrescuetruehistory.com; Isabel Wilkerson, "Drive Against Abortion Finds a Symbol: Wichita," *New York Times*, Aug. 4, 1991; "The Death of Dr. Gunn," *New York Times*, March 12, 1993; "Dr. David Gunn Is Murdered by Anti-Abortion Activist," History, history.com; "Michael Griffin, Murderer of Pensacola Abortion Doctor David Gunn, Is Denied Parole," *Pensacola News Journal*, Oct. 31, 2017; Seth Faison, "Abortion Doctor Wounded Outside Kansas Clinic," *New York Times*, Aug. 20, 1993; Dirk Johnson, "An Abortionist Returns to Work After a Shooting," *New York Times*, Aug. 21, 1993; Violence Statistics, National Abortion Federation; Gwen Ifill, "Clinton Signs Bill Banning Blockades and Violent Acts at Abortion Clinics," *New York Times*, May 27, 1994; "Freedom of Access to Clinic Entrances (FACE) Act," National Abortion Federation, prochoice.org.

With their blockades limited: Veronica Puente, "Anti-Abortion Group Leasing Next to Clinic," *Dallas Morning News*, April 1, 1995; McCorvey, *I Am Roe*, pp. 176–184; Milbauer, pp. 7–9; Joe Drape, "*Roe v. Wade* Plaintiff Says She Lied About Rape," *Dallas Morning News*, Sept. 9, 1987; Gayle Reaves, "'Jane Roe' Says Views on Abortion Changed," *Dallas Morning News*, Aug. 11, 1995; Sam Howe Verhovek, "New Twist For a Landmark Case," *New York Times*, Aug, 12, 1995; Bill Minutaglio, "Effect of McCorvey Baptism Unclear in Abortion Debate," *Dallas Morning News*, Aug 12, 1995; Whitehill, personal note, April, 23, 1994, Whitehill personal papers; Prager, "Accidental Activist"; Norma McCorvey with Gary Thomas, *Won by Love*; Garrow, pp. 602–603; "Court Rejects Motion to Overturn *Roe v. Wade*," CNN.com, cnn .com/2004/LAW/09/14/roe.v.wade/; Harlan, "*Roe v. Wade*."

Pregnant Pause: Pregnancy and Abortion

Dr. Willie Parker, *Life's Work*, pp. 91–112; American College of Obstetricians and Gynecologists, "Practice Bulletin: Medical Management of First-Trimester Abortions," no. 143, March 2014 (reaffirmed 2016) and "Practice Bulletin: Second-Trimester Abortion," no. 135, June 2013, Reaffirmed 2019; "Induced Abortion in the United States," Guttmacher Institute, Sept. 2019.

Restrictions

By the early 2000s: Ceci Connolly, "Access to Abortion Pared at State Level," *Washington Post*, Aug. 29, 2005; Michael D. Shear, "New Abortion Restrictions Upheld," *Washington Post*, April 3, 2003; Parental Involvement in Minors' Abortions, Guttmacher Institute, July 1, 2019, guttmacher.org/state-policy/explore/parental -involvement-minors-abortions; "What Kinds of Questions Will the Judge Ask Me," Jane's Due Process, janesdueprocess.org/what-kinds-of-questions-will-the-judge -ask-me/; Kate Coleman-Minahan, Amanda Jean Stevenson, Emily Obront and Susan Hays, "Young Women's Experiences Obtaining Judicial Bypass for Abortion in Texas," *Journal of Adolescent Health*, 2019; Molly Redden, "This Is How Judges Humiliate Pregnant Teens Who Want Abortions," *Mother Jones*, Sept./Oct. 2014.

Teens weren't the only ones: Diana Greene Foster and Katrina Kimport, "Who Seeks Abortions at or After 20 Weeks?" *Perspectives on Sexual and Reproductive Health*, doi.org/10.1363/4521013; "Induced Abortions in the United States," Guttmacher Institute, Jan. 2018, guttmacher.org/fact-sheet/induced-abortion-united -states; American College of Obstetricians and Gynecologists, "Practice Bulletin: Second-Trimester Abortion"; Tracy A. Weitz, "Lessons for the Prochoice Movement From the 'Partial Birth Abortion' Fight," *Conscience*, catholicsforchoice.org/issues _publications/lessons-for-the-prochoice-movement-from-the-partial-birth-abortion -fight/; David Stout, "President Signs Bill That Prohibits Type of Abortion," *New York Times*, Nov. 5, 2003; *Gonzales v. Carhart*, Justia, supreme.justia.com/cases /federal/us/550/124/#tab-opinion-1962402; Joe Stumpe and Monica Davey, "Abortion Doctor Shot to Death in Kansas Church," *New York Times*, May 31, 2009; Monica Davey, "Abortion Foe Found Guilty in Doctor's Killing," *New York Times*, Jan. 29, 2010.

The murder also put the women's: Elizabeth Nash, Rachel Benson Gold, Zohra Ansari-Thomas, Olivia Cappello, and Lizamaria Mohammed, Policy Trends in the States: 2016, Guttmacher Institute, Jan. 2017, guttmacher.org/article/2017/01 /policy-trends-states-2016; *Whole Woman's Health v. Hellerstedt*, Justia, supreme.justia .com/cases/federal/us/579/15-274/#tab-opinion-3590956; Emergency Contraception Website, Office of Population Research, Princeton University, ec.princeton .edu/pills/planbhistory.html; "What's the Plan B Morning After Pill?" Planned Parenthood, plannedparenthood.org/learn/morning-after-pill-emergency-contraception /whats-plan-b-morning-after-pill; Julia Belluz, "The Historically Low Birthrate, Explained in 3 Charts," *Vox*, May 15, 2019, vox.com/science-and-health/2018/5/22 /17376536/fertility-rate-united-states-births-women; Joerg Dreweke, "U.S. Abortion

Rate Reaches Record Low Amidst Looming Onslaught Against Reproductive Health and Rights," *Guttmacher Policy Review*, vol. 20, 2017; Amelia Thomson-Deveaux, "The Abortion Rate Is Falling Because Fewer Women Are Getting Pregnant," Fivethirtyeight, fivethirtyeight.com/features/the-abortion-rate-is-falling-because-fewer-women -are-getting-pregnant/; Alanna Vagianos, "Women Aren't The Only People Who Get Abortions," *Huffington Post*, June 7, 2019; huffpost.com/entry/women-arent-the-only -people-who-get-abortions_n_5cf55540e4b0e346ce8286d3; "Induced Abortion in the United States," Guttmacher Institute, Jan. 2018, guttmacher.org/fact-sheet/induced -abortion-united-states; Sister Song, sistersong.net.

Pregnant Pause: Birth Control Today

Contraception, Centers for Disease Control and Prevention, cdc.gov /reproductivehealth/contraception/index.htm#Contraceptive-Effectiveness; "Contraceptive Use in the U.S.," Guttmacher Institute, July 2018, guttmacher.org/fact -sheet/contraceptive-use-united-states.

Epilogue

Almost daily: Boyd, "The Morality of Abortion"; Boyd interview; "An Overview of Abortion Laws," Guttmacher Institute, July 1, 2019, guttmacher.org/state-policy /explore/overview-abortion-laws; Williamson and Taylor, "The Hyde Amendment."

Republican Donald Trump: Sarah Kaplan, "'I'm a Warrior for the Babies,' Planned Parenthood Suspect Declares in Court," *Washington Post*, Dec. 10, 2015; Violence Statistics, National Abortion Federation; John T. Bennett, "Trump's Federal Judge Pace Matches Recent Presidents—But With a Big Twist," *Roll Call*, May 8, 2019; Justices, Oyez.org; Adam Liptak, "Kavanaugh and Gorsuch, Justices With Much in Common, Take Different Paths," *New York Times*, May 12, 2019; Timothy Williams and Alan Blinder, "Lawmakers Vote to Effectively Ban Abortion in Alabama," *New York Times*, May 14, 2019; "State Policy Updates," Guttmacher Institute, guttmacher .org/state-policy; Ariana Eunjung Cha, "21 States Sue to File Suit to Block Trump Administration's Abortion 'Gag Rule,'" *Washington Post*, March 4, 2019; Parker, pp. 103-104; "Texas Women's Experiences Attempting Self-Induced Abortion in the Face of Dwindling Options," Texas Policy Evaluation Project Research Brief, Nov. 17, 2018; Author interviews with Geoffrey Stone, law professor, University of Chicago, Feb. 20, 2019, and Sanford Levinson, law professor, University of Texas, April 2, 2019; Megan Brenan, "Nearly Two-Thirds of Americans Want *Roe v. Wade* to Stand," Gallup, July 12, 2018; Michael C. Bender, "Record 71% of Voters Oppose Overturning *Roe v. Wade*," *Wall Street Journal*, July 23, 2018.

PHOTO CREDITS

p. 6: Photo by Norbert Scott, courtesy of Martha Scott; **p. 12:** Granger; **p. 15:** Drawn by Nicholas Hartsoeker in 1695; **p. 23:** Courtesy of the National Postal Museum, Smithsonian Institution; **p. 26:** Granger; **p. 31:** Bain News Service Collection, Library of Congress; **p. 32:** Social Press Association, New York World-Telegram and Sun Newspaper Collection, Library of Congress; **p. 36:** Arthur H. Estabrook Papers, 1908–1962. M.E. Grenander Department of Special Collections and Archives, University Libraries, University at Albany, State University of New York; **p. 41:** The Alan Mason Chesney Medical Archives of The Johns Hopkins Medical Institutions; **p. 43:** Meharry Medical College Archives and Special Collections; **p. 49:** Granger; **p. 51:** Advertisement in the Honolulu Star-Bulletin, July 8, 1930; **p. 55:** J. R. Eyerman, The *Life* Images Collection/Getty Images; **p. 57:** © Keystone Press Agency/ Zuma Press; **p. 67:** Bettmann/Getty Images; **p. 68:** Dittrick Medical History Center, Case Western Reserve University; **pp. 73, 82:** Bettmann/Getty Images; **p. 85:** John Lindsay/AP Images; **p. 94:** Henry Groskinsky, The *Life* Picture Collection, Getty Images; **p. 98:** Walt Zeboski/AP Images; **p. 101:** Most Rev. James T. McHugh Priest File - Archives & Special Collections, Seton Hall University; **p. 103:** Luigi Felici/ AP Images; **p. 105:** Bettye Lane, Schlesinger Library, Radcliffe Institute, Harvard University; **p. 110:** Vince Graas, Schlesinger Library, Radcliffe Institute, Harvard University; **p. 114:** Bettye Lane, Schlesinger Library, Radcliffe Institute, Harvard University; **p. 117:** Steve Starr/AP Images; **p. 120:** Bettmann/Getty Images; **p. 123:** Dittrick Medical History Center, Case Western Reserve University; **p. 128:** Vivian Castleberry Papers, DeGolyer Library, Southern Methodist University; **p. 132:** Courtesy, *Fort Worth Star-Telegram* Photograph Collection, Special Collections, The University of Texas at Arlington Libraries, Arlington, Texas; **p. 134:** SMU Archives, DeGolyer Library, Southern Methodist University; **p. 137:** Courtesy of Dr. Curtis Boyd; **p. 141:** Bill Janscha/AP Images; **p. 143:** Bettmann/Getty Images; **p. 146:** Courtesy of Linda Coffee; **p. 151:** Courtesy, *Fort Worth Star-Telegram* Photograph Collection, Special Collections, The University of Texas at Arlington Libraries, Arlington, Texas; **pp. 154–155:** Courtesy of Linda Coffee; **p. 159:** Photo by Doug Podd, used with permission; **p. 163:** AP Images; **p. 166:** http://www.chicagomag. com/Chicago-Magazine/April-2019/Chicagos-Forgotten-Pro-Choice-Warriors-the-Janes/; **p. 167:** Courtesy Judy Norsigian, Our Bodies Ourselves; **p. 172:** Courtesy Martha Scott; **p. 173:** Courtesy Jeanne Galatzer-Levy; **p. 180:** Courtesy, *Fort Worth Star-Telegram* Photograph Collection, Special Collections, The University of Texas at Arlington Libraries, Arlington, Texas; **p. 183:** Charles H. Phillips, The *Life* Picture Collection/Getty Images; **p. 193:** © Steve Wilson/*San Antonio Express-News* via ZUMA wire; **p. 198:** Harris & Ewing, Collection of the Supreme Court of the United States; **p. 202:** Franz Jantzen, Collection of the Supreme Court of the United States; **p. 204:** Courtesy, *Fort Worth Star-Telegram* Photograph Collection, Special Collections, The University of Texas at Arlington Libraries, Arlington, Texas; **p. 207:** State of Texas, *Roe v. Wade* case files; **p. 211:** Cheryl Bray/*Atlanta Journal-Constitution* via AP; **p. 213:** Harris & Ewing, Collection of the Supreme Court of the United States;

p. 220: Fred W. McDarrah/Getty Images; **p. 231:** The Richard Nixon Presidential Library and Museum; **p. 236:** Virginia Whitehill Papers, DeGolyer Library, Southern Methodist University; **p. 239:** Courtesy of *Austin American-Statesman*, [AS-78-99925], Austin History Center, Austin Public Library; **p. 243:** Bud Skinner/*Atlanta Journal-Constitution* via AP; **p. 247:** Harry A. Blackmun Collection, Manuscript Division, Library of Congress; **p. 255:** Lewis F. Powell Jr. Papers, https://scholarlycommons.law.wlu.edu/casefiles/16/, Washington and Lee University School of Law, Lexington, Virginia.; **p. 258:** AP Images; **p. 262:** Ted W. Powers, photographer, found in the *Fort Worth Star-Telegram* Archives; **p. 270:** Gary Settle/*The New York Times*/Redux; **p. 278:** Ira Schwarz/AP Images; **p. 281:** John Duricka/AP Images; **p. 288:** Joseph Bailey, *National Geographic*, Courtesy of the Supreme Court of the United States; **p. 297:** Louis DeLuca/© 2019 *The Dallas Morning News*, Inc.; **p. 306:** Mike Hutmacher/*The Wichita Eagle*, AP Images; **p. 312:** Photo by Andy Lyman, Courtesy of *New Mexico Political Report*; **p. 316:** Fred Schilling, Collection of the Supreme Court of the United States.

INDEX